Facilitating adoptions
from care

Facilitating adoptions from care

A compendium of effective and promising practices

Susan Livingston Smith and Donaldson Adoption Institute staff

THE DONALDSON
ADOPTION INSTITUTE

Published by British Association
for Adoption & Fostering
(BAAF)
Saffron House
3rd Floor, 6–10 Kirby Street
London EC1N 8TS
www.baaf.org.uk

Charity registration 275689 (England and Wales)
and SC039337 (Scotland)

© Donaldson Adoption Institute, 2014

British Library Cataloguing in Publication Data
A catalogue record for this book is available
from the British Library

ISBN 978 1 910039 10 6

Project management by Shaila Shah, Publisher, BAAF
Designed by Helen Joubert Associates
Typeset by Avon DataSet Ltd, Bidford on Avon
Printed in Great Britain by TJ International
Trade distribution by Turnaround Publisher Services,
Unit 3, Olympia Trading Estate, Coburg Road,
London N22 6TZ

BAAF is the leading UK-wide membership
organisation for all those concerned with
adoption, fostering and child care issues.

Contents

Acknowledgements

The funding for this compendium was provided by the New Brunswick Adoption Foundation and the Donaldson Adoption Institute.

The chapters in this compendium were authored by staff members of the Donaldson Adoption Institute – Susan Livingston Smith, Dr Jeanne A Howard, Dr Martha Henry and Dr David Brodzinsky – with assistance from two attorneys – Meredith Tenison and Elizabeth Lyons – who wrote entries on court practices. The compendium was edited by Adam Pertman, President of the Adoption Institute. We also would like to thank a number of scholars and adoption professionals who helped with this effort, particularly Dr Julie Selwyn of the University of Bristol and Dr John Simmonds of the British Association for Adoption and Fostering, who provided copious input on the outlined topics as well as feedback on the initial draft. Sincere thanks, too, to Shaila Shah and BAAF for their indispensable role in making this important book a reality.

Others who provided extensive input or reviews include Bruce Boyer, Loyola University School of Law; Howard Davidson, American Bar Association Center on Children and the Law; Pat Fenton, adoption social worker, Toronto; Cheryl Fix, Alberta Ministry of Human Services, Child and Family Services Authority; Suzanne Kingston, New Brunswick Adoption Foundation; Kathy Ledesma, AdoptUSKids; Dr Gary Mallon, Hunter College; Dr Ruth McRoy, Boston College; and Sarah Pedersen, Adoption Council of Canada.

The Donaldson Adoption Institute is a unique think tank based in the US that is the pre-eminent research, policy and education organisation in its field. Its mission is to better the lives of everyone touched by adoption by providing leadership that improves laws, policies and practices through sound research, analysis, education and advocacy.
www.adoptioninstitute.org

Executive summary

Developed, industrialised countries have systems of care to address the needs of children who cannot safely grow up in their original families. In recent decades, some of these countries have established permanency as a priority for children in care who are not able to return home. This is particularly the case in the United States, England and Canada, where drifting in non-permanent care is viewed as antithetical to the best interests of children. Adoption and guardianship are types of alternative permanencies that are emphasised in these countries, and the number of adoptions from care, in particular, has grown over recent decades. Despite ongoing national campaigns and increased success rates, however, permanency is not being achieved for all the children who need this.

Every year, tens of thousands of older children and young people who have been in care in the US, England and Canada go out on their own without a permanent family. Though there have been remarkable increases in US foster care adoptions in the past 15 years, the percentage of young people exiting through emancipation has increased in recent years. The most recent annual report indicated that over 23,000 young people "aged out" in 2012 (US Department of Health and Human Services [DHHS], 2013). In England, over 6,900 young people who had been looked after at age 16 left care at 19 (Department for Education [DfE], 2013a), and thousands of others did so in Canada. England reports that at least one-third of those leaving care at 19 are not in education, training or employment. Studies in the US show that a high percentage of these young people will face extreme difficulties in adulthood as they struggle with poor educational attainment, insufficient employment and low income, inadequate housing, early parenthood, involvement with the criminal justice system, substance misuse, and physical and mental health problems (Courtney and Dworsky, 2006; Berzin, 2008; Courtney et al, 2010; Howard and Berzin, 2011).

These realities raise important questions:

- **Would these young people be better off if permanent adoptive or guardianship families could be found for them?**
- **What can governments and professionals do to offer the best prospects for finding a permanent family for young people who cannot return home?**

This volume seeks to answer these questions by examining child welfare research, policy and practice across England, the US and Canada. The introduction analyses the body of research underlying the value of permanency – that children need a consistent, nurturing family to promote optimal development and emotional security, not only when they are young but throughout their lives. It reviews solutions for children in care who cannot safely return home, including permanency with kin, adoption, guardianship and long-term foster care. Research comparing adoption to long-term care supports the following conclusions about adoption.

- It offers greater stability.
- It offers optimal potential for resilience, particularly if it begins when children are younger.
- It best promotes children's emotional security, sense of belonging and general well-being.
- It offers children a lifelong family and support to assist them in the transition to adulthood.

Some specific child welfare practices are particularly important for providing children with the greatest likelihood of achieving permanency through adoption or guardianship. This compendium describes 22 specific practices linked with success in finding permanent families for children, along with research and practice knowledge and key resources related to each practice. These practices are important throughout a child's journey through placement. Some minimise the trauma experienced by girls and boys in the child welfare system; others assist children in coping with life experiences and transitions, thus facilitating their adjustment and placement stability; and still other practices help to find families and enhance their ability to commit and be successful in permanently parenting these children.

Organisational practices set the stage for achieving permanency – from the explicit requirement in law and policy to find permanent families for children who cannot return home, to valuing permanency in all aspects of agency culture and operations, to providing essential training, support and supervision to workers. Research indicates that with special efforts, permanent families can be found for older children and young people with very complex special needs, even for teenagers in residential treatment centres (Avery, 2010). Yet if a worker views a child as "unadoptable", it is unlikely they will make significant efforts to achieve this goal (Avery, 2000). Child welfare organisations also need systems for monitoring permanency outcomes and for reinforcing accountability in achieving them at all levels of the system.

There also are practices that maximise children's likelihood of achieving permanency through adoption, extending from the time they enter care to the services provided to their families after adoption. Placements with relatives support children's well-being by minimising the trauma of separation from the original family. Placements with relatives are likely to be more stable, and these caregivers are good prospects for adoption or guardianship if the child is unable to return home. Aggressive *family finding* practices that maximise the use of relative placements are in the best interests of children's well-being and permanency. Also, using *concurrent planning* strategies facilitates placing children as early as possible with caregivers who are open to adopting them if they are unable to return home, thus minimising moves in care and interrupted attachments.

Other practices also serve to minimise the trauma that children experience in the child welfare system, thereby promoting their healthy adjustment and reducing obstacles to adoption. For example, the initial removal from the birth family and subsequent moves in care are often traumatic experiences, reinforcing children's feelings of vulnerability and powerlessness, and creating and compounding difficulties in establishing trusting attachment relationships. Strategies for minimising the trauma of moves and for supporting children through transitions that need to occur, including *life story work*, are critically important.

Involving children in permanency work is not only their right but also important for achieving successful permanency. Facilitating active participation in decision-making and planning, rather than leaving them to be passive recipients of information, benefits children by fostering self-determination, understanding and acceptance. In addition, determining and working to achieve the level of openness that is in a child's best interests helps to minimise traumatic loss and maximise continuity of relationship and identity in life.

A range of practices related to recruitment and retention of adoptive or guardianship families is important for achieving permanency for children. This compendium includes strategies for general, targeted and child-specific recruitment, including research on strategies linked with successful outcomes. Research also indicates that many prospective adoptive families are not retained even after application due to various obstacles within the system, so that retention – in addition to recruitment – is a target for needed reforms (Geen *et al*, 2004; McRoy, 2007).

Given the traumatic life experiences that most children in foster care have endured, a substantial proportion of them will continue to have ongoing adjustment issues that may intensify as they age. Preparing and supporting adoptive and guardianship families both before and after placement not only help to preserve and stabilise at-risk placements but also offer children and families the best opportunity for success. A continuum of adoption support and preservation services is needed to address the information, support and therapeutic needs of children and their families. The overall body of adoption research generally has linked receiving post-adoption services with more positive outcomes and unmet service needs with poorer outcomes (Barth and Berry, 1988; Groze, 1996; Leung and Erich, 2002; Reilly and Platz, 2004; Child Welfare Information Gateway [CWIG], 2012c).

Adoption provides a lifetime of benefits for children who cannot return to their families of origin, including the emotional security of caring adults and a committed family to ensure that their needs are met. Gaining a family for life not only transforms the futures of children in care, but also brings benefits to child welfare systems, governments and communities. For example, one US economist found that every dollar invested in the adoption of a child from care returns about three dollars in public and private benefits (Hansen, 2006). Adoption also delivers societal benefits once these children become adults, such as a reduced likelihood of their receiving public assistance, having criminal or substance abuse involvement or experiencing a range of other difficulties affecting individuals, their families and the communities in which they live. Child welfare systems across all jurisdictions need to regularly assess their performance in achieving permanency for the young people in their care and to search for ways to better meet their needs, including incorporating the practices described in this volume.

PART I

INTRODUCTION

Introduction

I was in a foster home for eight years so I was drawing that distinction between adoption and foster care. I didn't have that permanent family. If I had an adoptive family maybe things would have been different and I would have someone I could go to, to talk to, for certain things and I'd feel like I belonged somewhere and that I meant something to someone. Alisha Bowie

Permanency equals a sense of belonging. When it comes to permanency for youth in care, there's one simple fact: it's a basic human need that everyone should be entitled to. We should all know where we go at Christmas. Lisa Davis

The goal of permanency for those children in out-of-home care who cannot return to their original families has evolved in recent decades into a priority among some national child welfare systems. This goal is rooted in the belief that all children need a consistent, nurturing family to promote optimal development and emotional security, and these family connections are important in sustaining them throughout their lives. The introductory quotes from young people providing testimony to a Canadian parliamentary committee (HUMA Committee, 2012, p. 1) underscore the overwhelming and essential nature of belonging in a family – something most of us take for granted and can scarcely imagine being without.

Family Connections (Adoptions Unlimited, 2008),[1] a DVD made by older children and young people who were in foster care or adopted from care, poignantly captures the importance of family connections.

---

1 This DVD was developed for a federally funded Adoption Opportunities grant project and can be viewed in its entirety on the internet or ordered from Adoptions Unlimited in Chicago, Illinois.

One young man, Jeremy, who was still in care while he attended university, vividly described what it is like to go through life without a family:

> *I know that my friends who have families talk about how great it is to see their grandparents and their aunts and uncles. To have the ability to connect with my own family, I don't know how that would feel. I think I'm missing something, definitely. I always feel like there's something I'm missing out on. It's taxing to know that I have a family that I don't know. Yeah, I think it will continue to affect me – it's something I'll probably have to deal with my whole life.*

Jeremy's ties to his biological family had been severed, but no other permanent family had been found for him.

This report examines, from an international perspective, the concept of permanency for young people separated from their original family; it reviews what we have learned from research about the outcomes of various care options for these children, examines permanency policies and practices in several countries, and identifies practices that facilitate achieving permanency, through adoption or guardianship, for children in care.

International approaches to protecting children

Developed countries with advanced economies have systems to protect children whose welfare is challenged by maltreatment or their parents' inability to provide for basic needs. Gilbert's (1997) comparative analysis of child protection systems in the mid-1990s delineated two contrasting orientations of countries toward protecting children – the child protection and family service orientations. Primarily English-speaking or Anglo-American countries (England, the US and Canada) were oriented toward child protection. They viewed child abuse primarily as harm from "deviant" parents, requiring investigation in a legalistic and adversarial manner, and child placements were primarily without the parents' consent. In contrast, the continental European and Nordic countries approached child maltreatment from a *family service orientation* – that is, abuse was viewed as arising from family conflict or dysfunction due to social/psychological difficulties that needed to be addressed with help or support. In countries with a family service orientation, protecting children emphasised prevention, participation and family support, and most out-of-home placements were voluntary. In Sweden, for example, around 85 per cent of those entering care do so under voluntary arrangements agreed upon with parents (Thoburn, 2007).

There are obvious relationships between the societal safety net provided for families involving basic services – such as health care, family allowances, day care, maternity and parental leave and others – and the level of child poverty and maltreatment; that is particularly the case in relation to neglect, which is a primary reason that children come into care in Anglo-American countries. In comparing child welfare systems in 10 countries, the US has the lowest level of government spending on family policies, the lowest UNICEF ranking of child health and safety, and the highest rate of child maltreatment deaths (Gilbert *et al*, 2011). In the Scandinavian countries, where spending is higher on income maintenance, housing support, day care and health, the rate of young children entering care due to neglect is low.

In 2010, Gilbert and colleagues repeated a comparative analysis of child welfare systems, finding that their approaches to child welfare intervention had begun to converge (Gilbert *et al*, 2011; Gilbert, 2012). For example, in the US, the number of children receiving preventive services increased dramatically, and family support became more of a focus in England. Many (although not all) countries with a family service orientation introduced mandatory reporting of child abuse and adopted more stringent and compulsory child protection measures, leading to the conclusion that these 10 countries now have a blend of orientations. One other similarity among all countries except the US was that their rates of out-of-home placement had increased since the mid-1990s.[2] Generally, there was an expansion of

---

2 Some out-of-home placement figures in Table 1, particularly for Scandinavian countries, include not only child abuse cases but also children engaged in delinquency, criminal acts and substance abuse, or having mental illness.

these modern child welfare systems, with a broadening of their mandates and the numbers of families served. In the US, however, even though the number of children receiving preventive services multiplied five-fold from 1997 to 2007, the number in out-of-home care declined by 25 per cent (see Table 1).

Table 1
Children in out-of-home care per 1,000

	Time A		Time B	
US	8	(1997)	6	(2007)
Canada	4	(1991)	9.7	(2007)
England	4.5	(1994)	5.5	(2009)
Sweden	6	(2000)	6.6	(2007)
Finland	8	(1994)	12	(2007)
Denmark	9.5	(1993)	10.2	(2007)
Norway	5.8	(1994)	8.2	(2008)
Germany	9.5	(1995)	9.9	(2005)
Belgium	7.9	(2004)	8.6	(2008)
Netherlands	8.4	(2000)	10	(2009)

Source: Data drawn from Gilbert *et al*, 2011, p. 247

The primary reasons for the decline in the child welfare population in the US were: more adoptions; less time that young people stayed in care prior to achieving permanency; and an increased use of kinship care, sometimes as a diversion from formal placement (Gilbert, 2012). Conversely, the rise in out-of-home care rates for Canada and England was explained primarily by children staying in care for longer periods, not by greater numbers of children entering care. Beginning in 2008, however, after a scandal in England involving the death of Baby Peter Connolly, there was a small increase in the number of children entering care (DfE, 2013a). Also, in England and Canada, the proportion of children adopted from care was lower than in the US (Gilbert *et al*, 2011).

It is difficult to make some comparisons between child welfare systems since so many of the outcomes are embedded in contextual factors that vary significantly from one country to another. Just as countries vary in their approach to protecting children from maltreatment, they also differ in their views on how to address children's needs when they are not able to be safely reunited with their original families. Most countries use foster or residential care to meet the needs of these children; only a minimal number of children are adopted annually from the child welfare systems in most Nordic and European countries – for example, on average 15 a year in the Netherlands and 27 in 2007 in Norway (Gilbert *et al*, 2011). In contrast, as observed by child welfare researchers in England, 'The continuing commitment since the 1980s to adoption from care (or "special needs adoption" in the USA) as the preferred route to permanence outside of the birth family has over this period separated the USA, Canada and the UK from most of the rest of the developed world' (Schofield *et al*, 2012, p. 245). In the US, about seven of every 10,000 children in the general population are adopted from the child welfare system annually, whereas in England and Canada this number is about four per 10,000 (Gilbert *et al*, 2011).

What is in the best interests of children who cannot safely return to their families of origin?

The belief that permanency is in the best interests of children in care who cannot safely return to live with their original parents is a central tenet of child welfare reforms in Anglo-American countries. The primer of the permanency planning movement was a slim volume by Goldstein and colleagues (1973) – *Beyond the Best Interests of the Child*. This work, and a subsequent one by the same authors, *Before the Best Interests of the Child* (1979), confirm the sanctity of the parent–child bond and the reality that the state should only intervene in the most serious circumstances, but it advances principles that should be followed when a state does intervene to assure the best interests of the child, including that:

- placement decisions should safeguard the child's need for continuity of relationships;

- placement decisions should reflect the child's sense of time;
- placement decisions should utilise the least detrimental alternative or the least restrictive setting for safeguarding the child's development;
- children should have full-party status in decision-making and the right to be represented by counsel; and
- the child's welfare should be the paramount consideration.

The permanency planning movement, with a focus on adoption as a primary alternative to remaining in care (when children could not safely return to their families of origin), became established in the US and England around the same time in the 1970s; it arose out of the recognition that many children were remaining in "temporary" circumstances for long periods and that "drifting" in care had harmful effects on them (Rowe and Lambert, 1973; Fanshel, 1976, 1978). For example, in Fanshel's study of children in foster care in New York City, 36 per cent were still in care five years after their initial placements, and those who were emancipated from care when older had been in care close to 10 years, on average. Over the past three decades, child welfare systems in the US, England and Canada have instituted changes in laws, policies and practices aimed at achieving permanency for these children, although they differ somewhat in the types of permanency alternatives that are considered and emphasised. (Adoption law and policy are becoming increasingly divergent in each of the four countries comprising the UK, and the focus here is England.)

In *England*, the Children Act 1989 established the welfare of the child as paramount. It sought to encourage local authorities to partner with parents, consult with children and keep them all informed. The Looked after Children system was developed as an assessment, care-planning and review process that was embedded in an ecological perspective. The principles and many procedures of this system have been exported to other countries, including Canada (Thomas, 2011). During the 1990s, government inspections of local authorities revealed very variable approaches to using adoption; the Adoption and Children Act 2002 sought to ensure that adoption was considered early and delays minimised (Monck *et al*, 2004). When the court issues a care order, the local authority assumes primary parental responsibility, the birth parents retain some parental rights and the court approves a plan for permanence. That plan can aim to reunify the child with the parent or place him/her with a relative or in long-term foster care; these placements can ultimately be secured by a legal order such as a Residence or Special Guardianship Order. Where the local authority plan is adoption and the court makes a Placement Order, the child will leave care once the final Adoption Order is granted. Adoption is considered primarily for children under the age of five, many of whom have special needs (Schofield and Simmonds, 2009; Schofield *et al*, 2012).

The *United States* has enacted a series of successful legislative reforms promoting adoptions from foster care, leading the number to more than triple since the late 1980s. The Adoption Assistance and Child Welfare Act of 1980 sought to limit foster care drift by requiring the court to determine the child's future status within 18 months of initial placement, establishing a hierarchy of preferred outcomes – reunification, adoption, guardianship and long-term foster care – and offering subsidies in an adoption assistance programme. The Adoption and Safe Families Act of 1997 (ASFA) accelerated permanent placements by requiring states to initiate court action to free children for adoption after they have waited in care for 15 of the previous 22 months, allowing children in extreme cases to be freed more quickly, and providing adoption incentive payments to states for increasing adoptions from care. It also required states to develop permanency plans – which could no longer include "long-term foster care" – for children within 12 months of their entering care. The Fostering Connections to Success and Increasing Adoptions Act of 2008 provided funding for a broader range of permanency options, including subsidised guardianship, as well as more consistent federal funding for adoption subsidies (Barth and Berry, 1987; CWIG, 2011a).

Canada's child welfare system is made up of 13 separate jurisdictions, and there are no federal child welfare policies or official, nationally collected statistics. Periodically, national studies are issued that collect detailed provincial information, such as the Canadian Incidence Study in 2003; however, there are no national statistics on the number of waiting children or of adoptions, only estimates. Each jurisdiction sets its own child welfare policies, although they are guided by principles such as a primary focus on the best interests of the child, intervening in the least intrusive ways and mandating citizens to report child maltreatment (Swift, 2011). Canada's Waiting Kids website (2012a) reports an estimated 78,000 children in out-of-home care in that country, and it is estimated that only about 2,000 children are adopted each year from the public care system (HUMA Committee, 2012).

Research comparing outcomes of adoption and other forms of care

It is important for child welfare professionals and policy-makers to have a true understanding of the outcomes of adoption and other care arrangements, as evidenced by research, so that they can use this knowledge to inform policy and practice. The most substantial studies examining adoption outcomes in relation to other types of care are reviewed briefly below. Two rigorous studies comparing outcomes from different forms of substitute care originated in Sweden, where national data are readily available on a range of variables.

Bohman and Sigvardsson's longitudinal Swedish study

These two researchers studied a group of children (around 600 who were registered before or after birth with a Stockholm adoption agency in the mid-1950s). Ultimately, 168 were adopted as infants, 208 were returned to their birth mothers, and 203 were in long-term foster care. They were followed up at ages 11, 15, 18 (boys only) and 23. At ages 11 and 15, teachers and parents were interviewed, while the data at age 18 involved IQ tests for military registration and, at age 23, the percentage showing up on criminal or drug abuse registries. At age 11, a significantly higher percentage of children in all three study samples were rated as "problem children" than among the controls (classmates); however, by age 15, the differences between adopted boys and girls and their classmates had disappeared, whereas the reunified and fostered groups contained two to three times more children receiving maladjustment ratings than those in the control groups. At age 18, adopted males did not differ significantly from controls on IQ, whereas the other two study groups scored significantly lower. At age 23, there were not significantly more adopted young people on the criminal and drug abuse registries; however, there were twice as many from the fostered groups, compared with their peers (Bohman and Sigvardsson, 1990).

Swedish national cohort study

Vinnerljung and Hjern (2011) used data from 10 national registers to follow children born from 1972–1981 who entered out-of-home care before age seven; they compared 899 who were adopted by age seven (mean time in care = 1.6 years) to 3,062 who grew up in foster care (mean time in care = 15.7 years). Children in the general population served as an additional comparison group. Negative outcomes were far more common for those in long-term foster care than for the adopted group or the general population. For all outcomes, the adoptees fell between the ex-foster young people and their peers in the general population. For example, cognitive test scores at military conscription for adopted males were the equivalent of five IQ points lower than the national comparison group, but the disparity between ex-fostered males and the national group was twice that size. A regression analysis controlled for birth mother's education, birth parent risk indicators, and age at entry into out-of-home care. When compared with adoptees, those who had been in foster care had a 60 per cent higher risk of having only a primary school education by age 26 and a 60 per cent lower likelihood of graduating from university. They also had lower grades in school and were 2.4 times more likely to have received social welfare by age 25. The authors concluded: 'These results provide additional support for the wisdom of the US and UK child welfare policy with adoption as an important component of permanency planning … results can be used as arguments for reconsidering adoption – with or without parental consent – as an optional intervention for pre-school age children that otherwise will grow up as wards of public care' (p. 1909).

Triseliotis's Scottish study and review

John Triseliotis (1980, 1983) conducted in-depth follow-up studies of 44 adopted children (placed with their parents between the ages of three and seven, originally perceived as "at risk," so placements were delayed) and 40 who grew up in long-term foster care (average 11 years, with same foster parents). In interviews with these individuals as young adults, Triseliotis asked them to rate the quality of their childhood experiences in growing up adopted or fostered; he found that only nine per cent of adoptees rated their experiences as poor or very poor, compared to 25 per cent of those fostered. For ratings of current closeness to their adoptive or foster parents, 27 per cent of fostered and only two per cent of those adopted reported "poor or very poor". On measures of competence, adopted individuals obtained higher educational achievement, more secure and skilled jobs, and better housing than did the fostered group.

Triseliotis (2002) also conducted an in-depth review of research on outcomes of long-term foster care and adoption for children in care. When combining results from many studies, he found an overall breakdown rate (disruption) of around 43 per cent for those in long-term foster homes at 2–5 years post-placement as compared with around 19 per cent for adoptive placements, 2–8 years post-placement. He also cited a more recent study of British foster placements, reporting that only six per cent of the young people were in the same placement for six years or more (Sinclair *et al*, 2000). Referring to his own research, Triseliotis perceived more of a safety net for adopted individuals as they transitioned to adulthood, in that one-third of the fostered young people had lost all contact with their caregivers, whereas adoptees who had fallen out with their parents did not sever contact altogether. He reported: 'The main defining difference found between these two forms of substitute parenting appears to be the higher levels of emotional security, sense of belonging and general well-being expressed by those growing up as adopted compared with those fostered long term' (p. 23).

British studies comparing adoption and long-term foster care

Through analysis of data on 374 children, surveys of caregivers and social workers for close to 200 children in foster care in 1998/99, and interviews with a subset of children and caregivers, researchers at the University of York sought to assess the success of three types of placement in providing permanence and positive adjustment outcomes for children (Biehal *et al*, 2009). The foster care population was separated into a stable group who had remained in long-term foster placements (n = 120) and an unstable group who had left foster placements after living in them for three or more years (n = 86). (The remaining children had reunified with birth parents or had Residence Orders.) Among the group of 135 children who were placed for adoption or were adopted, 13 per cent had experienced an adoption disruption at some point in their lives, so that stability for those in long-term foster care (where 42% experienced disruption) was much less than for adoption. Scores on a standardised measure of emotional and behavioural problems were available for 38 per cent of children, with the unstable foster care group scoring significantly worse than the others. Children who were in stable placements were more likely to have entered them at younger ages, underscoring the importance of timely planning to give children the best chance of success.

Selwyn and Quinton (2004) followed 130 British children with a goal of adoption, comparing those placed for adoption with those who ended up in long-term foster care. In their initial report on this study, they concluded: 'There were many similarities in the experience of offering an adoptive or foster home to the young people, but some key differences were in the stability of placements, the amount of autonomy the adoptive parents/carers had, and their views of how close they were to the child and their assessment of the child's closeness to them' (p. 6). They observed that there was a link between the security of adoption felt by the caregivers and the children and their ability to commit wholly to the relationship. Of 96 adoptive placements, 17 per cent were not intact 6–11 years later, and of the children ending up in long-term foster care, 46 per cent disrupted (Quinton and Selwyn, 2009). Overall, studies find a lower rate of breakdown in adoptive placements than in other types of permanency.

National Survey of Child and Adolescent Well-Being
Using data from this nationally representative longitudinal study of children receiving child welfare services in the US, Lloyd and Barth (2011) analysed the developmental outcomes of 353 children who were less than 13 months old when they entered care. Data, including seven standardised measures, were collected at baseline and at 18-, 36- and 66-month follow-ups. Outcomes were compared for three groups – 191 who were adopted, 63 who returned to birth homes and 99 who were still in foster care – on child developmental measures and the HOME (Home Observation for the Measurement of the Environment) scales assessing the quality of the parenting environment. Both the bivariate and multivariate analyses clearly indicated that the children's development at ages 6–7 was influenced by their long-term child welfare placement; this was particularly salient given that the children in care had been in their current placements for 4.3 years, on average, yet had the poorest developmental outcomes on all measures except adaptive behaviour. The children who had returned home had less responsive parents and greater poverty but more positive developmental outcomes than those still in foster care. The adopted children, despite having the highest percentage (79%) assessed as high risk for neurodevelopmental problems soon after entry into care, had the highest developmental achievement overall, and their parents scored significantly better on most HOME scales than did both birth and foster parents. The authors concluded: 'Results support the longstanding tenet of child welfare services policy that remaining in foster care is less developmentally advantageous than having a more permanent arrangement of return home or adoption' (p. 1383).

If a child cannot be safely reunited with his or her original family, the body of research supports the following conclusions related to the benefits of adoption.

Adoption offers greater stability than other permanency alternatives. Any type of placement, including reunification, can result in failure or impermanency. Several US studies indicate that around 30 per cent of children who are reunified with their parents eventually return to foster care (Berrick, 2009). In England, one study found that nearly half of reunifications had broken down within two years (Farmer and Lutman, 2010), while another reported 59 per cent of reunified children returned to care at least once within four years (Wade *et al*, 2010).

Studies across the United States and England show a lower breakdown rate for adoptions than for long-term foster care. In the US, adoption breakdown is described as "disruption" before placements are legally finalised and "dissolution" when a legal termination of the formal adoption occurs. Studies of large child welfare populations in the 1980s generally reported disruption rates of 10 to 15 per cent (Urban Systems Research and Engineering, 1985; Festinger, 1986; Barth and Berry, 1988). Since 1990, most US studies show overall ranges of adoption disruption from about six to 11 per cent (Coakley and Berrick, 2008). The most recent large-scale study conducted in Illinois of almost 16,000 adoptive placements found an overall disruption rate of 9.5 per cent, with another 3.6 per cent awaiting finalisation (Smith *et al*, 2006).

British studies of adoption breakdown do not distinguish between disruption and dissolution, and most report slightly higher long-term failure rates. For example, the study discussed above by Quinton and Selwyn (2009) reported a failure rate of 17 per cent six to 11 years later, but a 46 per cent failure rate for long-term foster care placements. In another study, the mean rate of disruption for placements made by 34 local authorities in the previous three years was four per cent (Dance *et al*, 2010). This somewhat higher disruption rate may be due to a higher proportion of new matched adoptions (with strangers rather than previous caregivers) in England than in the US.

Very little research exists on adoption dissolution or on post-adoption placement into foster care or residential treatment. Festinger (2002) reported that 3.3 per cent of 516 adopted children in New York had been in foster care or other out-of-home placements within four years of their adoption; however, many if not most of these children were expected to return home. Also, Festinger and Maza (2009) used Financial Year (FY) 2005 AFCARS data (Adoption and Foster Care Analysis and Reporting System) to analyse the outcomes of 3,166 previously adopted children (from any type of adoption) who had entered care and were exiting that year (comprised 1% of those leaving care). For this group, most young people (59%) were reunited with adoptive parents and the rest were dissolutions, of whom 88 per cent were re-adopted.

The reality that adoption is linked with family stability and perm-anence to a much greater degree than continuing in foster care is poignantly illustrated by a DVD made by the Adoption Council of Ontario Youth Network (2011), which can be viewed on the internet.[3] Ten young people, holding up signs with numbers, take turns stating: 'It's not how many pieces of gum I chew . . . this is not how many pages of homework I have' and other similar comments, followed by this statement from all of them: 'It's how many times I've changed families', averaging about seven per child. At the conclusion, they all hold up cards with the number "0" saying: 'This is the number of new families I've had since I was adopted.'

Adoption offers children optimal potential for resilience, particularly if it occurs when they are younger. Most children adopted from care have elevated risks for developmental, emotional or behavioural challenges due to adverse experiences in their early lives; these range from unhealthy prenatal environments, such as exposure to toxic substances, to abuse or neglect, to multiple placements and other emotional conflicts related to loss and identity issues. Adoption clearly benefits children who otherwise would likely grow up in less stable or nurturing situations. As a group, adopted children from higher-risk early environments are resilient and make rapid gains in their adoptive

---

3 www.youtube.com/watch?u=c4+N3i_Drgsadoptontario.ca/Public/Default. aspx?l=165andn=Youth+Network

families. Indeed, research indicates that the majority of young people adopted from care are in the normal range on standardised measures of behavioural/emotional functioning, and well over 90 per cent of parents are satisfied with their adoptions (Rosenthal and Groze, 1992, 1994; Howard and Smith, 2003; Howard *et al*, 2004; Dance and Rushton, 2005; Simmel *et al*, 2007).

The negative impact of earlier experiences, however, does not disappear with adoption, and some young people continue to struggle with ongoing challenges throughout childhood. Research indicates that cumulative trauma experiences are associated with greater complexity and severity of symptoms (Briere *et al*, 2008); many of the behavioural symptoms of adopted children who are seen in mental health settings stem from the effects of trauma (Berry and Barth, 1989; Rosenthal and Groze, 1994; Simmel *et al*, 2001; Howard and Smith, 2003; Simmel, 2007). The physiological consequences of maltreatment also involve changes in the neurochemistry and physiology of the brain, as well as deficits in some brain functions (Perry, 1998; Lansdown *et al*, 2007), and recovery potential in the neural systems is greatest when children are very young (Fisher and Gunnar, 2010). Lloyd and Barth's study (2011, reviewed above) of the development of at-risk infants in three types of placements underscores the superior parenting of adoptive parents and developmental recovery of children who had achieved permanency, particularly through adoption.

Children's best prospects for maximising their recovery from early trauma, deprivation or other maltreatment, and for realising their developmental potential, come from living in adoptive families that provide a healing environment and remain committed to them in the face of challenges. Furthermore, research generally finds better outcomes for children placed for adoption at earlier ages and with fewer moves in care (Festinger, 1986; Barth and Berry, 1988; McRoy, 1999; Howard and Smith, 2003; Simmel, 2007). In all families, good parent–child relationships promote positive outcomes for children, but this is particularly true for children coming from high-risk situations, when parental sensitivity and responsiveness are critical for fostering a healing environment. Research on adoptive families establishes the importance of specific positive parenting qualities and the impact that these have on helping children to overcome early adversity (Steele *et al*, 2003; Kaniuk *et al*, 2004; Smith-McKeever, 2005; Simmel, 2007).

Adoption best promotes children's emotional security, sense of belonging and general well-being. One of the most harmful aspects of entering foster care is the lack of continuity in caregivers, which undermines children's ability to develop a secure attachment and a sense of emotional security. Studies find that foster placement instability has more of a negative impact on children than the single event of removal from original family and placement into foster care (Ryan and Testa, 2005; Lewis *et al*, 2007). Foster care instability predicts an increase and intensification of behaviour problems and other developmental deficits, increased usage of and costs for mental health services, pervasive and ambiguous loss, and development of internal barriers to closeness, such as distancing behaviours and distrust (Rubin *et al*, 2004, 2007; Lawrence *et al*, 2006; Samuels, 2008).

For foster children who are subsequently adopted, multiple moves in care prior to adoptive placement are linked to adoption instability and greater likelihood of adjustment problems (Festinger, 1986; Barth and Berry, 1988; McRoy, 1999; Howard and Smith, 2003; Simmel, 2007). While adoption does not automatically lead to emotional security and well-being, studies reviewed for this compendium found that young people in adoptive families are more likely to report feeling a sense of belonging and closeness to parents than are those who remain in care (Triseliotis, 2002; Selwyn and Quinton, 2004).

Adoption offers children support to assist them in the transition to adulthood and a lifelong family. Over the past few decades, the time between adolescence and independent adulthood has lengthened as young adults take longer to complete their education, become established in careers and repay university loans, and get married and have children. A significant minority of young people who were adopted from care or who aged out of care have serious learning or developmental challenges, which means they are not ready for independence at age 18 or soon thereafter, and need help to transition to adulthood. We know that young people who leave foster care often face difficulties in early adulthood as they struggle with poor educational attainment, insufficient employment and low income, inadequate housing, early parenthood, involvement with the criminal justice system, substance abuse, and physical and mental health problems (Courtney and Dworsky, 2006; Berzin, 2008; Courtney *et al*, 2010). For many, there is no dependable adult to serve as a safety net, such as the example of a former fostered young person who was filling out a job application and was asked to give an emergency contact person: 'He wrote 911. He had no one else' (Holtan, 2004, p. 35).

Research and experience teach us that permanent, emotionally sustaining and committed relationships with adults are imperative for young people to reach self-sufficiency and to thrive in early adulthood. The body of research reviewed earlier indicates that adopted young people are more likely to have sustaining parental relationships and also attain more positive outcomes (education, employment and self-support) in adulthood than do their counterparts in long-term foster care (Triseliotis, 1980, 1983, 2002). Furthermore, family connections beyond age 18 count for a lot more than a financial safety net; a family for life means sustained emotional support and belonging, a home to return to on holidays, siblings who typically are the longest relationships sustained in their lifetimes, parents to consult on difficult decisions, grandparents and aunts and uncles for children, and a secure sense of belonging.

Use of a range of permanency options in England, the US and Canada

Before focusing on the range of placement alternatives used to meet the permanency needs of children in care, we first need to focus on the meaning of permanency. The guidance and regulations on care planning in England state: 'Permanence is the framework of emotional permanence (attachment), physical permanence (stability) and legal permanence (the carer has parental responsibility for the child) which gives a child a sense of security, continuity, commitment and identity'

(Butler and Hickman, 2011, p. 128). A comprehensive definition of permanence developed by Casey Family Services (2007) in the US asserts that achieving "permanence" means having an enduring family relationship that:

- *is safe and meant to last a lifetime;*
- *offers the legal rights and social status of full family membership;*
- *provides for physical, emotional, social, cognitive, and spiritual well-being; and*
- *assures lifelong connections to extended family, siblings, other significant adults, family history and traditions, race and ethnic heritage, culture, religion, and language . . . In achieving permanency outcomes, the objective is the optimal balance of physical, emotional/relational, legal, and cultural dimensions of permanence within every child's and youth's array of relationships'* (p. 3).

Using this definition, permanency means a family for life. As we consider each alternative form of permanency, we need to assess to what extent it provides these elements.

When birth parents are provided with a range of services and resources but are still unable to adequately care for their children, then the objective is to move these children from foster care into permanent families. The three countries that are the focus of this compendium approach this objective somewhat differently, although children attaining permanency or remaining in care reside in the same types of placements. These include placements with relatives, adoption, guardianship, ongoing foster care with stability as the ideal, and residential care for those who require it. This compendium explores variations in the use of these permanency alternatives and examines research regarding their benefits and limitations.

Permanency with relatives

The use of kinship care has increased in recent years, particularly in the US, where over one-third (37%) of foster families are relatives (28% of all placements), 30 per cent of adoptions are by relatives and an additional number of young people exiting care go into guardianships with relatives or are discharged from care to live with them (USDHHS, 2013). There is considerable variation among states, however, in their reliance on kinship care for state-supported foster placements, ranging from six to 46 per cent (Annie E Casey Foundation [AECF], 2012). The Family Connections Act requires states to make good-faith efforts to locate and inform relatives as soon as possible after a child enters care, and to consider relatives as resources for placement. This is particularly important since relatives are more likely to adopt or become guardians of older children and young people. While some professionals may harbour a negative bias towards utilising relatives, these caregivers compare favourably to non-relatives on many factors, including the quality of parenting and their neighbourhoods (measured by a Community Environment Scale) (USDHHS, 2010).

It is important to recognise that most children cared for by relatives are not part of the child welfare system – only four per cent in the US and five per cent in England (AECF, 2012; Selwyn and Nandy, 2012). Formal foster or adoptive placements with relatives are used less often in England; according to the most recent statistics, ending March 2013, 14 per cent of foster placements were with relatives or friends – or 11 per cent of total out-of-home placements (DfE, 2013a). The proportion of adoptions or "special guardianships" with relatives is not reported in England's national statistics; however, a study of the first two years of implementation of special guardianships in eight local authorities reported that 86 per cent were with relatives (Wade *et al*, 2010).

Kinship care, both within and outside of the child welfare system, is increasing in Canada, but specific data on these placements are not available nationally (Swift, 2011). Some Canadian provinces or territories, such as British Columbia, use a "kith and kin" arrangement for aboriginal children. This is described as 'a written agreement between a social worker and a child's extended family member or other person known to the child, to care for and financially support the child's living arrangement. The child is not under government care and the parent remains the legal guardian. The parent agrees to this arrangement and is involved in the child's care plan' (Federation of BC Youth in Care Networks [FBCYICN], 2010, p. 10). Kinship care is preferred among many Canadian child welfare systems and is heavily used; for example, a study contrasting kin and non-kin care in Ontario reported that over 30 per cent of placements studied were with relatives. Ontario uses two types of such placements: "kin service" placements, which undergo an assessment, but the standard of approval is lower and they do not typically receive financial support; and "kin care" homes, which meet the same standards as other foster homes and are eligible for financial and other supports (Perry *et al*, 2012).

Many studies find that kinship placements are much more stable than others (Barth *et al*, 1994; Testa, 1997; Koh, 2010). For example, a Canadian study found non-relative placements were four times more likely to end within the first month, while kinship placements continued to remain more stable long term (Perry *et al*, 2012). In Ontario, "kin" is defined broadly to include friends and members of the child's community, but placements with unrelated "kin" were not as stable as relative placements. A British meta-analysis of factors associated with outcomes for looked after children reviewed 92 studies, finding that kinship placements were linked not only to greater placement stability, but also to fewer total placements, fewer emotional and behavioural problems and less mental health service usage (Jones *et al*, 2011). A US study found that, even after controlling for baseline risk and placement stability, children initially assigned to kinship care had fewer behaviour problems than those in other kinds of foster care or those moved to kinship care after significant time in other foster homes (Rubin *et al*, 2008).[4]

Studies have also found that most relatives will consider adoption when they are properly informed and supported (Testa *et al*, 1996; Testa, 2001; Geen, 2003). Indeed, relatives – who often had been ignored or deliberately excluded – have been the major source of new adoptive homes since the implementation of the Adoption and Safe

---

4   For a comprehensive review of research on kinship care, see Winokur *et al*, 2009.

Families Act in 1997, accounting for dramatic increases in adoptions of children from care (Testa, 2004). For example, 16 per cent of adoptions were by relatives in 1998, doubling to 32 per cent by fiscal year 2009 (USDHHS, 2013). A study matching kin and non-kin samples on a number of factors, and including subsidised guardianship as a permanency outcome, found that kinship placements were as likely to result in permanency as non-kinship placements (Koh and Testa, 2008). Another benefit of kinship adoption is that disruptions or dissolutions are less common; for example, one study found 35 per cent less likelihood of kinship adoptions failing than other types (Fuller *et al*, 2006).

Kin caregivers (whether foster, adoptive or guardians) are older, poorer and less educated than their non-kin peers, and they are disproportionately single and African American (Needell and Gilbert, 1997; USDHHS, 2000; AECF, 2012). Relatives are particularly important resources for older African American young people; Maza (2006) found 64 per cent of adoptions of these children aged 9–17 were by unmarried female relatives. In addition, kin were more likely to have adopted more children, so their limited incomes had to support more people. The economic disadvantage of many kin adopters is exacerbated by some states' policies of providing lower subsidies to relatives than to other adoptive parents.

Adoption or guardianship by relatives appears to benefit children, and it also seems to be good for the adults as well, i.e., when relatives adopt from foster care, they report a higher level of satisfaction and better child outcomes than do other adopters (Howard and Smith, 2003; Fuller *et al*, 2006; Ryan *et al*, 2010). A more recent study of nearly 1,700 adoptive families also found positive outcomes in kin adoptions. While relatives were less positive about the adoption's effect on the family overall, they were more likely to report that they would adopt the child again given what they now know, to be satisfied with the overall adoption, and to report a positive relationship with the child (Ryan *et al*, 2010). Another advantage is that children adopted by relatives are more likely to have ongoing relationships with siblings and birth parents. Howard and Smith (2003) found that the majority of children adopted by relatives (64%) had contact with birth parents more than once a year. This was rare in foster (13%) and matched (9%) adoptions. Kin-adopted children were also more than twice as likely as those in other types of adoptive families to have contact with their siblings.

Adoption

The most common type of adoption today in the United States, England and Canada is of children placed from their child welfare systems. In the US this number has soared since ASFA was passed and federal adoption incentives to the states were implemented in the late 1990s – increasing from about 15,000 in 1988 to 31,030 in 1997 and peaking at 57,466 in FY2009. The most recent figure is 52,039 for FY2012. In the 10 fiscal years preceding ASFA (1988–1997), about 211,000 children were adopted from care (Maza, 2008); in the most recent 10 years (FY2003–2012), 524,891 adoptions were reported – roughly two-and-a-half times as many. According to the most recent statistics, 30 per cent of the adoptions were by relatives, another 56 per cent were by foster parents, and 14 per cent were by new or matched adopters (USDHHS, 2013).

Despite increases in the number of children adopted from care in the US, there is one area in which real progress has not been made: reducing the number of young people who leave foster care each year without a permanent family. On average, just under 28,000 young people were emancipated from care each year, peaking at 29,730 in FY2007. The percentage of young people being emancipated grew steadily, from seven per cent in FY1998 to 11 per cent in FY 2011, though it dropped to 10 per cent in FY2012 (USDHHS, 2012).

In 1998, the UK government took measures to increase the use of adoption, and a subsequent Prime Minister's report highlighted that over half of adopted children had entered care under 12 months of age but were not adopted until several years later (Performance and Innovation Unit, 2000). Parliament established a goal to increase adoptions by 40 per cent in 2004/05 and by 50 per cent in 2006. The number of children adopted from care rose from 2,200 in 1998/09 to

3,770 in 2005, more than meeting the target set; the numbers slowly declined after 2006, however, to 3,050 in 2011. The most recent national data showed 3,980 adoptions in the year ending March 2013, and 10.4 per cent of adoptions from care in England were by foster carers (DfE, 2013). The explanation for the decline in the number of adoptions after 2006 has been hypothesised as systemic inertia, severe delays in the court system, and the introduction of Special Guardianship orders (Selwyn and Sturgess, 2002; Selwyn et al, 2006a).

Canada's Waiting Kids website reports that 22,000 of the more than 78,000 children in government care are waiting for adoption, and a parliamentary committee report estimated that approximately 2,000 children are adopted each year from care (HUMA Committee, 2012). Some provinces report data on their own child welfare populations – British Columbia reported 294 adoptions in 2008 (16.6% of waiting children); Alberta reported 298 adoptions in 2007–08; Ontario reported adoptions for about one-third of the estimated 2,500 children needing adoption in 2009–10 (Swift, 2011).

One interesting difference between these three countries is the proportion of adoptions that are from other nations, with Canada having a much larger proportion of total adoptions from outside its borders. The latest intercountry adoption statistics reported for 2012 are 120 for the UK, 1,367 for Canada, and 8,668 for the US (Selman, 2013). The number of children adopted from care in England and the US is five to 13 times greater than the number of intercountry adoptions, whereas in Canada the number of intercountry and child welfare adoptions are very similar. The table below reports the most recent statistics on adoptions from care in the three countries (HUMA Committee, 2012; DfE, 2013; Canada's Waiting Kids, 2013; USDHHS, 2013).

Table 2
Adoptions from care

	# in care	# adopted	% of total	% of exits	Mean age
England	68,190	3,980	5.8%	14.0%	3.8 yrs
US	399,546	52,039	13.0%	21.5%	6.3 yrs
Canada	78,000	2,000 (est.)	2.6%		

Factors linked with likelihood of adoption

Considerable research has examined the factors linked with the achievement of completed adoptions for children in care, and the most consistent one across all studies is the younger age of the child (Barth, 1997; Snowden *et al*, 2008; Akin, 2011). Other child-related factors linked with increasing the likelihood of a child in care being adopted include: being white, having no diagnosed mental health problem, having a physical disability, no sexual abuse history, an intact sibling group, early placement stability, and fewer moves in care (Barth, 1997; Smith, 2003; Snowden *et al*, 2008; Akin, 2011).

The older a child at care entry and the longer a child remains in care, the less likelihood that he or she will be adopted (Barth, 1997; Selwyn *et al*, 2006a; Snowden *et al*, 2008). Some of the time on this ticking clock is caused by organisational factors, such as changes in workers or placements; for example, a US study of foster care drift after termination of parental rights (Cushing and Greenblatt, 2009) found that for each year a child spent in foster care after termination of parental rights, the likelihood of adoption was reduced by 80 per cent, and children who experienced a change in case worker after termination of parental rights were 44 per cent less likely to be adopted. This study also found that rejection of the foster home as an adoption resource decreased the likelihood of adoption by 66 per cent, and foster parent ambivalence about adopting reduced the odds by 52 per cent.

An English study of 130 children with a goal of adoption found that delay was a major factor in whether adoptions actually took place, particularly delayed decision-making prior to entry into care (identified for 68% of children) and the length of time between entering care and the adoption recommendation. For example, the odds against adoption increased 1.7 fold for each additional year of age on entry into care (Selwyn *et al*, 2006a). For this sample of children, 79 per cent had been referred before 12 months of age and most came from very vulnerable families who were well known to social services; however, most did not enter care for longer than a six-week period until after the age of three, during which time they experienced multiple forms of maltreatment and multiple caregivers. After care entry, there were additional delays in planning, legal hold-ups, further required assessments, professional disagreements and other delays. The authors concluded:

Overall the study highlighted that delay in decision-making and action has an unacceptable price in terms of the reduction in children's life chances and the financial costs to Local Authorities, the emotional and financial burden later placed on adoptive families and future costs to society. (p. 575)

Other child-related factors that shape adoption outcomes include the internal barriers that young people may have related to gaining a new, permanent family and their involvement in planning for their own futures. Child welfare policy and practice in England gives special respect to the voices of children in permanency planning; a study in one English local authority found that children and young people were present at 62 per cent of reviews and planning meetings (Thomas and O'Kane, 1999). In the US, nearly all states require that older children and young people give consent to their adoptions, with 25 states setting the age of consent at 14; 18 states at age 12; and six states at age 10. In 16 states, courts can decide to dispense with children's consent if it is deemed in the latter's best interests (CWIG, 2010b). Sometimes workers have taken a child's "no" to adoption as a permanent barrier; however, as discussed in Chapter 16 of this volume, such ambivalence needs to be explored and revisited.

The availability and amount of financial subsidies is another predictor of the likelihood of a child in foster care being adopted (Barth *et al*, 2003; Dalberth *et al*, 2005; Children's Rights, 2006; Hansen and Hansen, 2006; Hansen, 2007). Hansen and Hansen (2006) found that the amount of the assistance payment was the most important determinant of such adoptions, and a British study found that availability of financial and post-adoption support is linked to foster carers' willingness to adopt (Kirton *et al*, 2006). The lack of post-adoption services was identified by both agency staff and adoptive parents as a barrier to adoption from foster care in McRoy's study (2007), with 43 per cent of parents responding to a survey reporting that this represented a major barrier for them.

Finally, broader, contextual aspects of the child welfare system itself influence children's likelihood of adoption, including the specific locality in which they reside. For example, one US study found that the state had an impact on adoption rates when controlling for child and family variables (Snowden *et al*, 2008). Another study showed that across a specific state, the child's district of residence was the single most important predictor of successfully exiting to permanency, with geography accounting for a seven-fold difference in the rate of successful permanency (Becker *et al*, 2007). Significant variations identified in local authority rates of adoption in England have resulted in the introduction of adoption "scorecards". These measure a number of key indicators in a local authority's performance and compare them to overall national rates. A news story on this initiative reported that, 'Children in some areas spend more than twice as long in care as those in others and in one corner of London the difference can be up to 15 months depending on what side of a street they live on' (Bingham, 11 May 2012).

Guardianship

In many cases, guardianship is a more achievable permanency alternative than adoption, particularly if there is a provision for financial support, such as subsidised guardianship in the US or special guardianship in England and Wales. Guardianship creates a legal relationship between a child in care and a designated adult (usually, but not necessarily, a relative). This judicially created relationship is intended to be permanent and may offer financial and other support similar to that for adopting from care. The child gains permanency and security, and the child welfare system reduces its caseload and oversight obligations. Other benefits of this form of permanency are that guardianship:

- does not require termination of parental rights or the extended time period required to accomplish termination;
- provides for permanency when reunification is not safe, but there is insufficient basis to meet the evidentiary standard to terminate rights (Testa, 2004);
- honours the wishes of children who do not want to irrevocably break legal ties to their first/birth parents through being adopted;
- respects the cultures of groups such as African Americans, Native Americans, or First Nations peoples with traditions of extended family involvement in child rearing;
- reduces conflict and pain within the family of having one member declared as an unfit parent while another relative assumes the parental role;
- gives guardians legal decision-making authority for children;
- offers more flexibility than adoption – for instance, if parental circumstances improve, they can be reinstated as the legal parent.

Guardianship orders do have limitations. For instance, they provide less protection against further litigation than do adoptions, which confer full parental rights on the new parent; guardianship also expires when the child reaches 18.

In the US, the Fostering Connections Act of 2008 made it possible for states to receive federal funds to assist with payments to guardians; today, most but not all states offer subsidised guardianship (Generations United, 2010). To qualify for federal reimbursement through the Guardianship Assistance Program, states must have their subsidised guardianship plans approved by the federal government, which imposes eligibility criteria such as a requirement that the applicant is a licensed foster home. The number of young people exiting US foster care through guardianship has risen significantly over the past 10 years, from 5,916 in FY1998 (2% of those leaving care) to 16,421 in FY2012 (7% of exits) (USDHHS, 2013).

Prior to the Fostering Connections Act, 11 states had federal demonstration waivers to provide subsidised guardianships and test their efficacy in improving permanency outcomes for children in care. A synthesis report on the evaluations of these projects indicated that several states demonstrated significant boosts to their net permanency rates (from 6.6% to 18%) among children in the experimental groups as compared to those in control groups (USDHHS, 2011). Some evaluations indicated that the availability of subsidised guardianship reduced the time children spent in care by 80 days to 9.5 months. Generally, research has indicated that subsidised guardianship is as stable as adoption, especially after controlling for age at entry (Howard *et al*, 2006; Testa, 2008).

Beginning in December 2005 in England, special guardianship became an additional permanency option, providing a formal family bond for children until they reach 18 without legally severing the relationship with their birth parents. The Special Guardianship Order removes the child from "looked after" status, although local authorities still have a duty to assess needs and, if possible, to link with a range of services and support as they would to those adopting from care. (There is a duty to assess needs, but no corresponding requirement to provide for any identified need.) A study of the implementation of this provision in eight local authorities involved a survey of 81 guardians of 120 children, as well as interviews with professionals, carers and a few children (Wade *et al*, 2010). As noted earlier, the large majority of the carers were relatives (86%) and most children had been in care with the guardians prior to their application. The low rate of unrelated foster carers was attributed to concerns about financial uncertainty and loss of social work support. The original guidance had specified guaranteeing financial support for two years, but some local authorities offered support packages for the duration of the guardianship. At the time of the study, 90 per cent of guardians were receiving a regular allowance, although many received less money than they did as foster carers due to means testing. Guardians said the arrangement met their expectations by providing sufficient legal security and the ability to exercise parental responsibility. By 2013, 2,740 children left the care system through special guardianship, comprising 9.6 per cent of all those leaving care (DfE, 2013a).

Long-term foster care

England regards long-term foster care as an option – along with adoption – when deciding the best fit for a child's permanency needs. A care plan is developed through an in-depth process of social work assessment and consultation with the child, parents and other relevant parties, and is approved by the court if a Care Order is made. It is then the responsibility of the local authority to implement the care plan and review it every six months thereafter. Generally, long-term foster care is used more often than adoption as a permanency option for children aged five or older, as well as for those with links to birth relatives that are deemed important to preserve or that might still lead to reunification. While a long-term foster home is intended to last until the child reaches the age of 18, many young people still continue to move around the system (Sinclair, 2005; Bullock *et al*, 2006; Schofield *et al*, 2012).

Several studies indicate that long-term foster care can provide a security arrangement that is viewed by both the young person and the parents as a permanent family; that is, they have a sustained commitment to one another and expect to continue their relationship beyond its legal termination (Triseliotis, 1983; Biehal *et al*, 2009; Schofield *et al*, 2012). Triseliotis's (2002) review of eight studies on long-term fostering, however, found that about 43 per cent of placements broke down within two to five years, while young people did not sustain their relationships after emancipation in some placements that continued until age 18. Also, a substantial minority (over 30%) of them lost contact with birth families in a two-year time span in Schofield and colleagues' study (2012) of over 190 young people in long-term foster care in England. This study also reported that in some long-term placements, local authorities still insisted on authorising decisions – from haircuts, school trips and overnight stays to medical treatment, and some caregivers felt they were not allowed to establish reasonable family norms, such as physical contact or the amount of a young person's pocket money. The families also continued with six-month reviews that were sometimes perceived as intrusive, and authors recommended greater flexibility in agency oversight to allow greater latitude for caregivers to function as normal parents. The concept of agreed "delegated authority" for foster carers has become an important part of improving current practice.

In the US, ASFA eliminated long-term foster care as an acceptable permanency plan; despite this policy, however, the case goal for over 20,000 young people is still long-term foster care, and an additional 20,251 have a goal of emancipation (USDHHS, 2013). ASFA added APPLA (another planned permanent living arrangement) as a case plan designation for children for whom there is no goal of placement with a legal, permanent family. Workers were to first explore all possible legal, permanent family options for the child before moving to APPLA, and even when it was the case goal, they were to work towards building in sustaining relationships and support for the young person, such as mentoring or an advocate.

There is widespread concern among many in the US about the overuse of APPLA as a case goal and about insufficient attention being paid to the permanency needs of older children and young people in care. At a Senate Caucus meeting in June 2012 on APPLA's use as a default goal, two child welfare scholars expressed the view that insufficient attention was being paid to the permanency needs of young people in care, saying, in part:

> ...permanence is about locating and supporting a life-long family. For young people in out-of-home placement, planning for permanence should begin at entry into care and be youth-driven, family-focused, continuous, and approached with the highest degree of urgency. Child welfare agencies, in partnership with the larger community, have a moral and professional responsibility to find a permanent family relationship for each child and young person in foster care. (Renne and Mallon, 2005, p. 498)

Research examining teens aged 15 and older from 12 states, who exited care in the years 2000–2005, indicated that permanency was not achieved for about one-third of them (Maza, 2009). Another study reported that for young people in care on their 16th birthday, only about 10 per cent had entered care before the age of 13, so it is uncommon for a child to grow up in foster care in the US (Wulczyn and Hislop, 2001).

Focus of this compendium

Debates continue over the best pathways to permanence for children in care who cannot safely return home, but one reality remains across the three countries that have been examined by the Adoption Institute: far too many girls and boys remain in temporary placements and transition to adulthood without an enduring family to sustain them. Much work remains to be done to adequately meet the permanency needs of these children. This compendium identifies practices that have shown promise as a means to that end, primarily through adoption or guardianship. Though adoption is the term primarily used throughout the ensuing pages, the concepts discussed also apply to permanency through guardianship. Salient knowledge and research related to these practices are presented, as are descriptions of model programmes and key resources related to each practice. The practices are grouped into the following categories:

- organisational practices;
- court practices;
- recruitment and retention of families;
- pre-adoptive casework processes;
- supporting and preserving adoptive families.

There are differences in terminology across the countries addressed in this volume. In the US, professionals use the term child welfare or foster care system, whereas in the UK the care system is the common terminology. Whereas adoption breakdowns at any time are called disruptions in the UK, in the US adoptive placements that fail prior to legal finalisation are called disruptions and dissolution is used to refer to those in which the legal parent–child relationship is dissolved after adoption. To the extent possible, we have tried to clarify terminology where it is different.

The authors of this volume consulted with adoption professionals and reviewed scholarly adoption literature in all three countries in order to gain information about the research, initiatives, and innovative services that are used to illustrate the 22 practices described. However, we want to emphasise that these are examples only and in no way include a comprehensive review of all, or even most, exemplary practices that exist throughout England, the US and Canada. Because the authors reside in the US, by far the largest of these three countries, there are likely more American-based examples; however, we believe that adoption professionals in one US state have much to learn from those in other states, as well as from one country to another. We hope this review of practices can expand the knowledge and perspectives of adoption professionals across Anglo-American and other countries so that more waiting children can have families for life.

Part II

ORGANISATIONAL PRACTICES

1 Valuing permanency through adoption or guardianship

Description and overview

Child welfare organisations represent a complex web of social, political, legal, policy and cultural environments. The interplay among these factors has significant influence and can impact the rates of adoption for children and young people. Research has demonstrated that complex contextual factors influence the likelihood of adoption for children in the custody of child welfare (Snowden *et al*, 2008). These factors vary from agency to agency, country to country. At a general level, the United States, Canada and England have been committed for decades to the principle that adoption is a positive alternative for children who are unable to return to their families of origin (Schofield *et al*, 2012). This movement toward adoption as a permanency option is highlighted by federal legislation in both the US and England, while Canada has not yet enacted overarching national child welfare policies. In the US, the Adoption and Safe Families Act of 1997 strongly established adoption as the top priority for children who cannot be reunited with their birth family in a timely manner, and the Fostering Connections Act of 2008 established subsidised guardianship as an alternative form of legal permanency. In England, adoption is the most common permanency option for any child under five years who cannot return home or be placed permanently with extended family, while long-term fostering is more often the plan for older children. The plan that is made is shaped to some extent by what is thought to be deliverable and by the child's point of view (Julie Selwyn, personal communication, 16 October 2012).

Leadership at all levels of the system must embrace permanency for all children and value the role of adoption in permanency planning. In the US, adoption rates vary significantly from one state to another, and the state of residence is a predictor of the likelihood of adoption even after controlling for child and family factors (Snowden *et al*, 2008). Adoption rates also vary by jurisdiction within individual states (Courtney and Hook, 2012).

A range of factors pertaining both to the children and to their experiences in the foster care system helps to shape their likelihood of achieving permanency through adoption or guardianship. Some of these include age, length of time in placement, moves in care, level of behavioural or emotional problems, type of caregiver, changes in case workers, rejection of the foster family as an adoption resource, and ambivalence toward adoption (Barth, 1997; Snowden *et al*, 2008; Cushing and Greenblatt, 2009).

Central to achieving permanency outcomes are staff dedication and their belief, from leadership to case workers, that every child is "adoptable" – as well as an agency culture that supports this belief (Avery, 1999a, 1999b). Worker views that children over a certain age or with certain conditions cannot be placed in new families create a significant barrier to adoption for older children (Avery, 2000). In her study of the children in New York City who had waited the longest for an adoptive placement (a mean of 11.8 years), Avery found that only 26 per cent of their workers believed that the child was adoptable, and approximately 70 per cent of workers had carried out none of seven identified recruitment activities on behalf of these children (Avery, 1999a). Thus, it appears that a lack of belief in a child's prospects and a lack of effort to achieve adoption go hand in hand.

Agencies must create a commitment to permanency for young people at every level of the child welfare system – including but not limited to lawmakers, court personnel, child welfare directors, supervisors and workers, as well as the young people themselves – to improve adoption outcomes for the girls and boys who are without legal, permanent families (Ford and Kroll, 2005). The availability of training on achieving permanency and the provision of ongoing support to accomplish this are also aspects of operationalising this commitment.

One model intervention that reinforces the commitment to permanency of those at all levels of the child welfare system is the

Permanency Roundtable process, initiated in January 2009 through the Georgia Division of Family and Children Services (DFCS) and Casey Family Programs. This initiative was piloted with approximately 500 young people the first year; the perceived success of the process led to its implementation state-wide in the second year. The project utilises a collaborative approach to achieve permanency for young people who are at risk of being "stuck" in foster care, i.e., those who have been in the system for at least two years. Roundtables are structured meetings where intensive exploration of children's situations takes place, with the goal of removing barriers to permanency and moving children out of care. Each team is made up of a case manager, supervisor, master practitioner, administrator and permanency expert. At the roundtable, the facts of a young person's case are presented and, using a structured format, the team identifies barriers, explores strategies and develops an action plan. Additional experts are available by phone to immediately address a range of legal, policy and adoption issues (Rogg *et al*, 2009).

Case progress is tracked through special project evaluation forms. After the roundtables, all case summary and consultation data are entered into a tracking system, coupled with individual action plans and follow-up activities. To ensure follow-through after the roundtable, monthly meetings are held during which master practitioners, case managers and supervisors assess individual cases. A state-wide permanency co-ordinator monitors and tracks progress overall. (Research findings on the impact of roundtables on permanency are in the Outcomes section.)

Key programme elements

Organisational factors supporting the aggressive pursuit of adoption include:

- **Leadership:** Personnel with leadership roles within an agency must value adoption as a permanency option for all young people and must clearly communicate an expectation for achieving permanence. The culture of an organisation must support active permanency planning, encourage young people's participation, and promote recruiting, and matching children with families prepared to address their needs and nurture their strengths.

- **Legislation and policy:** Laws and policies at all levels should promote timely achievement of alternative permanency (adoption or guardianship) for children and young people who are unable to safely return to their birth families. Additionally, laws and policies should provide for pre- and post-adoption support for adoptive families to enable them to be successful.
- **Practice:** Core practice values and principles should embody the belief that permanency through adoption is an option for all legally available young people, even those with severe special needs or who are close to adulthood.
- **Dedicated adoption workers:** Reorganising staff to create adoption-specific units or positions, providing specialised training on adoption, and creating permanency task forces or committees can help reduce barriers to child welfare adoption (Urban Institute, 2002).
- **Training:** In addition to focused training for designated adoption workers, child welfare personnel and collateral child- and family-serving professionals (e.g., mental health, court workers) would benefit from a deeper understanding of adoption and related issues. Topics that would be appropriate for designated personnel include but are not limited to talking about and preparing children and young people for adoption, working with first/birth families and siblings, preparing prospective parents, the impact of and recovery from trauma, openness, adoption support and preservation, and other focused/relevant topics.
- **Data-informed decision-making:** Collecting data about the characteristics, placements, permanency plans and recruitment efforts is vital to preparing staff and tracking efforts made for individual children in need of permanent families. Monitoring children's progression towards permanency and building in methods to strengthen accountability for outcomes link data analysis with goal achievement.

Lessons learned

The tone set by child welfare administrators and supervisors facilitates or constrains permanency achievement. Coyne (1990) found that successful adoptive placements were related to the commitment of agency staff at all levels to adoption for children, and special training for recruitment and placement was important for succeeding with the hardest-to-place children.

An example of the change in culture that can come from an aggressive, system-wide focus on permanency is Georgia's Permanency Roundtable initiative. The first-year evaluation found a significant increase in achieving permanency state-wide, not just for the young people whose cases went through the process (see Outcomes). The reason was thought to relate to factors such as a state-wide emphasis on permanency values and practice, as well as addressing systemic barriers that were identified in the roundtables. In two-thirds of the cases, systemic barriers were identified, including appeals of termination of parental rights findings or delayed court hearings. Some of these were addressed system-wide, for example, only supervisors had access to search databases for family finding before the roundtables; after this was identified as a systemic barrier, case managers were given access and training (O'Brien et al, 2012).

Finally, the voices of those who experience the child welfare system can have a powerful impact both on legislation that promotes permanency for all young people and on an individual's permanency planning activities. Recommendations based on research include establishing agency guidelines and procedures to help dedicated child welfare staff carry out permanency policies, including ones that prioritise young people's participation, give several permanency options, and limit independent living and long-term foster care as case goals (Ford and Kroll, 2005). In addition to examining bias about adoptability, professional development opportunities must underscore the advantages of permanency for children and young people, explore the impact of trauma on behaviour and development, and identify best practices for finding permanent families for young people specific to their needs and circumstances (e.g., Coyne, 1990).

Outcomes

Research examining the factors linked with the achievement of adoptions from foster care consistently reveals a number of child-related factors as key predictors; however, non-child-related factors have also been shown to play a role in adoption practice and outcomes. The organisational context of child welfare adoption practice is powerful when it comes to improving outcomes. When prejudices against permanency for older children and young people exist in the child welfare system (Avery, 1999a, 1999b), they can hamper efforts to find adoptive families for some of the most vulnerable young people. Both agency policies and staff who lack specialised training create barriers to successful recruitment of families for children with distinct needs (Rodriguez and Meyer, 1990).

In the United States, the historic unwillingness of some agency personnel to place children transracially led to specific legislation and policies (Multi Ethnic Placement Act of 1994, with amendments in 1996) that forbid agencies which receive federal funding to base adoption placement decisions solely on race, culture or national origin. Research suggests that agency practices and staff attitudes can create barriers to the recruitment of minority families for minority children, and reveals that staff bias has led to African American families being screened out during the recruitment process (McRoy et al, 1997) or perpetuation of the myth that minority families are unwilling to adopt (Mason and Williams, 1985; Sullivan, 1994).

McRoy's (2007) *Barriers and Success Factors in Adoptions from Foster Care* study of 200 families who engaged in the process of adopting from foster care (102 discontinued and 98 finalised) demonstrated that *attrition was most often attributed to agency-related factors*. These factors are discussed in more detail in the section on adoption recruitment, but overall, working to develop a consumer-friendly and responsive service system is an organisational factor that is central to finding families for waiting children.

Georgia's Permanency Roundtable initiative, described earlier, was piloted with about 500 cases of young people who had been in care over four years on average, with the outcome of 31 per cent of them achieving permanency within 12 months of this intervention (9.1% adopted, 13.3% guardianship and 8.3% reunification). Descriptive data on the young people served in the pilot indicated that 69 per cent were aged 10 or older, the vast majority (92%) were African American, and 40 per cent lived in restrictive settings. Analysis of data on more than 9,000 children in care state-wide found a significant improvement in permanency achievement for the year in which roundtables were piloted compared to the previous year – 51 per cent achieved permanency in 2009 compared to 45 per cent in 2008 (Rogg *et al*, 2009; O'Brien *et al*, 2012). As noted earlier, the project appeared to have a spillover effect in shaping the culture of moving aggressively toward permanency and addressing systemic barriers.

Based on the process and outcome evaluations of the Georgia permanency project, the following recommendations were advanced (O'Brien *et al*, 2012).

- Diligent family searches should be implemented as soon as children come into care. Children in the project who had not had a diligent search completed earlier were 63 per cent less likely to achieve permanency during the project.
- Child participation is a key factor. Young people who had not been engaged in permanency planning were 87 per cent less likely to achieve permanency during the project.
- Leadership must establish and maintain the urgent goal of achieving legal permanency, make this a top priority, and make sure it is reinforced within the organisation.
- Case managers should not be overburdened with initiative overload, but need to be supported in sustaining aggressive casework until permanency is achieved.

Selected resources
National Resource Center for Foster Care and Permanency Planning and Casey Family Services (2004) *Permanence for Young People Framework*. Access at: www.hunter.cuny.edu/socwork/nrcfcpp/downloads/permanency/ Permanency_Framework.pdf

2 Using data to track outcomes

Description and overview

Understanding the factors that influence permanency through adoption is critical to child welfare practice. This is not only true in relation to the child, but is also critical to both assess and enhance the system itself (Snowden *et al*, 2008). This can be achieved through comprehensive and uniform data collection and sharing. Information collected by public child welfare agencies on various characteristics of children, their placements and their length of stay can be used to study what factors may predict the practices and policies that support greater chances of permanency for children and families.

In addition to understanding predictors that lead to adoption, data are critical to improving transparency and accountability. Comprehensive data and assessments provide valuable and necessary evidence to inform policy and practice at multiple levels of the system (Snowden *et al*, 2008; Lyons, 2009).

At a national level, both the United Kingdom and the United States collect annual child welfare statistics, including specifics about adoption; currently, a national data collection system is still unavailable in Canada (Gough *et al*, 2009). While studies have been conducted to collect provincial-level information, such as the Canadian Incidence Study in 2003, the comparison of Canadian provincial and territorial data is difficult due to divergent child protection legislation across jurisdictions, so that terms and data are not always analogous (Child Welfare League of Canada, 2003). Capturing information at a national level facilitates an understanding of how many children are in need of permanent families, where they reside, what their needs are, and the factors linked with achieving permanency in order to better inform policy, practice and resource management.

In the US, the federal government attempts to support positive outcomes for children and families by monitoring state child welfare programmes through mechanisms such as, but not limited to, Child and Family Services Reviews (CFSRs) and the Adoption and Foster Care Analysis and Reporting System (AFCARS). The CFSRs are designed to 1) ensure that states are conforming with federal requirements for child protective, foster care, adoption, family preservation, family support and independent living services; 2) analyse what happens for children and families when they are engaged with services; and 3) help states to improve their capacity to help children and families achieve positive outcomes (US Children's Bureau, 2012). The combination of a comprehensive self-assessment, gathering and submitting data, and a site visit allows a joint federal-state team to review case records; interview children and families involved in services, as well as community stakeholders (family and service providers, courts and others); and assess conformity with federal standards. If a state does not meet those standards, a Program Improvement Plan (PIP) is established and an opportunity is provided to address concerns before penalties are imposed. This final phase of the CFSR allows states to implement strategic programme improvements and undergo assessments of progress. The CFSR is designed as a continuous quality-improvement model, so the three-phase process begins again once states have completed their two-year PIP.

AFCARS, a federally mandated data-collection system, provides case-specific information on all children in public child welfare. Data are also collected on children in state custody who are placed for adoption, and urged for children placed for adoption privately. The goal of AFCARS is to use data both federally and locally to inform policy, fiscal and programme considerations (National Data Archive on Child Abuse and Neglect, 2013). The key data categories collected include demographics of young people, biological family, foster family; physical and behavioural status; disability; funding sources; reason for removal; and placement(s). Various summary reports and data files per fiscal year, one for foster care and one for adoption, are available and distributed by the National Data Archive on Child Abuse and Neglect. The files for adoption contain 37 elements, including demographic variables and dates of case-related events.

The UK Statistics Authority collects annual data on the adoption of looked after children, and reports are produced by designated governmental agencies (Office for National Statistics, 2010). Due to legislative differences, terms may not be defined the same in all four UK countries; there are some differences in the data elements collected and each country has a different administrative body that produces the reports (DfE, 2010a). Many local authorities in England also have permanency tracking panels – groups of senior managers who meet regularly to check looked after children's progress toward permanency and to identify delays as early as possible.

Beginning in 2012, the Department for Education in England has published a publicly available performance scorecard for each local authority (DfE, 2012). Using three key indicators, the adoption scorecard shows how quickly children in need of adoption are placed, and graphs shows the local authority's performance in relation to the country as a whole. These scorecards contain detailed data, including the number of gay and lesbian adopters, and give local authorities and adoption agencies the opportunity to monitor their own performance and compare it with that of others. To better understand the circumstances of each local authority's performance, data are collected to indicate the timeliness of the jurisdiction's family justice system, the number of older children being adopted, and the number of waiting children for whom a family has not been identified. Additional information will be collected in the future to capture the engagement time with prospective adopters.

In England, in addition to using data to track outcomes, all adoption services must meet a set of minimum standards established in law. Minimum standards do not mean standardisation of provision but focus on delivering achievable outcomes for children, adopted adults and their adoptive and birth families. Each standard is preceded by a statement of the outcome to be achieved by the agency. The standards are intended to be qualitative in that they provide a tool for judging the quality of life experienced by service users, but they are also designed to be measurable.[5] Every registered provider is inspected

---

5   www.education.gov.uk/publications/eOrderingDownload/Adoption-NMS.pdf

for delivery of these standards by Ofsted (an independent evaluative and regulatory body reporting to Parliament), and a publicly available report is published, including a grading of that service.

Overall, the collection and sharing of data provide the opportunity at multiple system levels to inform decision-making and resource management. At a national level, aggregate data have allowed for a broader understanding of who is in need of a permanent family through adoption, and researchers are able to review the information to better understand child, family and system-related factors influencing adoption and other forms of permanency (Avery, 1999b).

Key programme elements

Important variables to track in data-collection systems include the following:

- **Details about removal:** The type of maltreatment children experi-ence in families of origin and other reasons for placement are important data to retain – they inform future planning and have been found to be associated with the likelihood of being adopted or achieving other types of permanency (Connell *et al*, 2006).
- **Child characteristics:** These include key demographic data on children, including sex, age, race/ethnicity, birth family inform-ation, place of residence, legal status, sibling status and others. It is also important to capture significant conditions of the children, such as the presence of a range of disabilities, in order to understand their developmental trajectory and factors associated with perman-ency. Ideally, variables from child assessments on standardised measures would be included.
- **Significant events throughout time in care:** It is important to track the steps in a child's journey through placement such as court determinations and legal status and placement events (including when a foster placement becomes an adoptive placement). Both the number and type of placements have been associated with adoption and higher levels of care (Courtney and Wong, 1996). Tracking the length of time between termination of parental rights and perm-

anency is important for providing targeted case management to children waiting for long periods. Research suggests that those in care for longer than 18 months are less likely to be adopted (Connell *et al*, 2006). Additionally, keeping records of how long it takes for children to be adopted after termination of parental rights is critical to informing local and jurisdictional policy and practice.

- **Characteristics of caregivers:** Capturing parent-specific data, including the child's relationship to the caregiver, is useful for understanding the characteristics of the parent and child that result in successful permanency. Research suggests that the characteristics and types of families who adopt young and healthy children differ from those who adopt older children and those with pronounced special needs (Coyne, 1990).

- **Provision of specific services to child and adoptive family:** Tracking the provision of adoption subsidies and other support or services would enable policy-makers to better understand the needs of children and families and the services that help them to sustain permanency.

- **Child's identity when discharged from care:** In order to track adoption dissolution or disruption (in England) or the child returning to care after adoption, child welfare systems need to be able to match the identity of a foster child to her/his identity as an adopted child.

Lessons learned

Without national statistics about children in the care of child welfare agencies in Canada, it is difficult to create effective adoption policies and service arrays (HUMA Committee, 2012). While the collection and sharing of uniform data have informed policy and practice decisions in the US – and states and agencies are being held accountable – critics argue that post-service outcomes, a key aspect of child welfare, have been basically ignored (Barth and Jonson-Reid, 2000). It is vital that child welfare agencies capture post-service outcomes to aid in targeting scarce resources, promoting interagency co-ordination, and identifying areas of programme and policy improvement or development.

Going beyond basic statistics is critical to understanding which practices and policies are effective in finding safe and permanent families for children. For instance, by 2004, all US states had undergone the CFSR assessment and on-site review, but no state was found to be in substantial conformity with all seven systemic factors relating to safety, permanency and well-being. Every state was required to create a performance improvement plan to address deficits. Furthermore, while the AFCARS data are critical to having a national picture of the population being served by the child welfare system, because of its crude presence-or-absence code, it falls short of understanding young people from a longitudinal perspective. Thus, the two main critiques of the AFCARS data system include no link between young people from year to year, creating an inability for longitudinal review, and the binary nature of the data fields (e.g., presence or absence), which provide little to no descriptive information that could be valuable in providing more detail to inform policy and practice at a richer level (Wulczyn, 1996; Smith, 2003).

Some scholars caution that using outcome measures to set performance standards can create pitfalls as well as benefits; they suggest using strategic planning and logic models to determine the desired interventional practices that lead to desired outcomes (Wells and Johnson, 2001). They also suggest that measuring outcomes to the exclusion of "process" and quality-assurance measures can lead to inappropriate practices that focus too narrowly on the measure rather than the experience of the child and family.

Outcomes

In the US, there is no single child welfare system. Instead, it is composed of many state and local components, unified by overarching federal laws and regulations (Berrick, 2011). Critical federal regulation includes the national collection of child welfare data, inclusive of information about public adoptions. While the data have limitations, they also have strengths that inform practice initiatives and policy development (Snowden *et al*, 2008). For example, collecting and analysing information about children who are free for adoption can reveal factors that predict permanency outcomes.

Data collected by states and reported to the federal government have provided a better understanding of the children and young people in care, their permanency goals and their departures from the system. For instance, research has found key factors that can affect permanency for a child, including age, race, disabilities, abuse experiences, poverty and mental health issues (Becker *et al*, 2007). Research has also shown that place of residence is a predictor of permanency outcomes (Becker *et al*, 2007; Snowden *et al*, 2008). While that level of data analysis may not reveal the reasons for the effect of geography, it offers an opportunity to focus attention on understanding how a child's place of residence (both state and local) may influence their chances of a permanent family. Furthermore, recent research suggests that jurisdictional differences in the likelihood and timing of juvenile court involvement for young people can influence their achievement of legal permanency (Courtney and Hook, 2012).

Collecting and reviewing data elements that capture the interactions of different agencies responsible for the welfare of children, young people and families also provides a mechanism to hold them accountable for achieving permanency for children in need.

Both child recruitment and matching processes benefit from well-informed workers who have useful data on the needs of the children, such as medical and mental health and behavioural and emotional issues, among others (Crea *et al*, 2011). When data are collected on the specific characteristics and needs of children, opportunities to create targeted recruitment, which is discussed in more detail later in this book, can lead to more stable and successful placements. Aggregating and sharing the data offers information about how best to support permanency achievement for children across jurisdictions.

Selected resources

National Data Archive on Child Abuse and Neglect (2013) Adoption and foster care analysis and reporting system (AFCARS). Access at: www.ndacan. cornell.edu/ndacan/datasets/dataset-details.cfm?ID=168

UK National Statistics (2012) Gateway to UK national statistics. Access at: www.statistics.gov.uk/hub/children-education-skills/children-and-early-years-education/child-safety-and-well-being/index.html

Wells S. J. and Johnson M. A. (2001) 'Selecting outcome measures for child welfare settings: lessons for use in performance management'. *Children and Youth Services Review*, 23:2, pp. 169–199.

3 Providing essential training and support to workers

Description and overview

Adoption is a special area of child welfare that requires specific training regarding recruitment and retention of families, preparation of children and families for adoption, and supporting and preserving placements. Experts suggest that creating designated adoption units and staff who have case management responsibilities specific to the adoption process and who work in collaboration with children, families, courts and other service providers can help to address complex barriers to adoption (Urban Institute, 2002). The responsibilities of dedicated adoption units or staff are to oversee the many aspects of the process for children in need of permanent families, including securing adoptive placements (family finding within the child's extended family and significant attachment figures and recruiting adoptive families); assessing and approving prospective families; linking and matching families and children; participating in the necessary legal proceedings; establishing adoption subsidy and/or additional service needs; preparing and transitioning both children and families for adoption; and identifying and securing post-placement services.

A well-trained and competent workforce is critical to managing the complexity of child welfare adoption, which is often burdened by limited resources and a lack of clarity and focus on the child. In addition to the core ingredients of successful practice (e.g. adequate resources, dedicated leadership, community support and informed practice strategies), professional development and support are fundamental to preparing staff to achieve outcomes for children that balance safety, permanence and well-being. While the rates of disruption are low in comparison to the number of public adoptions each year, the impact of unsuccessful adoptions on the parties involved – including the agencies – are significant and long term (Coakley and Berrick, 2008). Improving the skills, knowledge and attitudes of professionals responsible for child welfare adoptions is fundamental to placement stability and positive outcomes (Hill-Tout *et al*, 2003).

Good staff retention rates and satisfaction in child welfare agencies have been attributed to professionally educated and trained workers, ensuring that they have a sound understanding of the service arena (Whitaker and Clark, 2006). Professionally educated and trained social workers remain in their jobs, report high satisfaction with their work, and have a solid understanding of the child welfare field. In England, researchers have found that, when specialised adoption workers quickly took over case management, the work quality was better and the matching of children occurred more quickly (Farmer and Lutman, 2010).

There are three main areas of child welfare training – pre-service, in-service and professional education (Collins *et al*, 2007a). Pre-service training provides new staff with basic knowledge, attitudes and skills to work with complex families and children with histories of abuse, neglect and out-of-home care. In-service or continuing education is designed to support the implementation of changes in practice or promote competencies in particular methods or practice areas, such as adoption. Finally, professional education offered in colleges and universities is intended to provide current and future child welfare workers with theory-grounded coursework and field experience to understand high-quality practice, including comprehensive clinical, programmatic and administrative decision-making. Quality training programmes must focus on improving performance and outcomes for children and families.

One example of the strategic use of specialised adoption staff is the Swift Adoption Services unit within Oklahoma's Department of Human Services. This unit within the Child Welfare Division is made up of approximately 100 staff focused solely on adoption or post-adoption work. They receive a computerised monthly report that identifies all children across the state with a goal of adoption and consult with permanency-planning staff to move these cases along more quickly. Once the child is placed, the case is shifted to the adoption unit, which is responsible for recruitment and responding to inquiries; home studies and adoptive parent training are contracted out to other agencies (Deborah Goodman, personal communication, 12 September 2012).

Another example is an initiative in New Brunswick stemming from the provincial government's commitment to increasing adoptions of children from foster care. The newly formed New Brunswick Adoption Foundation blitzed the province with an adoption advertising campaign, and the province employed 25 social workers to focus solely on adoption, leading to a major increase in the number of children adopted each year (see Outcomes).

Key programme elements

There are several crucial components of the adoption process in child welfare that designated adoption staff, or those with specialised training, need to implement to ensure that the process is well managed from its beginning to post-placement. It is critical that staff members work in collaboration with several key stakeholders during the adoption process. Responsibilities of the relevant personnel include the following:

- **Casework services for the target child:** A social worker works with the child to explore and establish permanency goals, create plans to achieve the goals, and monitor progress. Elements include exploring the child's expectations and concerns related to permanency, helping the child understand the reasons for separation from their birth family, addressing loss and grief issues, processing life events, including life story work, and focusing on the future. Planning for maintaining significant attachment relationships to the extent possible is also a goal of work with the child, birth family and current caregivers.
- **Recruitment of adoptive families:** Adoption workers provide a customer-service approach to finding and recruiting families for waiting children.

- **Approving prospective adoptive families (home study process):** Social workers trained in adoption assess potential parents and families for their readiness for adoption, and address their needs and concerns.
- **Linking and matching children and families:** Adoption workers are actively involved in finding potential families to consider adopting a specific child and selecting the family that best meets the child's needs.
- **Participating in the legal proceedings for adoption:** Staff work with court personnel to fulfil legal mandates, protect the child's best interests, and minimise unnecessary delays.
- **Establishing adoption subsidy and/or additional service needs:** Based on a child's current and projected needs, adoption workers help determine his/her eligibility for financial assistance or other resources (e.g., health insurance, mental health services).
- **Preparing and transitioning children and families for adoption:** Pre-service and ongoing training, support and counselling are provided to all parties to prepare them for adoption.
- **Identifying potential post-placement service needs:** Based on the needs of children and families, adoption staff identify post-placement service needs.
- **Providing or co-ordinating referrals for services:** Adoption staff help the family find and secure appropriate services to address needs (e.g., therapeutic counselling, support groups, respite care).

In the area of adoption, staff must be trained in techniques that promote permanency and prevent or address instability. Training must be encouraged at all levels, including leadership, and should be designed to improve staff performance and outcomes. The training programme for adoption staff should be comprehensive, covering a wide range of issues. In addition to understanding the impact of loss and trauma and how to promote healing, adoption staff should be trained in the following areas:

- comprehensive child and family assessment, including needs and strengths;

- the adoption life cycle and critical aspects of adjustment for children, parents and siblings;
- cultural competency, including the exploration of bias and assumptions;
- recruitment and matching for child-specific needs and parental capacities;
- therapeutic parenting and strategies for promoting secure attachment;
- planning and supporting optimal levels of openness;
- post-placement and post-adoption services.

When adults in educational situations are engaged as independent and reflective learners, they have the opportunity to challenge assumptions, interact with and learn from others, and apply their knowledge to real situations. This is critical to ensuring that educational opportunities indeed improve performance. Moreover, training adoption supervisors offers additional opportunities to provide support and mentoring, while the supervisory relationship can be used to reinforce in practice the knowledge and skills learned in training (Collins *et al*, 2007b).

Lessons learned

Child welfare workers perform myriad functions to achieve the safety, well-being and permanency of children and families. In a single day, they may address a concern about a child being maltreated in his birth family, provide support to a foster family to prevent the disruption of a sibling group placement, go to court on a case involving termination of parental rights, and counsel a foster teenager about a truancy problem. Crises occur frequently, and the most critical need often gets in the way of seemingly less essential but very important tasks, such as returning phone messages on matters that seem less pressing. Effectively achieving permanency for hard-to-place children requires hundreds of hours of active recruitment and assessment of applicants. It requires specialised knowledge and skills to carefully prepare and serve children and families, make appropriate matches in selecting families, and work to support and stabilise adjustment of children within adoptive families. Adoption staff need to assist caseworkers in completing many of these tasks, such as carrying out diligent searches for relatives or exploring inquiries from interested families about waiting children.

Well-trained and supported staff are fundamental to achieving positive child and family outcomes, and training is an important factor in facilitating greater satisfaction and retention within child welfare agencies (Mor Barak *et al*, 2006). Organisations need to consider the investment of workforce development activities, and ensure that the costs are appropriate and in line with productivity and output. Additionally, organisations that promote competency practice must have cultures that support and cultivate learning and effective performance. Utilising multiple approaches to training (e.g., supervision, coaching, mentoring, peer support) offers additional opportunities for practice-based reinforcement of desired knowledge, skills and attitudes that promote effective permanency practice (Collins *et al*, 2007a). While assessments of training programme effectiveness are useful, agencies often lack the resources to conduct rigorous evaluations. Furthermore, traditional methods of evaluation (e.g., knowledge testing) may be counter-intuitive to adult learning and hamper ability to accurately gauge effectiveness (Collins *et al*, 2007b).

In the US, the federal government provides states with financial resources for training for child welfare workers. A provision under the Social Security Act, Title IV-E, allocates funding for both pre-service and in-service training, as well as higher education coursework for state child welfare agency employees (both current and future). This funding is a benefit to states to encourage well-trained and well supported workforces.

Outcomes

Examples were cited earlier of specialised adoption units within Oklahoma's Department of Human Services and the addition of 25 social workers hired by New Brunswick to facilitate adoptions across that province. The Swift Adoption Services unit in Oklahoma was created in 1999, and adoptions increased state-wide by 64 per cent over the next nine years, whereas nationally they rose three per cent over the same period (Coppernoll, 20 November 2011). Following this addition of adoption workers in New Brunswick, the number of adoptions from care quadrupled, from an average of 25 per year before 2002 to about 100 annually (Eggertson *et al*, 2009).

The complex activities and responsibilities associated with adoption require staff with specialised knowledge and skills to ensure that child placements are appropriate and successful. While there is limited evaluation of specialised child welfare training (Collins *et al*, 2007a), it has been shown to increase both knowledge and skills (Franke *et al*, 2009). Competent adoption practice requires advanced skills to navigate the complexities of multiple relationships (e.g., child, birth and adoptive families) and legal procedures, as well as to work diligently to secure permanent families for children who often have complicated histories. Also, research indicates that professionally educated and trained social workers demonstrate greater satisfaction and job stability than do child welfare caseworkers without this education (Whitaker *et al*, 2004).

Selected resources

Collins M. E., Amodeo M. and Clay C. (2007a) Review of the literature on child welfare training: theory, practice, and research. Access at: www.bu.edu/ssw/files/pdf/BUSSW_CSReport21.pdf

Title IV-E fact sheet can be accessed at: www.socialworkers.org/advocacy/updates/2003/081204a.asp

4   Availability of subsidies

Description and overview

For families who adopt or become guardians, financial subsidies help to care for children and thus minimise financial barriers to permanency. In the US, the Adoption Assistance and Child Welfare Act of 1980 provided federal funding for adoption subsidies; eligibility for federal funds was tied to the child being from a poverty-level birth family (a requirement that is being phased out by 2018) and to meeting their state's definition of "special needs". Each state sets its own criteria of what constitutes "special needs", but generally it applies to older age, certain ethnicities, sibling group status, or known medical, emotional and/or behavioural challenges. These criteria do not necessarily equate to a developmental delay or problem in the child; definitions vary widely from one state to another, as does the proportion of children receiving subsidies (from fewer than half to 100%). States can also receive federal funds to assist with one-time payments for adoption costs (CWIG, 2011a).

States receive matching federal funds for subsidies up to the amount of the maintenance payment the child would receive in foster care, and may receive federal funds for adoption assistance up to the age of 21 if the child has a mental, emotional or physical disability. In most states, subsidies routinely end at age 18 unless the child is significantly disabled, although some states extend this age for other circumstances. Federal policy specifies that eligibility for a subsidy is based on the child, and family income cannot be used as a basis for denying a subsidy. (It is legal, however, to use family income to determine the amount of the state-funded portion, although this is not customary.) In some states, parents can sign an adoption assistance agreement at the level of $0 or $1, with the option of increasing it if needs emerge later (deferred adoption assistance), and they can receive a Medicaid card for the child. Of the children adopted in 2010,

90 per cent received subsidies, but 16 per cent of subsidies were deferred assistance (CWIG, 2011a; North American Council on Adoptable Children [NACAC], 2012; Hansen, personal communication, 7 July 2012; USDHHS, 2013).

In England, the Adoption Support Services Regulations 2005 provide for the payment of support until age 18 if an assessment establishes financial need. In determining the amount of the allowance, the adoption agency assesses the needs of the child and the family's own resources; the amount cannot exceed the fostering allowance. The allowance, once awarded, is reviewed annually and may be reduced or withdrawn (UK National Archives, 2012). England's statistics on looked after children do not give data on adoption allowances. One study following 80 children adopted from care approximately six years later found that 68 per cent of families received adoption or fostering allowances in the first year of placement, but only 30 per cent were still receiving an allowance at follow-up (Sturgess and Selwyn, 2007).

All Canadian provinces and territories offer some adoption subsidies. Ontario instituted these province-wide in June 2012 for families with incomes below $85,000 who adopt children over age 10 and, in Alberta, all families adopting children from care can receive a subsidy. Canadian subsidies typically contain maintenance (from 50–100% of the foster care rate) and service components. In most jurisdictions, qualifying for a subsidy is determined by the child's special needs and the family's income level; however, Alberta, Newfoundland/Labrador and Nunavut territory do not base their subsidies on financial needs assessments. In most areas, the subsidy continues until age 19, subject to a review every two to three years; however, Alberta and Manitoba end subsidies at age 18. Some jurisdictions have provisions to extend the subsidies beyond age 19 and three (New Brunswick, Prince Edward Island and Saskatchewan) can continue subsidies to age 21, while British Columbia provides educational assistance up to 24 (NACAC, 2012).

Key programme elements

The following policies and practices are important in providing financial support to encourage adoptions or guardianships from care.

- **Educate parents about available financial support and the process for receiving it.** In the US, federal law requires states to tell prospective adoptive parents about the availability of adoption assistance and adoption tax credits (CWIG, 2011a).
- **Offer adequate subsidies to families.** The median adoption subsidy in the US for children adopted in 2010 was $485 a month, excluding the 16 per cent of subsidies that were $0 or $1 (Mary Hansen, personal communication, 7 July 2012). A US study analysing adoption subsidies and foster care payments from 2000 to 2006 reported that the average foster care payment was approximately $100/month higher than the average subsidy payment (Buckles, 2013), and additional expenses such as day care are covered for foster children but often not for adopted children. Research indicates that 57 to 63 per cent of adoptive parents receiving subsidies report that they are not sufficient to meet their children's needs, and some had to forego necessary services, go into debt or work extra jobs to meet these (Fuller *et al*, 2006; Children's Rights, 2006).
- **Establish reasonable eligibility criteria that are applied equitably.** The process for determining subsidies requires pre-adoptive parents to negotiate this rate with professionals, and surveys across countries have reported that some adoptive parents perceive the process as difficult, too discretionary and inequitable; a Canadian study described the outcome as 'the luck of the draw' (Sturgess and Selwyn, 2007; Ontario Ministry of Children and Youth Services [Ontario MCYS], 2009).
- **Provide consistent assistance until the child reaches a specific age.** When adoptive parents commit to assuming legal responsibility for a vulnerable child, they need to know what assistance they can count on until the child reaches adulthood. In the US, some states have attempted to withdraw or reduce existing

adoption subsidies, only to have these decisions overturned in federal courts.[6] A study of adoptive parents in England found that after a number of families lost allowances, several parents felt that the decline in income had a 'detrimental effect on their quality of life and the kind of compensatory experiences they could offer their children. Especially affected were those who had been unable to return to work because of their child's ongoing medical or behavioural needs (33%), although overall, 44 per cent of the families interviewed described themselves as struggling financially by that stage' (Sturgess and Selwyn, 2007, p. 20).

Unilaterally withdrawing or reducing a subsidy years down the road not only has a negative impact on the adoptive families affected, but it also undermines the trust of others seeking to adopt and other foster children's chances of finding permanent families.

- **Offer a process for increasing the subsidy if significant new needs develop.** It is impossible to predict, at the time of adoption, all the significant costs a family might incur in the future. Jurisdictions need to make provisions for obtaining funds to cover special needs or circumstances that become apparent as the child develops.

Lessons learned

- **Reducing the ongoing costs of adoption increases adoptions overall, especially for foster carers and relative caregivers**, who adopt 85 per cent of children from care in the US. These families have relatively low incomes, and their adoption decisions have significant economic consequences – forfeiting foster payments and supports and assuming legal responsibility for ongoing costs of services, education and other expenses. Research indicates that adoption subsidies are particularly important to enable foster

---

6   For example, Missouri sought to eliminate all existing subsidies for those above a specific family income level (*E.C. v Blunt*), and Oregon sought to reduce all existing subsidies by 7.5% (*A.S.W. v Oregon*); see National Center for Youth Law website (2012).

carers and older relatives to adopt (Argys and Duncan, 2008; Buckles, 2013). The former study found that reducing the disparity between monthly foster care and adoption allowances (more so than the levels of either payment) best predicts foster carers' decisions to adopt, particularly among those caring for children who are older and have behaviour problems. A recent US study found that for children adopted from foster care whose parents had previously fostered them, nearly one-third (30%) received an adoption subsidy lower than their previous foster care payment (Malm *et al*, 2011b). Such discrepancies provide a financial disincentive to adoption from the very pool of parents who are most likely to adopt.

An English study of almost 1,200 foster carers found that the loss of financial assistance and social support was the primary reason given by more than half of respondents who had considered but not pursued adoption. The same study also found that 62 per cent of those fostering for over 15 years had considered adopting, but only 38 per cent pursued it – a decision more likely taken by those with lower incomes (Kirton *et al*, 2006).

- **Reliable financial supports that take account of the child's evolving needs are important:** US courts have ruled that existing adoption assistance contracts cannot be unilaterally modified without the consent of adoptive families; however, states have succeeded in reducing the amounts for future subsidies in a variety of ways. NACAC conducted a comparison between 2001 and 2006 subsidy policies, finding that approximately half the states reduced their subsidy rates or tightened special needs criteria to exclude more families (Children's Rights, 2006). In Sturgess and Selwyn's (2007) study of adoptive families in England, parents indicated that losing their adoption allowances had detrimental effects on their quality of life and what they could provide for their children, and 'some were very angry that they had to deal with financial worries on top of the children's difficulties' (p. 20). Ontario's governmental study of adoption concluded that the current time-limited subsidy agreements given by some agencies around the province meant that prospective adoptive families could not count on ongoing financial assistance, and they recommended providing ongoing, reliable subsidies (Ontario MCYS, 2009).

Outcomes

Studies of families after adoption indicate that receiving financial and health benefits are their most pertinent need (Rosenthal *et al*, 1996; Barth *et al*, 2001; McDonald *et al*, 2001; Howard and Smith, 2003; Reilly and Platz, 2004; McRoy, 2007). Financial subsidies for families adopting from care contribute to the following outcomes.

- **Necessary support for families**: Many families adopting from the US child welfare system – the vast majority of whom are foster parents (51%) or relatives (30%) – have very low incomes. Nationally, nearly half (46%) of families adopting from care are at or below 200 per cent of the poverty level. State data reveal a similar trend. In Illinois, one study found the majority (56%) of families had annual incomes under $35,000 (excluding subsidies) and another that nearly one-third (30%) had annual incomes below $20,000 (including subsidies). In Oregon and Washington, nearly half (47–48%) of families adopting from care had incomes under $40,000 (Fine, 2000; Howard and Smith, 2003; Fine *et al*, 2006; Fuller *et al*, 2006).

- **Permanency for more children who cannot return home**: Subsidies are critical to enabling families to adopt vulnerable children from foster care. Research consistently indicates that the availability and size of financial subsidies are significant predictors of the likelihood of a child in care being adopted (Barth *et al*, 2003; Dalberth *et al*, 2005; Hansen, 2005, 2007; Hansen and Hansen, 2006). Many parents report that they could not have afforded to adopt without a subsidy (Malm *et al*, 2011b). In a multi-state study of adoptive and prospective adoptive parents of foster children, most (81%) indicated that subsidies were important to their decision to adopt, and 65 per cent of those who had already adopted reported that they could not have done so without a subsidy (Children's Rights, 2006). In a study of success factors associated with adoption of children from care, two-thirds (66%) of parents said they needed the subsidy to be able to adopt (McRoy, 2007). Two of the top three barriers to foster care adoption by African American families are lack of financial resources both to support children and to complete adoptions; these are also among the top reasons cited by professionals (Ledesma *et al*, 2011).

Economic analyses indicate that subsidies have a significant positive effect on adoption rates and conclude that subsidy policy is the most important determinant of adoptions from foster care that is under the control of policy-makers (Hansen and Hansen, 2006; Hansen, 2007; Buckles, 2013). According to the authors of one study, 'Adoption subsidies are perhaps the single most powerful tool by which the child welfare system can encourage adoption and support adoptive families' (Dalberth *et al*, 2005, p. 1).

- **Greater well-being and stability in adoptive families**: Financial support is among the factors significantly associated with higher satisfaction in parenting children with special needs (Reilly and Platz, 2004). There is also some evidence linking adoption subsidies with adoption stability (Berry and Barth, 1990; Sedlak, 1991; Barth, 1993). The link between financial support and stability also applies to kinship care and subsidised guardianships. Research on the stability of kinship care suggests that lower rates of disruption are associated with the provision of financial support and the availability of post-placement services. Few ruptures occur when relatives become legal guardians and receive financial subsidies and post-permanency support; placements without such assistance are less stable (Testa, 2004).

- **Financial savings for governments**: Research consistently shows that governments save money when children are adopted rather than remaining in care. One economist found that every dollar invested in the adoption of a child from foster care returns about three dollars in public and private benefits (Hansen, 2006). Another study concluded that government savings for the 50,000 children adopted annually from US foster care ranges from $1 billion to $6 billion (Barth *et al*, 2003). According to a government study in Ontario, a cost-benefit analysis of doubling adoptions in five years, while providing subsidies, would save $18 million at the end of that time period and $413 million for the life of these adoptions. 'The problems and barriers in adoption services are costing Ontario in lost opportunities for waiting children and families and in high social costs,' the authors reported. 'It costs at least $32,000 a year to keep a Crown ward in care. It costs significantly less to provide supports and subsidies to help adoptive families parent children' (Ontario MCYS, 2009, p. 9).

Selected resources

Child Welfare Information Gateway (2011a) *Adoption Assistance for Children Adopted from Foster Care*. Website also includes links to information on adoption assistance for families and professionals, including state-specific information for all states. Access at: www.childwelfare.gov/adoption/preplacement/adoption_assistance.cfm

Dalberth B., Gibbs D. and Berkman N. (2005) *Understanding Adoption Subsidies: An analysis of AFCARS data*, Washington, DC: Office of the Assistant Secretary for Planning and Evaluation, US Department of Health and Human Services. Access at: aspe.hhs.gov/hsp/05/adoption-subsidies/report.pdf

North American Council on Adoptable Children (2012) Adoption subsidy website. US state profiles and Canada provincial profiles. Access at: www.nacac.org/adoptionsubsidy/adoptionsubsidy.html

Part III

COURT PRACTICES

5 Monitoring timeframes

Description and overview

Moving children quickly and efficiently from foster care to permanency has long presented challenges to courts in the US, England and Canada. In England, there has been a great deal of concern about the length of time it takes to obtain the legal order that allows a child to be placed for adoption. Delays have been increasing, so the government has committed itself to a statutory six-month limit on the duration of cases. Achieving this goal requires a major overhaul of, as well as cultural changes in, the family justice system. Beginning in the summer of 2012, a number of recommendations were introduced for implementation in the ensuing year, including having judges set the timetable and pathway for a case at the beginning, with the standard being 26 weeks, and also including implementation of a case management/tracking system.

In the US, the Adoption and Safe Families Act of 1997 (ASFA) transformed the child welfare priority for achieving permanency by requiring permanency hearings to occur within 12 months (rather than 18 months) of a child's placement in foster care, revising permanency goals by eliminating long-term foster care, and establishing a time limit for states to initiate proceedings to terminate parental rights for children in foster care for 15 of the most recent 22 months (ASFA, 1997). The US Department of Health and Human Services monitors the performance of states through Child and Family Services Reviews (CFSRs) and Title IV-E Foster Care Eligibility Reviews.

While ASFA and the reviewing systems have provided some improvement, permanency proceedings often move at a snail's pace, largely due to overburdened and, in some states, poorly managed court systems. Children can remain stalled in the system for alarmingly long periods of time. According to Children's Rights (2012), 1,200 children enter foster care in the US *each day* and remain there for more than two years on average. According to the Congressional Coalition on Adoption, 40 per cent of these children will wait over three years for adoption, and many will never find a permanent family.

In most states, the caseloads of judges handling foster care cases are exceptionally high. In Virginia, for example, each Juvenile and Domestic Relations court judge in 2005 averaged 2,450 juvenile cases and 5,429 juvenile hearings (National Conference of State Legislatures [NCSL], 2007). The day-to-day demands of the job often make it difficult for judges or their staff to recognise when cases have stalled or deadlines have been missed. In addition, attorneys representing these children are often overburdened, and therefore request postponements that further delay many cases. For example, in Arizona, court-appointed lawyers represent an average of 130 children in foster care (Reinhart, 26 May 2012). Workers responsible for drafting reports and co-ordinating with attorneys and courts to move cases along are also severely overloaded. These resource strains often result in failure to co-ordinate cases, which further contributes to harmful delays for children.

Technological advances offer help. Case-tracking software and case-management databases can help court personnel monitor progress, keep track of deadlines, and move cases through the system more efficiently. For example, the US Statewide Automated Child Welfare Information System (SACWIS) can assist courts in moving children to permanency more quickly. SACWIS is a comprehensive, automated case-management tool that supports social workers' foster care and adoption practice. The Adoption and Foster Care Analysis and Reporting System (AFCARS), developed in 1993, requires the mandatory collection of adoption and foster care data, so states are required to modify their child welfare information systems to be consistent with federal reporting requirements. The Court Improvement Program of the US Children's Bureau offers grants to states for the development of data collection and performance measurements to achieve quality improvement in court performance, and the US Justice Department offers a toolkit for improving court performance in child abuse and neglect cases (Office of Juvenile Justice and Delinquency Prevention [OJJDP], 2009).

Jurisdictions have developed a variety of strategies for overcoming unwarranted delays in the court process. Electronic case monitoring can facilitate the standardisation of procedures at hearings, helping judges follow guidelines to move cases forward. With electronic monitoring and other technology, assessment data can be collected and analysed from various courts to inform states where additional judicial resources are needed.

Key programme elements

The following are examples of strategies used to monitor timeframes in court proceedings concerning foster children.

- **Generate electronic reports to automatically notify judges of the status of cases.** In West Virginia, 'all circuit courts are required to report periodically on the status of every pending child abuse and neglect case. West Virginia's circuit court judges are now providing these reports electronically, and the reports generated from these data can be used to bring to the attention of judges cases on their docket[s] which are not compliant with the appropriate timeframes so that appropriate corrective action can be taken' (West Virginia Court Improvement Project [WVCIP], 2012).
- **Collect workload assessment data to ensure timely processing of cases, control caseload size and illustrate need for funding.** Often, heavy caseloads cause judges to rush through proceedings, failing to move cases along to the next stage. The National Council of Juvenile and Family Court Judges' Resource Guidelines recommend that judges spend an hour on preliminary protective hearings, for example. However, 'Florida courts reported in 1999 that the majority of its preliminary hearings lasted only four minutes' (NCSL, 2007). Tracking systems that help control judges' caseloads can enable them to handle cases more thoroughly and effectively.

Court-granted continuances are another common source of delay in foster care cases because the caseloads of child welfare attorneys are often overly burdensome. The National Association

71

of Counsel for Children (NACC) 'recommends that a full-time attorney represent no more than 100 individual clients at a time, assuming a caseload that includes clients at various stages of cases, and recognising that some clients may be part of the same sibling group' (NACC, 2001). Likewise, the American Bar Association (ABA) recognises the court's role in preventing attorneys from becoming overburdened. ABA standards provide that, 'trial court judges should control the size of court-appointed caseloads of individual lawyers representing children, the caseloads of government agency-funded lawyers for children, or court contracts/agreements with lawyers for such representation' (ABA, 1996). Data-monitoring programmes can also be used to track the workload of attorneys representing children in foster care.

- **Use tracking systems to help courts monitor data and co-ordinate between child welfare and legal systems.** Sometimes judges grant continuances due to poor co-ordination among lawyers and social work agencies. Teams may not have enough time to prepare documentation before trial or conduct adequate searches for missing biological parents (who must be provided with sufficient notice of hearings). Social workers often do not provide attorneys with copies of their reports or their clients' health or educational records before a hearing. Information technology can be used to help ensure that necessary documents are properly processed and electronically provided to all the necessary parties in a timely fashion (Annie E Casey Foundation [AECF], 2001). While granting that some continuances may be necessary, it has been found that, 'missed deadlines between the initial protective hearing and termination of parental rights translated on average to nearly an additional year that a child spent waiting for a permanent home' (NCSL, 2007).

  The potential uses for monitoring software are numerous. Courts could receive automatic notice when the 12-month deadline for conducting a permanency hearing was approaching. Reports could indicate when children had not been appointed counsel or guardians ad litem. Where no diligent search had been conducted, the software could flag the file. Collecting data about court performance can help facilitate collaboration between courts and agencies, and increase accountability to children.

- **Hold monthly hearings and team meetings.** One national policy organisation focusing on infants and toddlers in foster care recommends a successful model of co-operation in foster care cases developed by the Miami-Dade juvenile court. The model involves, among other things, monthly "court team" meetings and hearings to carefully monitor the movement of cases (Hafford and DeSantis, 2009).

Lessons learned

The Supreme Court of Georgia Committee on Justice for Children allocated funds to improve outcomes for children who had been in foster care for years, deemed "cold cases". Trained as child welfare attorneys, Supreme Court fellows reviewed 214 such cases to evaluate what barriers to permanency existed, including issues with families and guardians, child welfare agencies and the courts. The fellows found that, 'for one in three children, the courts presented barriers to permanency such as time delays, missing or inaccurate petitions and motions, lack of attorney action, and lack of judicial oversight' (Meredith *et al*, 2010).

From the legal review

- Fewer than half (46%) of files had legal documentation to indicate that a permanency hearing was held within one year of a child coming into care.
- The majority of files (71%) contained "reasonable efforts" (to achieve permanency) language, but some would likely not survive a federal audit.
- Roughly one-quarter (27%) of children in cold cases had an attorney.
- There was no evidence of a diligent search in 41 per cent of files.

The case monitoring and tracking technology noted above could provide a solution to many of these barriers. However, states and individual courts have often been slow to utilise available methods. The Pew Commission on Children in Foster Care (2004) identified potential barriers preventing courts from implementing the emerging technologies to track and manage data, including lack of access to information about the technology; lack of training on its use; concern that they would require expensive management systems; and concern about how information would be used by state court leadership, elected officials and the media. In response to these concerns, the American Bar Association, National Center for State Courts, and National Council of Juvenile and Family Court Judges developed a set of outcome measures for courts to assess their performance (American Bar Association's Center on Children and the Law *et al*, 2004 (see Selected Resources).

Outcomes

- **Improvements in Missouri – the Fostering Court Improvement Project**: Missouri implemented a Fostering Court Improvement Project (FCI) in 24 of the state's counties in autumn 2005. This collaborative, multidisciplinary team approach utilises case-management best practice and agency and court data systems to improve case handling and child outcomes. The project provided intensive, data-focused interaction and training for personnel in selected judicial circuits. Courts and child welfare agencies use these data to improve outcomes in five key areas: timeliness, due process, safety, stability and permanency. It is now fully funded through the CIP Data and Technology Grant (Pew, 2009).
- **Improvements in Montana – reducing the number of days to resolve cases**: In 2006, Montana held a State Leadership Summit on the Protection of Children. Judges, attorneys and other stake-holders created joint goals, action plans and timelines for improving the performance of courts and child welfare agencies. The state's Supreme Court followed up with groups at 90-day

intervals to monitor progress. Through this action, Montana reduced the number of days taken to resolve cases at appellate level by 25 per cent (Pew, 2009).

Selected resources

The American Bar Association's Center on Children and the Law, National Center for State Courts, and National Council of Juvenile and Family Court Judges (2004) *Building a Better Court: Measuring and improving court performance and judicial workload in child abuse and neglect cases*, Los Altos, CA: The David and Lucile Packard Foundation.

Office of Juvenile Justice and Delinquency Prevention (2009) *The Toolkit for Court Performance Measures in Child Abuse and Neglect Cases*, Washington, DC: US Department of Justice. Access at: www.ojjdp.gov/publications/courttoolkit.html

6   Permanency mediation

Description and overview

Mediation has been used in child welfare and custody cases in the US since the mid-1980s, when Connecticut and California developed pilot programmes. Mediation has wide acceptance in Canada as well (Stack, 2003). Neutral, trained mediators lead parties in confidential discussions of their interests and concerns, with the goal of resolving cases outside of the courtroom; agreements are submitted to judges for approval. In general, the confidentiality of mediation, which occurs off the record, allows a child's family of origin or prospective family to discuss their concerns and interests more freely than if conversations were on the record and in a courtroom before a judge. In addition, mediation provides a less adversarial, more co-operative environment in which to resolve cases that are often highly emotional and stressful for all parties. Mediation can be a powerful tool to lessen confrontation and thereby achieve more desirable results for children.

Mediation has been used at all stages of the legal process, including at review hearings, permanency hearings and petition filings to terminate parental rights, as well as for post-termination issues (Thoennes, 2009). It is a useful tool to reduce the length of time a child remains in the foster care system, and states increasingly view mediation as a cost-saving tool that can help reduce the amount of time courts spend on contested hearings and lengthy appeals. Mediation also has been described as a technique 'to minimize loss to children' (Consortium for Children, 2012).

Participation in mediation is usually voluntary, though judges will often refer parties to mediation and strongly recommend it to resolve their differences. Whether mediation is voluntary or court-ordered, parties are not required to reach an agreement, and they may resolve some issues but not others. It is important to note that exceptions to the guarantee of confidentiality exist. For example, a mediator may have a statutory obligation to report communications of child abuse.

While it is usually voluntary, mediation can raise ethical concerns when it involves the prospective termination of parental rights. Often, parties are referred to mediation when it has become clear that reunification is not likely, but before termination proceedings have commenced. Etter (1988, 1993) pioneered the CAMP (Co-operative Adoption Mediation Project) model to build relationships between birth and potential adoptive parents and to develop written post-adoption communication agreements. CAMP has been applied when reunification was unlikely, and most cases have ended with voluntary relinquishments and co-operative adoption agreements.

It is important for mediators to be well trained and supervised to ensure that any relinquishments obtained in the process adhere to ethical standards of informed consent, and that birth parents do not feel pressured to terminate their rights in exchange for ongoing contact. Nolan-Haley (1999) set forth three conditions for informed consent to be valid: 1) pertinent information has been fully disclosed to birth parents; 2) birth parents understand the information; and 3) birth parents grasp the actions and repercussions of the mediation process throughout it.

Another concern with mediation is the inherent imbalance of power between the birth parents and potential adoptive parents or the state. A trained, ethical and skilful mediator will understand how to support birth parents in a mediation setting. For example, credential-ing and training requirements for a Massachusetts permanency mediation programme included a professional degree and at least three years' experience related to child welfare, 35 hours of mediation training, 20 hours of co-operative mediation training, a course on ethical mediation, participation in an ongoing supervision group, and ongoing continuing education (Mary LeBeau, personal communica-tion, 24 April 2013). The Association of Family and Conciliation Courts (2012) offers guidelines for mediation, including strategies for addressing power imbalances between the birth parents and the child welfare agency.

Key programme elements

Mediation can be requested by judges, child welfare agencies, children's attorneys, birth parents, prospective adoptive parents, guardians ad litem or Court Appointed Special Advocates (CASAs). When it is initiated, the following are important elements.

- **Qualified mediators:** Professionals with experience and training can best facilitate permanency mediations. Experienced social workers who mediate bring an important understanding of the emotional and psychological aspects of child welfare cases to the table. Evaluations have found no differences in outcomes based on whether the mediator is a court employee or a contractor, but the mediator must be familiar with the child welfare system, respected by professionals who participate in mediation, and skilled in carrying out these sessions (Thoennes, 2009).
- **Protecting parties' rights:** Mediators cannot offer legal advice to the parties or answer legal questions. Rules vary from state to state, but parties generally may request that their lawyers be present during mediations. Birth parents or prospective adoptive parents may not be able to afford the legal fees, but ethical concerns may exist where only one party has counsel before or during the process. Disparities also exist when one attorney has never participated in mediation previously and another, such as a child welfare agency attorney, has done so.
- **Flexibility within a defined structure:** Mediators usually meet independently with each party to hear their concerns and to discuss their interests before convening the parties to sit down together. Sometimes, participants are welcome to have relatives or friends present at the mediation for support. Most often, these individuals do not join the discussion unless at the invitation of the mediator. A non-profit organisation in California, Consortium for Children (2012), which conducts mediations at the request of courts or attorneys, reports that its permanency mediation usually takes place for about 30 hours over the course of two to three months.
- **Input and feedback:** It is important that a wide variety of stake-

holders provide input to states, counties or court systems designing mediation programmes. In addition, programmes should have built-in feedback systems to improve the process and outcomes. Another important component is that mediated agreements must be ratified by courts, which ensures that the agreements comply with applicable laws.

- **All necessary parties must be included.** In a survey in Essex County, New Jersey, almost a quarter of birth parents who had engaged in mediation believed that someone had been missing from the process who should have participated (Dobbin *et al*, 2001). In order for the parties to have faith in the outcomes of their mediation, it is important for them to feel that all necessary parties and concerns were heard. In addition, it is critical that everyone involved is made aware of the terms of any agreements that are made.

Lessons learned

Having at least one champion for mediation is important. The Michigan Permanency Planning Mediation Pilot Program (PPMP) evaluation reported that 'the most common insight from professional participants was that having at least one judge who supported mediation was crucial to implementing a mediation program' (Anderson and Whalen, 2004). The enthusiasm of judges for mediation may stem from its effect in reducing their caseloads, reducing the time until permanency is achieved, and/or improving the relationships among caseworkers, litigants and attorneys. Four out of nine judges who responded to the Michigan PPMP survey 'noted a positive impact attributable to an enhanced spirit of co-operation and lessening of confrontation and antagonism between caseworkers and family members and between caseworkers and attorneys' (Anderson and Whalen, 2004, p. 38). A review of research conducted on 16 mediation programmes found that most of them started slow and struggled to get referrals. This problem was alleviated somewhat if judges ordered specific cases to the programmes, and few parents failed to participate when there were judicial orders for mediation (Thoennes, 2009).

Funding may be hard to secure initially until results are demonstrated. Court systems often face overcrowded dockets and constrained budgets. One objective of permanency mediation is 'to identify high-conflict parties early and move them to trial expeditiously, while giving them access to justice through case conferencing while they wait for their court date' (Canadian Forum on Civil Justice [CFCJ], 2010). While high-conflict parties often need mediation services, the court may view them as unlikely to reach a mediated agreement. When a programme is in its pilot stage and funders are evaluating mediation as a tool, it therefore could be helpful to include families experiencing varying degrees of conflict.

In designing a programme, 'it is critical that the parties to mediation are provided clear information in advance about the process and their options'. Parties should be given ample time to ask questions and be fully informed. In one evaluation of a mediation programme, both prospective adoptive and birth parents found it stressful to learn about mediation just as they were asked to participate in it. Some people felt they did not have enough information to make informed decisions, in part because 'they were not privy to the inputs of the courts and the child welfare agency, which they viewed as major stakeholders in their mediation' (Maynard, 2005, p. 520). Maynard suggested building in a scheduled opportunity for participants to consult with their lawyers or others before reaching any agreement. In the Michigan PPMP, the majority (53%) of foster and adoptive parents did not know what steps other parties were to take following the mediation (Anderson and Whalen, 2004). If mediators help clarify the next steps, then the parties may have a better sense of where they stand after mediation.

Participants 'may need additional support during or after mediation' to help them understand and manage open adoptions, address their own concerns and feelings, and develop effective communication in the relationship (Maynard, 2005). In her qualitative study of open adoption and permanency mediation, Maynard found that almost all birth parents and pre-adoptive parents expressed confusion about their agreement, and almost all birth parents were unprepared to cope with the grief and guilt related to relinquishing parental rights.

A 2002 study conducted interviews with birth parents and prospective adoptive parents in permanency mediation pilot programmes
in Massachusetts (Maynard, 2005). Birth parents expressed concerns
about how their voluntary termination of parental rights would affect
their children, i.e., they worried that their children would view it as a
failure to fight for them. In terms of facilitating a level of openness in a
child's best interests, mediation may promote or impede birth parents'
contact and visitation goals. Ethical concerns exist when, from a birth
parent's perspective, future contact seems predicated on the
"voluntary" termination of parental rights. Trained and sensitive
mediators may help alleviate some of these concerns.

Outcomes

Evaluations of permanency mediation programmes reveal some
benefits for participants, in part based on their roles in the process.
Outcomes and observations include the following:

- **Mediation is effective in producing agreements**: Thoennes's
  (2009) review of 16 evaluations of mediation programmes found
  that 60–80 per cent of cases ended with agreements that addressed
  all the issues before the court, and another 10–20 per cent reached
  partial agreements. Only about 10 per cent were unable to reach
  any agreement.
- **Improved case-processing timeliness, fewer continuances and
  more timely permanencies**: An evaluation of a pilot programme in
  King County, Washington, compared mediated and non-mediated
  child abuse and neglect cases on the basis of case processing and
  efficiency, finding that mediated cases were adjudicated 34 days
  sooner than non-mediated ones. In addition, fewer continuances
  were required at adjudication for mediated cases (Summers *et al*,
  2011). A Louisiana study found a higher rate of achieving permanency within 12 months among mediated cases as compared with
  non-mediated ones (Center for Policy Research, 2005), and a
  Washington DC programme reported a shorter timespan for
  mediated versus non-mediated cases in the time from the initial

hearing to permanency (Gatowski *et al*, 2005). More research is needed on how mediation affects continuances, contested hearings, appeals and litigation costs.

- **Positive perceptions of the mediation process and mediated agreement**: In a Michigan Permanency Planning Mediation Pilot Program (PPMP), most foster and prospective adoptive parent participants felt the process had given them an opportunity to be heard and a chance to provide input into case planning. Two-thirds (67%) of these participants agreed that the result of the mediation was fair, and more than half (60%) said they would use mediation again and recommend it to others. Roughly 73 per cent of participants felt that their mediators did a good job explaining mediation, listening to them, and remaining neutral (Anderson and Whalen, 2004).

- **Varied effects of the mediation process in improving communication between parties**: When parties convene for mediation, their relationships do not always improve. In the Michigan PPMP evaluation, 57 per cent of foster and prospective adoptive parents surveyed found mediation did not help improve relationships with one or more persons in the room. While one objective of mediation is to help parties better understand the issues, 60 per cent of foster and adoptive parents stated that they did not gain a better understanding of each other's perspectives. Fifty per cent of lawyers and 63 per cent of child welfare case workers surveyed reported that their relationships with one or more persons at the mediation improved as a result of it (Anderson and Whalen, 2004).

- **Mediation yields financial savings**: Thoennes's review (2009) reported that evaluations have struggled to quantify the cost savings of mediation programmes, with figures ranging from $637 to over $10,000 per case; however, it seems reasonable to conclude that mediation saves money.

Selected resources

Association of Family and Conciliation Courts (2012) *Guidelines for Child Protection Mediation*. Access at: www.afccnet.org/Portals/0/Guidelines%20for%20Child%20Protection%20Mediation.pdf

Child Welfare Information Gateway (2011b) *Mediation for Permanency Planning*, Washington, DC: US Department of Health and Human Services, Children's Bureau.

Stack K. (2003) Information Packet: Child Welfare Mediation, *National Resource Center for Foster Care and Permanency Planning*. Access at: www.hunter.cuny.edu/socwork/nrcfcpp/downloads/child-welfare-mediation.pdf

Thoennes N. (2009) 'What we know now: findings from dependency mediation research', *Family Court Review*, 47:1, pp. 21–37.

7 Assuring continuity in judicial decision-making

Description and overview

Continuity in judicial decision-making, such as through the practice of "one judge, one family", can promote permanency for children. Embraced as a key principle for a "holistic approach to families" by the US National Council of Juvenile and Family Court Judges (NCJFCJ), this process allows children and families to appear "exclusively and continuously" before the same family or dependency court judge for the duration of a child welfare case relating to neglect or abuse, juvenile delinquency, custody or parental rights (Flango *et al*, 1999, p. 23; NCJFCJ, 2012). The one-judge, one-family practice differs from the conventional approach in which families are assigned to whichever judge is responsible for presiding over hearings that day, regardless of the case history or issues (Fidler *et al*, 2013).

For the most part, case continuity is not a particular focus in Canada, as 'family proceedings are dealt with in both levels of trial courts, with federally and provincially appointed judges dividing responsibility' (Bala and Birnbaum, 2010, p. 10). Federal and provincial action would be needed to appoint judges 'who have a comprehensive jurisdiction over family matters, including domestic, child welfare and enforcement issues' (Bala and Birnbaum, 2010, p. 10).

When a one-judge, one-family approach is not used, families may attend dozens of hearings before many different judges during their involvement with the justice system. Reporting to a domestic relations court, juvenile court, criminal court and probate court may result in a more fragmented experience than consistently appearing in a family or dependency court (Supreme Court of Ohio, 1997). Where cases go before multiple courts and judges, '[f]requent changes in judicial officers can lead to various interpretations of the case at critical points, leading to potential barriers to timely and appropriate permanency goals' (Department of Family Administration, 2007, p. 3).

The benefits of having a family appear before the same judge for all matters related to the child welfare case include familiarity and time savings. When a judge is familiar with a family's history, hearings can go more quickly. The family court in Lancaster County, Pennsylvania, has followed this best practice since 2000. There, a former family court judge stated: 'The hearings are much shorter. We can do it in two hours instead of doing it in two days' (Schweigert, 2012). Shorter hearings also may allow judges to better manage their caseloads and meet permanency deadlines (Mehaffey, 2012).

Key programme elements

A key element of all child welfare court proceedings is that the *judge emphasises timely permanency*. This is more achievable when one judge remains with a family and hears matters related to the case. From the very first hearing, a judge should underscore the importance of achieving timely permanency for children. In child protection cases, 'the work accomplished in the first few hours and days will set the pace and tone for all that follows' (Edwards, 2007, p. 10). It is also important that judges convey urgency and demonstrate their vested interest in helping to achieve timely permanency (Edwards, 2007). The following are also important components of the one-judge, one-family approach.

- **Judges get to know families and their case histories by consistently presiding over their hearings.** Time can be saved when a judge already knows 'which issues have been previously litigated, what the parents have done that brought the child to the attention of the authorities, and what the plans for the family are' (Edwards, 2007, p. 18).
- **Parents and children become familiar with their judge.** Appearing before the same judge helps families recognise a court's expectations and 'anticipate a judge's or master's response to their future conduct' (Department of Family Administration, 2007, p. 3).

A working relationship develops between judges and families that appear before them repeatedly (Edwards, 2007).

- **Judges assess progress early and often.** It is helpful for judges to meet with families frequently to review their case progress and to make sure they have complied with court orders. Dependency courts participating in a Pennsylvania project called Permanency Practice Initiative (PPI) hold court reviews every three months, as opposed to every six months. These hearings are intended to 'increase awareness of the changing needs of children and families and thereby better provide needed services in a timely manner' (Office of Children and Families in the Courts, 2009).

- **Judges help facilitate communication and co-ordination among stakeholders.** The National Council of Juvenile and Family Court Judges (NCJFCJ, 2012, p. 1) recommends that courts 'should develop protocols for communication and co-ordination to ensure that case plans and dispositions are integrated, reasonable, and achievable'. For example, at the first available opportunity, judges should order that families receive services; later in a case, they should confirm that the families have received the ordered services and should ascertain caseworkers' findings and opinions (Department of Family Administration, 2007).

- **Families understand where they stand and how a judge is likely to rule.** Additional benefits of "one judge, one family" include consistency and reinforcement. Judges help to hold families accountable for making changes and implementing orders over the span of their cases – and they define consequences for failing to comply. Compliance with judicial orders may increase when a family can anticipate how a judge will react to their behaviour (Flango *et al*, 1999; Bala and Birnbaum, 2010). After a final decision has been issued, parties may be less inclined to appeal if they know they will appear before the same judge (Schweigert, 2012).

Lessons learned

The actions of a dependency or family court judge have an enormous impact on the children to whose cases they are assigned. English child welfare advocate and social worker Chris Beckett has written that one effect of legal delays is that 'While children wait for court decisions, their childhood ticks by' (Beckett, 2001, p. 60). Judges differ in their orientation to assuming responsibility over child welfare cases. Some feel called to serve on the dependency bench and spend their careers helping children; others view this assignment 'as an initiation into the system – an early assignment until they can move "up" to civil or criminal court' (Pew Charitable Trusts, 2004, p. 47).

In a one-judge, one-family system, it is also important to outcomes for jurists to stay in place long enough to shepherd their cases through litigation. When judges rotate quickly out of family court assignments, continuity and timeliness are compromised. The Pew Charitable Trusts recommends that judges interested in devoting their careers to dependency court should be allowed to remain there, rather than be rotated to other assignments (Pew Charitable Trusts, 2004). Over time, dependency and family court judges can become experts on child welfare and related issues. Through judicial education, training and first-hand experience, judges develop expertise that benefits their communities. 'Judges who remain in the juvenile court for extended numbers of years are in a better position to take control of their dockets and move cases along expeditiously' (Edwards, 2007, p. 18).

Since some children are engaged in court proceedings for several years, it is beneficial for experienced, dedicated judges to remain in their positions for long tenures as well. In the US, the length of terms served by judges hearing child welfare cases differs by jurisdiction. In Delaware, family court judges serve 12-year terms; in California, judges who preside over dependency cases serve six-year terms (Delaware Family Court, 2006; California Judges Association FAQ, 2012). The California Blue Ribbon Commission on Children in Foster Care (2010) recommended that judges be assigned to hear dependency cases for at least three-year rotations. In other jurisdictions, long-term assignment to the juvenile court bench is considered best practice (Edwards, 2007).

It is not clear how much funding is required to implement a one-judge, one-family system (National Center for State Courts [NCSC], 2006). In some rural jurisdictions, including in South Dakota, judges may be required to travel great distances to hear dependency cases (NCSC, 2006). Texas uses "cluster courts", in which multiple counties are combined into one dependency docket; a single judge hears all of the cases on that cluster's dependency docket (Pew Charitable Trusts, 2004).

In Lancaster, Pennsylvania, six family court judges work in teams of two. If a family's regularly assigned judge is unavailable, the other one can provide assistance. The Lancaster County system combines the benefits of "one judge, one family" with the advantages of special-isation. The family court judges devote at least one day a week to cases in a specialised area, including child abuse and neglect, protection from abuse orders, and delinquency of minors. The court also design-ates one "family business court day" each week for addressing issues that necessitate a quick response (Schweigert, 2012). This system may help maximise case continuity while also providing for specialisation and rapid responses.

Large jurisdictions with heavy caseloads may have difficulty up-holding the one-family, one-judge practice (Supreme Court of Ohio, 1997). Scheduling all the hearings relating to a family's case can require 'an excellent automated information system (or a very small court), an adaptable calendaring system, and a highly skilled judge capable of dealing with a multiplicity of possibly unrelated issues' (Flicker, 2005, p. 14).

Some experts recommend that "one judge, one family" be modified when necessary to "one family, one treatment team" (Flango et al, 1999, p. 30). Treatment team continuity would likely confer benefits when families have to appear before more than one judge. If families can rely on the same team of attorneys, social workers, guardians ad litem and others to help manage their cases and shepherd them through in a timely fashion, that may help counteract delays arising from changes in judges.

Outcomes

- **A pre-post comparison of one family/one judge implementation in Baltimore found a decrease in the number of continuances per case.** A collaboration between the Baltimore Juvenile Court, the University of Maryland School of Social Work and the NCJFCJ resulted in a broad-based assessment of how this practice affects children and families. Their evaluation found that every additional judge on a case increased the number of continuances per case. Stakeholders believed that the practice improved fairness and consistency of decision-making (Summers, 2013).
- **Pilot projects can ultimately lead to partial reorganisation of the court system.** In 1991, a family court pilot project called One Judge, One Staff, One Family, was established in Jefferson County, Kentucky. Three circuit court judges and three district court judges were assigned to the project. The same judge was assigned to hear every matter concerning each family (Annie E Casey Foundation [AECF], 2001). Since the debut of the pilot project, the family court has become a division of the Circuit Court of Kentucky, based on popular vote (Kentucky Court of Justice, 2011).

    The majority of attorneys and families involved in Kentucky's One Judge, One Staff, One Family project felt positively about family court. Jefferson County community members served on advisory and focus groups and responded to surveys regarding this pilot project. Approximately two-thirds (68%) of practising attorneys surveyed believed that Family Court was an improvement for families (AECF, 2001, p. 45). Two-thirds (67%) of litigating families thought the court's ruling met their needs (AECF, 2001, p. 45).

Selected resources

Bala N., Birnbaum R. and Martinson D. (2010) 'One judge for one family: differentiated case management for families in continuing conflict.' *Canadian Journal of Family Law*, 26, p. 395.

Center for Court Innovation (2012) New York, NY: Center for Court Innovation. Access at: www.courtinnovation.org/research/browse/all/popular

National Council of Juvenile and Family Court Judges (2012) Project ONE. Reno, NV: The National Council of Juvenile and Family Court Judges. Access at: www.ncjfcj.org/our-work/project-one

PART IV

RECRUITMENT AND RETENTION OF FAMILIES

8　Family finding within child's kin and social network

Description and overview

The family-finding model discussed below provides techniques in permanency planning efforts for identifying and engaging relatives and other adults who care about a child. It was originally developed in 1999 by Kevin Campbell at Western Washington Catholic Community Services to reconnect older children and young people, who had been in care for many years, with their relatives, to facilitate permanent, sustaining relationships and, if possible, to identify potential adoptive homes. Over the following few years, the agency found relatives for all but one of nearly 500 young people, and 85 per cent were either reunified with parents or placed with relatives. This success led to Washington state passing legislation requiring intensive relative searches for all children in foster care. The model began attracting national attention in the US in 2003, when it was implemented in a seven-year California Permanency for Youth Project and then spread to other states and to British Columbia (Shirk, 2006).

The successes of the family-finding model in reconnecting older children and teens to relatives have led to applying these search techniques at earlier stages. Ideally, the discovery process begins as soon as possible, with a focus not only on placement resources but also on other ways in which relatives can support children (respite, emotional support, mentoring, connections with culture, etc.). Family finding needs to be carried out intensely and be revisited over time, because circumstances change and relatives who may not be resources at one point may step up later.

Beyond informing relatives that they can help, family finding involves acquainting young people and relatives with each other, vetting adults who may have direct involvement in the child's life, and helping structure relationships that best meet the young person's needs (Bissell and Miller, 2007). In many states, such as Pennsylvania, family finding is used in conjunction with a model for family group decision-making. Family search and engagement involves a variety of strategies, including mining the case record, interviewing young people and their significant others, and conducting internet searches. In the US, the most common search engine that family finding utilises is US Search, but others include social media, genealogy sites, local government systems and child-support enforcement agencies (Allen *et al*, 2011).

The underlying philosophy is that everyone should have lifelong connections to help them succeed; kinship bonds matter, and a permanent set of sustaining connections enables young people to develop trust, self-respect and the capacity for healthy adult relationships and roles. Campbell (2007) believes that the best way to respond to the challenges of non-permanence for young people is to utilise strategies developed by groups that are successful at times of emergency – such as those used by the Red Cross to reunite people after natural disasters. Most young people have between 100 and 300 living relatives, many of them genetically and geographically distant. Campbell asserts that relatives have a right to know when children in their extended families are in or headed for foster care, and they should be given the opportunity to help. Family finding involves casting a wide net, including using internet-based tools and finding paternal relatives, who have often been overlooked in the child welfare world (Campbell *et al*, 2003).

The Fostering Connections to Success and Increasing Adoptions Act (2008) in the US mandated early family finding by requiring that 'within 30 days after the removal of a child from the custody of the parent or parents of the child, the State shall exercise due diligence to identify and provide notice to all adult grandparents and other adult relatives of the child (including any other adult relatives suggested by the parents), subject to exceptions due to family or domestic violence'. It is crucial that child welfare staff be thoroughly trained in relative search procedures, including across geographic or cultural boundaries within country and internationally (Northcott and Jeffries, 2012). Judges can reinforce these efforts by making the identification of family members a high priority, requiring agencies to search for relatives from both sides of the family, and rendering 'no reasonable efforts' findings when an agency fails to do this (Edwards, 2008).

In England, the law requires that family finding is the first option, and local authorities are required to use family group conferences to engage the wider family early in their work to find solutions to identified problems. Relatives may be approved as foster carers, apply to adopt or seek special guardianship orders.

Key programme elements

Campbell's (2007) original family-finding model involves six steps:

- **Discovery:** Mine the case file, interview children and maternal and paternal family, and use internet search tools as needed to identify at least 40 relatives of the child, including other adults who have been significant in his/her past.
- **Engagement:** Contact and engage family members and others important to the child by sharing information and inviting them to participate in providing support.
- **Preparation and planning:** Meet with the parents, family members and others who have been identified to plan for the child's future.
- **Decision-making:** Include the young person, team and social worker in determining how the child can be integrated safely into a relationship with one or more family members and what support is needed to facilitate a lifelong connection.
- **Evaluation:** Determine if there is a plan to achieve legal and emotional permanence with a timeframe and an adequate level of support for the child and caregivers, as well as a Plan B and C if Plan A is unsuccessful.
- **Follow-up support:** The team actively supports the child and carers to access formal and informal support and services, particularly natural and community support.

The National Resource Center for Permanency and Family Connections offers a practice guide for family search; it recommends that the process be youth-driven and begin with "setting the stage" – an opportunity for the child, social worker, supervisor, carers and other professionals to discuss the process and any fears or concerns, as well as how all will be involved. The guide suggests that a social worker and supervisor decide who has the best relationship with the child for working on permanence (social worker, independent living pro-gramme social worker, foster carer, therapist, group home staff, etc.). Many tools have been developed for work with children and their relatives to assist in assessing family connections, such as ecomaps, mobility mapping, a connectedness map, and others (see Louisell, in Selected Resources and Allen *et al*, 2011).

Locating family in other jurisdictions requires collaboration with other agencies within the same country or possibly outside of it; for example, at least one in five children in the US have a foreign-born parent. Over 40,000 offspring of immigrants are in foster care, and the number of such children with relatives outside the US is much larger still. Legal scholars recommend that policies and training reflect best practice in international family finding and that states use international family-finding resources at ISS-USA (International Social Service) in order to identify relatives for foster or adoptive placements (Northcott and Jeffries, 2012). In 2009, New Jersey began a federally-funded three-year project in partnership with ISS-USA on family finding for cases with a transnational component.

Lessons learned

Finding, contacting and engaging relatives takes considerable time; experience in implementing family finding in a thorough manner underscores that this be a shared responsibility and not the sole duty of frontline workers. Possible sources for assisting with relative search include CASAs (court-appointed special advocates) or other trained volunteers, designated search staff or specialised search units, clerical and support personnel, retired workers, private agency contractors or search services, court officials, federal parent-locator services, and others. Examples of successful internal and external arrangements include the following.

- Los Angeles County hired 80 retired social workers to work part time on family finding.
- Sonoma County, California uses 20 hours per week of a clerical worker's time to conduct internet searches.
- The Illinois Department of Children and Family Services (DCFS) contracts with a private agency to conduct database searches for relatives when workers have been unable to locate them. The firm emails contact letters to the caseworker, who sends them out and follows up.
- The San Francisco Department of Social Services (DSS) partners with the local Mexican consulate, where a staff member assists in locating Mexican relatives.
- The Washington child welfare agency works with the state child support office on relative searches.

Also, it is essential to document all search activities and findings so that this information is available in the future (Bissell and Miller, 2007). Furthermore, it is important to provide training, supervision and support for effective practice with relatives.

Challenges include workers' negative attitudes about relatives, parental resistance to contacting relatives, and complex dynamics involving deep conflicts and tensions in some extended family networks. The recommended resources at the end of this section provide tools and strategies for working with extended family networks to address these challenges.

Finally, older children and young people may be fearful about reconnecting with relatives or taking steps toward permanence. The practice guide on family search and engagement (see Louisell, Selected Resources) recommends explaining and discussing family and permanency with the child or teen. They may have misconceptions about what adoption means, such as assuming they would have to change their names or lose contact with siblings and birth or foster family members. They also may fear rejection. It might be helpful for them to hear from teenagers who have been adopted and others who have aged out of care without family. "Unpacking the No" in this practice guide offers strategies for being sensitive to the young person's feelings, while gradually helping them to recognise the value of permanent adult connections that they can count on into adulthood. Also listed among the resources are curricula developed by the Family Connections Project (2008) in Chicago for helping young people explore their need for permanency.

Outcomes

The evaluation of Georgia's Permanency Roundtable initiative illustrates the key relationship between thorough relative searches and eventual permanency. This evaluation found that children in the initiative who had not had a diligent search completed soon after care entry were 63 per cent less likely to achieve permanency during the project (O'Brien et al, 2012).

Many projects using family finding have reported positive outcomes, but a rigorous evaluation has not yet been published. In 2008, Child Trends began an experimental design evaluation of the family-finding model in nine counties in North Carolina and in San Francisco County. In 2009, three additional sites were added: Florida, Maryland and Wisconsin. Some sites use the model for children first entering foster care, while others use it for children lingering in care or for all children in care. The initial final evaluation reports on these sites will be released in 2013 or 2014. Preliminary reports on Child Trends' research address the differences in the implementation of family-finding approaches near the beginning of services and later for those children lingering in care (Malm and Allen, 2011), and client perspectives on family finding (Bringewatt et al, 2013).

Family finding inspired the California Permanency for Youth Project, which evaluated progress made with a study group of 276 young people for the seven years from 2003 to 2010. Overall, 206 permanent connections for these young people were established (most had been in care for many years, were in group homes, and had no ties to relatives). Fifty young people achieved legal permanency during the study period, with many more expected to achieve permanency after it ended. Over 350 more young people in sites that were not part of the official study group were also able to create permanent connections to caring adults as a result of these efforts. A permanent connection was defined as 'an adult who consistently states and demonstrates that she or he has entered an unconditional, lifelong parent-like relationship with the young people. The young people agree that the adult will play this role in his or her life' (Seneca Center, 2012).

Selected resources

Bissell M. and Miller J. (2007) *Making "Relative Search" Happen: A guide to finding and involving relatives at every stage of the child welfare process.* Silver Spring, MD: ChildFocus.

Detter E. and Winesickle R. (2010) *Family Finding: Planning.* Pittsburgh: Pennsylvania Child Welfare Training Program. Access at: www.pacwcbt.pitt. edu/curriculum/207%20Family%20Finding/Day%203/Cntnt/Dy3_Cntnt 121010.pdf

Family Connections Project (2008) *Youth Curriculum A* (for young people who are legally free with goal of adoption): www.nrcadoption.org/pdfs/ypc/ Youth%20Curriculum%20A.pdf *Youth Curriculum B* (for young people not legally free or with goal of independence): www.nrcadoption.org/pdfs/ypc/ Youth%20Curriculum%20B.pdf

Louisell M.J. (2008) *Six Steps to Find a Family: A practice guide to family search and engagement (FSE).* New York: National Resource Center for Permanency and Family Connections (NRCPFC) and the California Permanency for Youth Project. May be accessed at: www.nrcpfc.org/ downloads/SixSteps.pdf

McClure M. (2010) *Family Finding: Decision making standard curriculum.* Pittsburgh: Pennsylvania Child Welfare Training Program. May be accessed at: www.pacwcbt.pitt.edu/curriculum/207%20Family%20Finding/Day%204/ Cntnt/Dy4_Cntnt121010.pdf

Website of National Institute for Permanent Family Connectedness (2013) Seneca Family of Agencies. Contains a range of resources on family finding. May be accessed at: www.familyfinding.org/NIPFC.html

9 Maximising the range of adoption recruitment strategies and consumer-friendly practices

Description and overview

Looking first within the constellation of extended family for perm-anency resources for children who cannot be safely reunified is a priority within the child protection systems of the US, Canada and England. Jurisdictions and individual workers, however, vary in the extent to which they pursue placements with relatives; for example, in the US, the percentage of children in care who are placed with relatives varies from six to 46 per cent across states (Annie E Casey Foundation [AECF], 2012). When responsible family members cannot become permanent parents, it is the child welfare system's responsibility to find alternative permanent families for these children. The activities involved in accomplishing this goal include recruitment of prospective adoptive or guardianship parents, assessment and training of applic-ants, linking specific children with potential families, and matching the children with families who can best meet their needs.

A personal connection to adoption, including word-of-mouth messages from others who have successfully adopted, is the most common motivating influence for adoption. Recruitment messages and practice provide the opportunity or catalyst for potential parents to translate the motivation to adopt into action (Simmonds, 2001; Cousins, 2008). A US study found that, despite a 33 per cent increase in women's interest in adoption from 1995 to 2002, those who took steps to adopt decreased from 16 per cent to 10 per cent over the same period; these scholars recommended the use of innovative recruitment strategies and a shift in messaging from awareness to taking action (Macomber *et al*, 2005).

Many methods for recruiting have been categorised into three types of strategies: *general* (targets a large audience and builds public awareness of the need for homes); *targeted* (focuses on a particular group most likely to meet the needs of a category of waiting children); and *child-specific* (seeks a family for a specific child, typically one who is harder to place). While using one type of strategy will benefit some waiting children, a broad range is necessary to effectively recruit families for many who are harder to place. Research indicates that somewhere between one in 10 and one in 28 callers enquiring about adoption actually complete the process (Simmonds, 2001; Festinger and Pratt, 2003; Geen *et al*, 2004), so maintaining consumer-friendly practices that are responsive to applicants' needs is just as essential (if not more so) as recruiting them. (See 'Lessons learned' in this chapter for a description of Oklahoma's comprehensive approach to developing consumer-friendly practice.)

There are national adoption campaigns in all three countries examined in this compendium that seek to build public awareness and provide a foundation for efforts at state and local levels – campaigns that can mount expensive media productions, the involvement of high-profile celebrities, and public service announcements created by expert professionals. Beginning in 1997, the British Association for Adoption and Fostering (BAAF) has run National Adoption Week (NAW) every November. In addition to very successful TV events over several NAWs, an award-winning billboard was produced and moved to a new site each day; it stated: 'This poster has no permanent home. Like thousands of kids in care, this poster will be moved again tomorrow' (Cousins, 2008).

In both Canada and the US, November has been designated National Adoption Month, with a broad range of activities to raise the profile of adoption. The Dave Thomas Foundation, Freddie Mac Foundation, and Jockey International sponsor initiatives to promote adoptions from care in both countries. In the US, the federal Administration on Children, Youth and Families' Children's Bureau sponsors National Adoption Month activities each year that are designed and implemented by AdoptUSKids and Child Welfare Information Gateway.[7]

---

7 More information can be found at www.childwelfare.gov/adoption/nam/

Since July 2004, the Ad Council (a major non-profit organisation that provides marketing, communications and media expertise for social issues) has partnered with the National Adoption Month coalition on a national multimedia campaign to encourage adoptions from foster care. Since the campaign's launch, over 23,000 families have registered to adopt through AdoptUSKids, and the campaign has received over $341 million in donated media support across television, radio, print, outdoor and digital media (Ad Council, 2012, 2013). In addition to prompting prospective adopters to take action by ringing a free number or enquiring through the AdoptUSKids website, these general recruitment efforts attempt to educate the public about the variety of waiting children and their critical need for families; it uses a tagline, 'You don't have to be perfect to be a perfect parent', to try to dispel common myths and negative perceptions that sensational media coverage of adoption often perpetuates.

Media campaigns may also utilise celebrities or other advocates with an adoption connection to assist them in getting their message across to the public. For example, in England, the Adoption Champions initiative, launched and run by BAAF, has recruited over 400 adoption-experienced people as volunteers to find more permanent families for waiting children.

Key programme elements

The following practices are important for recruiting adoptive applicants, as well as for maximising retention of qualified candidates.

- **Develop a system for receiving and responding to calls in a timely, friendly and professional manner.** Enquiries should go directly to an adoption-knowledgeable staff member who can engage the callers, respond to their needs and concerns with accurate information, and help them feel welcomed and needed. Studies indicate that this often does not happen as less experienced personnel are assigned to phone duty and/or as callers get transferred several times or have to leave messages, many of which are not returned, or they receive dismissive or discouraging responses (Wilson *et al*, 2005; Wallis, 2006). The latter author advises that the agency's response, sense of urgency and support need to mirror the media messages.

- **Strike a balance between screening in and screening out applicants, especially early in the process.** At early stages, the focus should be on ruling potential parents in, not out; too often, they report feeling discouraged because they receive a lot of questions about their qualifications and interests, which seem focused on excluding them, or by hearing repeated messages about the challenges they will face in parenting waiting children without examples of successful adoptions or support that can be provided (AdoptUSKids, 2003).

  The reality is that many prospective adopters initially seek very young children, particularly infants; such girls and boys make up a very small percentage of waiting children, and many of them are ultimately adopted by relatives or foster carers. For example, in the US, AFCARS statistics report four per cent of children free for adoption are under age one and 13 per cent are under age two (US Department of Health and Human Services [USDHHS], 2012). AdoptUSKids has recently undertaken a new approach for responding to initial inquiries: providing current demographic data on waiting children in the caller's state and encouraging them to consider fostering as well as adoption, particularly if they hope to adopt young children (Kathy Ledesma, personal communication, 26 October 2012).

- **Provide key information** about the children needing families, the steps in the adoption process including an estimated timeline, possible criteria that might disqualify a family from adopting, and the support available to assist adopters.

- **Be accessible and responsive.** Information should be posted within a few days of a request. Informational or orientation sessions should be held on a regular basis at convenient times and accessible locations; for example, a London charity, The Adolescent and Children's Trust (TACT), offers a Saturday "Adoption Coffee and Cake Morning" about once a month. There should be opportunities for individuals to talk with workers to address their specific questions or concerns following such meetings. It is helpful to make follow-up phone calls to those requesting information or attending information sessions and to send reminder cards for orientation sessions. Workers need to receive training on how to be most responsive to clients' needs in the adoption process.

- **Create a really good website** that offers critical information and answers to commonly asked questions. Experts advise adhering to a "three-click rule" – that is, searchers need to get what they want within three clicks of the mouse (Cousins, 2008).

- **Dispel common myths and fears.** A primary barrier to pursuing adoption is fear of being rejected or of not being able to successfully parent. In fact, a follow-up survey of those requesting information packets during NAW 2003 in England found that only 10 per cent believed most people who apply to adopt are approved (Ward, 2011). Websites and printed materials need to convey that single males and females, lesbian and gay applicants, those who have birth children living at home, empty nesters, disabled people, and current foster carers can adopt from care. Standards related to housing and finances also need to be clarified. Parenting capacity is the essential qualification.

- **Provide non-biased and fair treatment of diverse clientele**, creating an open, welcoming environment that treats prospective adopters equally. It is important to convey this reality through printed materials and on websites, to reflect it with diversity among recruitment team members, and to recruit from diverse populations.

- **Consider ways to streamline the adoption process and reduce inefficiency**. As discussed in the Outcomes section, a Barriers and Success Factors study by McRoy (2007) found that the vast majority of both discontinued applicants and finalised adopters reported barriers related to adoption process logistics (bureaucratic red tape, the stress and time involved, and errors and inconveniences experienced, such as redundant, delayed or lost paperwork).

- **Clearly communicate the "adoption support" message.** As expressed by Cousins (2008, p 12), 'No one will come forward to care for children with complex needs (especially to adopt) if they fear they will be abandoned to deal with difficulties alone.' Research into enquiries in NAW in England indicated that the two main issues about which the public wanted more information are the approval process and what services/financial assistance are available after adoption. In the interests of transparency, it would be helpful to convey eligibility and the proportion of adopters receiving financial help.

- **Maintain connections with applicants and provide support to sustain them through the process.** Adoptive families need to feel that their social workers have their best interests at heart and are advocates for them. It is important to continue to check in at least monthly, even after the families have been approved. It also may be helpful to use experienced adoptive parents as team members in recruitment, information sessions and training, and as a support resource for those in the adoption process.

- **Work collaboratively with other professionals both within and outside the agency.** Workers need to guard against allowing their own needs and attitudes, as well as agency turf/political issues, to interfere with serving the best interests of prospective adoptive parents and children.

- **Track and monitor an applicant's progress through the adoption process and provide quality assurance measures.** Evaluate these outcomes collectively to see how many parents drop out at each stage and why. Look for ways to streamline the process wherever realistic. Periodically evaluate staff responsiveness, for instance, by using a "secret shopper" method, or having an independent evaluation with applicants who dropped out and those who completed the process (AdoptUSKids, 2003).

- **Consider an ombudsman or advocate with whom applicants in the process can consult.** A power differential is built into the adoption process, since workers have the authority to decide if someone can become a parent or not. In England, BAAF operates the Independent Review Mechanism of adoption determinations, under contract with the Department for Education (DfE). This allows prospective adopters who have not been approved to apply for a review of the agency decision. The case is heard by an independent panel and a recommendation is made by that panel to the originating adoption agency, which decides whether to change or uphold the original decision (DfE, 2013).

Lessons learned

The vast majority of people who express initial interest in adoption do not move forward, and most of those contacting agencies drop out early in the process. A number of studies indicate that internal barriers (fears, anxieties and misperceptions), as well as agency-related barriers, help to shape prospective adopters' progress toward adopting (Geen *et al*, 2004; Wallis, 2006; McRoy, 2007; Denby *et al*, 2011; Ward, 2011).

A social marketing study using telephone interviews with over 600 individuals analysed the factors associated with their likelihood of considering fostering or special needs adoption (Helm *et al*, 2006). Six distinct dimensions accounted for 52 per cent of the variance in responses: psychological barriers (social, privacy and financial issues); negative perceptions of the child; positive motives; self-reported knowledge; concerns about the process; and fear. By increasing individuals' knowledge about foster care and adoption, and by providing information or experiences that mitigate potential barriers and negative perceptions, the inhibiting impact of fear can be reduced. The goal in recruitment and retention should be not to let interested and qualified persons rule themselves out based on misinformation or inadequate responsiveness of the agency.

Wallis's (2006) study of individuals enquiring about adoption in England found that three-quarters of respondents were *concerned that they would not be eligible to adopt*, usually because of their age, income, housing, health or being single. Those with concerns about income and housing were less likely to express them with a social worker and less likely to begin the process. Even if they did raise these issues, they had difficulty getting clear answers. It is important to be aware that these issues can pose barriers to qualified adoptive parents continuing toward their goal, so prospective adopters need to be given every opportunity to share their concerns and to receive information that clearly addresses them.

Two US studies focusing on the attrition of prospective parents throughout the adoption process underscored the saliency of agency-related barriers (Wilson *et al*, 2005; McRoy, 2007). The first of these studies highlighted the *critical importance of the first phone call to the agency*, viewing this as a turning point from consideration to action. The researchers found that this first call was an intensely emotional experience for many, such as those who are infertile and who have experienced many setbacks in their attempts to become parents. Often this first call was not a positive experience – the caller was transferred to various people, left a message that was not returned, or felt the worker was not encouraging.

Another critical factor in maximising retention of qualified applicants is a *relationship with a caring, competent social worker who is accessible, maintains regular contact and provides support* throughout the process (Denby *et al*, 2011). Building trust that allows applicants to be honest about their concerns and doubts, and to believe that the worker understands their situation and will advocate for them, helps to reduce stress and build confidence.

An exemplary approach to developing and maintaining a consumer-friendly service orientation for effective recruitment and retention of foster and adoptive families is Oklahoma's Bridge to the Future project (2012). The project used data gathered through 12 focus groups with a range of stakeholders and surveys of current resource families to inform a required online training for child welfare staff ("Customer Service: Valuing Our Resource Families"); established a Bridge Resource Support Center and web portal to assist prospective and current resource families (including regular follow-up and data tracking); and instituted a process-improvement plan, including strategies such as "rapid-improvement events" and all-day training sessions focused on particular parts of the process, such as home studies. Some of the project's tools and those of 14 other diligent recruitment grant projects can be accessed on the website of AdoptUSKids (2012a).

AdoptUSKids (2013a) has advanced a PRO (processes, relationships and organisation) framework for supporting good customer service in child welfare organisations. This framework emphasises timely, relevant and consistent response; building mutual trust and partnership in relationships; and establishing customer service as an organisational priority as well as a culture that responds to both staff and families' needs. This AdoptUSKids publication, listed in the resources section, outlines principles and structure to support the PRO framework.

Outcomes

National recruitment campaigns in England and the US have tracked the response to advertising. For example, in England about 5,000 families requested information packets during NAW in 2003; a follow-up survey of 493 families one year later reported that 57 per cent took no further action, 20 per cent telephoned an agency but did not apply, 13 per cent applied, five per cent withdrew after application, and five per cent had a child placed with them (Ward, 2011). The Ad Council, which collaborates with AdoptUSKids on the national initiative on behalf of the US Children's Bureau, reported that a telephone operation already in effect prior to the initial campaign reported a little over 4,000 calls in the previous 18 months. In the 18 months following the campaign launch in July 2004, more than 14,000 calls were received – a 336 per cent increase. Also, recruitment campaigns that dispelled myths about who is eligible to adopt were effective (Bell *et al*, 2002; Wallis, 2006).

Studies consistently find that only *a small portion of those enquiring about adoption actually take steps to apply, with attrition at each successive step in the process* (Geen *et al*, 2004; McRoy, 2007; Ward, 2011). Agency-related factors are reported by many prospective parents (Wallis, 2006; McRoy, 2007; Ward, 2011).

McRoy (2007) conducted an in-depth study, for the US Children's Bureau, of families who engaged in the process of adopting from foster care (102 discontinued and 98 finalised). While family- and child-related factors were reported by families, *attrition was most often attributed to agency-related factors.* The primary reason for dropping out before the home study was most likely to be a family-related factor, such as change in circumstances; but those who dropped out prior to approval or between approval and placement cited agency factors as the top barrier they experienced. *The largest group of drop-outs was approved but had no child placed* (52%). The 98 parents with finalised adoptions also reported agency factors as the top barrier they experienced; overall, the longer that families stayed in the process, the greater the likelihood that they would report agency-related barriers. For the 53 families who dropped out between approval and placement, agency barriers reported were adoption process logistics (94%), communication/responsiveness (87%), agency emotional support (75%), jurisdictional and interjurisdictional issues (28%), level of agency bias and cultural competence (28%), and availability of services (26%).

A range of parent factors are associated with the likelihood of follow-through, and some types of prospective adopters are more vulnerable to poor agency responses. Those who drop out of the process are more likely to be single, be lower-income, be Hispanic, report altruism as a primary motivation rather than infertility, and be non-professionals (Simmonds, 2001; Hollingsworth, 2002, Geen *et al*, 2004; Wallis, 2006). Also, single people with no support or couples who were relying on each other for support were seven times less likely to embark on the process than those with a bigger support network (Wallis, 2006). Parent factors associated with greater likelihood of applying to adopt or with completing the process include being over 40, having a university education, being willing to adopt a child with learning or physical disabilities and sibling groups, having more positive percep-tions of the adoption process and being married (Geen *et al*, 2004; Wallis, 2006; Ward, 2011). Wallis (2006) emphasised that groups with lower socio-economic status and fewer resources are more vulnerable to dropping out and are often reluctant to raise questions with a worker.

There are mixed findings on whether *African American prospective parents* are more or less likely to adopt. Surveys of adoption interest have found greater interest in adopting from foster care among black and Hispanic families (Macomber *et al*, 2005; Center for Adoption Research and Massachusetts Adoption Resource Exchange [MARE], 2006); for example, the latter survey found that 33 per cent of black and 28 per cent of Hispanic respondents had seriously considered foster care adoption, compared to 19 per cent of Caucasians. The social marketing study on the likelihood of considering fostering or adopting found that the African American community is much more open to these; when compared with non-minority respondents, they reported more knowledge of foster care and adoption, more positive perceptions of the children, and fewer psychological barriers or fears; however, they were more concerned about the enrolment process itself (Helm *et al*, 2006).

The extent to which interest translates into action among prospective minority adopters is less clear. Historically, studies have found that African Americans experienced many barriers to adoption, particularly agency-related factors (Herzog *et al*, 1971; Festinger, 1972; Day, 1979; Rodriguez and Meyer, 1990; Gilles and Kroll, 1991). Wallis's (2006) study in England found that black enquirers appeared to experience extremes of good and poor practice, but overall reported more than three times the incidence of poor agency responses. McRoy (2007) found no differences in barriers experienced by families of colour and Caucasian families who finalised adoptions and no significant differences among those dropping out that indicated minority families experienced more agency barriers.

In summary, the body of research indicates that motivation to adopt is shaped by a complex array of knowledge, perceptions, feelings and life circumstances, some of which may be mitigated by receiving information or addressing fears. Recruitment campaigns are successful in increasing enquiries about adopting, but a small percentage of those who contact an agency actually apply within the subsequent year, and only about half of this group ultimately has a child placed with them. Myriad agency-related factors contribute to failure to retain a significant number of prospective adoptive parents, so improved agency practice is imperative to maximise permanency resources for waiting children.

Selected resources

AdoptUSKids (2003) *Practitioner's Guide: Getting more parents for children from your recruitment efforts*. Baltimore, MD: The Collaboration to AdoptUSKids. Access at: www.bit.ly/NPpYU0

AdoptUSKids (2011b) *National Adoption Month Capacity Building Toolkit*. Section 1: Supporting and retaining families (pp. 1–29). Access at: www.adoptuskids.org/_assets/files/NRCRRFAP/resources/national-adoption-month-toolkit-2011.pdf

AdoptUSKids (2012b) *Improving Customer Service: Prospective parent orientation sessions – 10 things you can do*. Access at: www.bit.ly/PcSBF6

AdoptUSKids (2013a) *Using Customer Service Concepts to Enhance Recruitment and Retention Processes*. National Resource Center for Diligent Recruitment at AdoptUSKids. Access at: www.adoptuskids.org/_assets/files/using-customer-service-concepts-to-enhance-recuitment-and-retention-practices.pdf

Cousins J. (2008) *Ten Top Tips on Finding Families*, London: BAAF.

Oklahoma Bridge to the Future Project (2012) Bridge to the Future Project Highlights and Products (including Resource Parent Satisfaction Survey). Access at: www.adoptuskids.org/about-us/diligent-recruitment-grantees/bridge-to-the-future

10 Innovative practices in targeted adoption recruitment

Description and overview

There is invariably a mismatch between the characteristics of waiting children and those whom adoptive applicants are seeking, not only in terms of demographics (such as child's age and minority status), but also in other respects. An analysis of England's 2006 Adoption Register revealed that there were 471 black and minority ethnic children, as compared to 212 prospective adoptive families for black and minority ethnic children (Cousins, 2008); and the following year's report indicated 240 sibling groups of three, but only 59 families willing to consider adopting this number of siblings (Dance et al, 2010). Targeted recruitment seeks to remedy such imbalances.

Targeted recruitment seeks to find homes for a specific group of children, such as older children and those with special health conditions, or to reach a specific group of high-propensity prospective adopters. The aim is to target agency resources and efforts towards families who are most likely to meet the needs of waiting children. To be most effective, these efforts are built on data that provide information about where and how to reach the targeted audience, as well as collaboration with representatives of that community who can assist in developing and executing strategies. It also requires steps to ensure that when prospective adopters respond, agency professionals are capable of engaging applicants in a culturally competent manner; for example, if Spanish-speaking families are targeted, Spanish materials, bilingual workers, adoption preparation classes in Spanish, and other steps are essential (AdoptUSKids, 2008).

A technique called "market segmentation" has been applied to adoption recruitment in recent years (Blackstone et al, 2008; AdoptUSKids, 2011a). It has been used in the business world for many years to analyse the profile(s) of consumers who use a certain product and to then figure out how best to reach and serve them. In relation to adoption, scholars argue that the "market" for waiting children is not a single pool, but is made up of segments of the population who are drawn to specific types of children (Blackstone *et al*, 2008). Four fundamental questions to address are: 'Who are the targets you most want to reach? What are they like? Where are they located? How can you reach them most cost-effectively?' (AdoptUSKids, 2011a, p. 2).

Some studies recommend targeting high-propensity groups of adopters; for example, an analysis of interest in adoptions from foster care in the US recommended targeting specific groups of women interested in such adoptions – 30–34-year-olds, black and Hispanic, and single and lower-income women (Macomber *et al*, 2005). Similarly, other studies recommend focusing on gay and lesbian prospective parents (Gates *et al*, 2007; Brodzinsky, 2011a).

Diligent recruitment of minority adopters: Probably the most common form of targeted recruitment involves outreach to minority groups that are over-represented in the child welfare system. While white people (non-Hispanic) make up the majority of the populations of the US (64%), England (87%) and Canada (80%), minorities are over-represented in the child welfare systems of all three countries. Minority ethnic groups make up 59 per cent of children in care in the US and 23 per cent in England. Also, in Canada, aboriginal and children of colour are over-represented (Swift, 2011); in British Columbia, for example, aboriginal children represent approximately five per cent of the population but 53 per cent of children in care (Federation of BC Youth in Care Networks, 2010).[8]

In the US, the Multi-Ethnic Placement Act requires that states carry out diligent recruitment of prospective foster carers and adoptive

8 Population and child welfare statistics taken from: www.census.gov/prod/ cen2010/briefs/c2010br-05.pdf; https://docs.google.com/spreadsheet/ccc?key= 0AonYZs4MzlZbdFJ6OVF1U3JZTXEyYnFjb0k1clJvOFEandhl=en#gid=0; http://en. wikipedia.org/wiki/Demographics_of_Canada#Visible_minorities_and_ Aboriginals; www.acf.hhs.gov/programs/cb/stats_research/afcars/tar/report 19.pdf; www.education.gov.uk/rsgateway/DB/SFR/s001026/index.shtml; www. bcstats.gov.bc.ca/StatisticsBySubject/AboriginalPeoples/CensusProfiles.aspx

parents who reflect the ethnicity of children in foster care, while at the same time mandating that ethnicity not be a barrier to adoption and forbidding ethnic matching. Recruitment of minority groups is common in all three countries. Tailoring the message to the needs and perspectives of the targeted population, and making sure that project staff and culture reflect the communities they are seeking to engage, are major components of these efforts (Cousins, 2008; AdoptUSKids, 2011b). In the US there are also a number of adoption agencies that specialise in serving minority families (see directory at AdoptUSKids, 2010).

A London-based project sought to find out why so few African and African-Caribbean people applied to adopt; it identified a range of barriers (misinformation, fears, cultural issues around discussing infertility and others) that provided helpful framing for recruitment efforts (Cousins, 2008).

An example of a diligent recruitment project in the US is Denver's Village (2012), which uses six community-based recruitment teams (CBRTs) to target specific geographic areas. CBRTs include resource families, young people, community members, faith-based organisations, schools, child welfare staff and others. Each team develops its own recruitment plan and strategies, which are informed by community-specific data and include about four activities a month, sometimes connected to local events.

Faith-based recruitment efforts: Faith-based organisations have focused on child welfare for centuries, but efforts to systematically engage them in recruiting families for children in care are more recent. These are occurring in all three countries with many different faith groups, including Protestant, Catholic, Jewish, Muslim and other faiths or organisations. An adoption attitude survey (Center for Adoption Research and Massachusetts Adoption Research Exchange, 2006) found that those most likely to prefer obtaining information from their place of worship were African Americans (75%). For several decades, efforts to recruit African American adopters have partnered with churches, beginning with the One Church/One Child programme started in Illinois in 1980 by Father George Clements; its goal was to find one family in every African American church who would adopt a child. This programme spread to over half of the states and has led to the adoptions of more than 140,000 children (AdoptUSKids, 2004).

Another poignant example of a faith-based collaboration is the Bennett Chapel Missionary Baptist Church in a rural area of East Texas known as Possum Trot. After the pastor and his wife adopted, they recruited other interested families and arranged for the child welfare department to train prospective resource parents at their church, eventually leading to the adoption of over 75 children (Belanger *et al*, 2008; Villalva, 2012). (See video clip on YouTube: www.youtube.com/watch?v=a8RRvzvw1SU.)

Recruitment of gay and lesbian parents: Child welfare professionals are making increasing efforts to engage and collaborate with lesbian, gay, bisexual and transgender (LGBT) communities and organisations. In England, an LGBT Fostering and Adoption Week (2013) and a charity, New Family Social (2012), are devoted exclusively to recruiting and supporting gay and lesbian adoptive and foster parents. In New York City, the Administration for Children's Services and private child welfare agencies collaborate with the Lesbian, Gay, Bisexual and Transgender Community Center on an LGBT Foster Care Project (2012) that seeks to enhance services for LGBT young people in care, as well as to increase the number of adoptive parents and foster carers from this community.

In addition to the types of targeted efforts described above, some agencies seek to recruit families for specific needs, such as large sibling groups, medically fragile children or teenagers.

Key programme elements

Myriad principles and strategies are offered for the targeted recruitment of a range of groups. Some of the foundational aspects include the following.

- **Analyse demographic and other data on children in care** to identify the types with the greatest unmet needs for permanency.

Some additional questions to explore include: What are the primary profiles of current adoptive families? From what areas of the community are most children removed and have these areas been targeted in recruiting?

- **Decide what types of parents are most likely to adopt these children** and where to target specialised recruitment efforts. (This may be based on an analysis of the characteristics of families who have already adopted such children.)
- **Cultivate relationships with members of the target community** and seek to engage them in supporting recruitment efforts.
- **Develop a recruitment team**, including current foster carers, adoptive parents, young people, staff and others who are members of the targeted community.
- **Identify other community organisations or partners** who are willing to collaborate by endorsing recruitment efforts or providing resources.
- **Frame messages** to appeal to the target group's values, meet its needs and reduce known barriers to taking action within that group.
- **Develop culturally sensitive and properly translated tools and materials**, including printed materials, media messages and web-based information. (Materials should contain images of adoptive families from the targeted community.)
- Plan and execute **strategies for messages to reach the target population**.
- **Provide outreach at events or venues** in the target community and develop and implement **orientation programmes** that reach specific communities.
- **Ensure that the adoption process is welcoming and inclusive** for prospective applicants who come forward from the targeted community. For example, this may mean providing training to staff on cultural competence in working with specific types of families, requiring training in a specific language, or asking if applicants have a partner instead of whether they're married.
- **Track and evaluate activities and outcomes**. Feedback will help in modifying strategies to be most effective.

Lessons learned

Many targeted recruitment projects have developed and issued recommendations for innovative strategies for reaching families – below are two examples.

- Project MATCH in Kentucky hired and trained experienced resource parents to work as diligent recruitment specialists. They identified a segment of the community to target and a local restaurant where such families were most likely to eat (a Ponderosa steakhouse). They partnered with the steakhouse to advertise on its sign, to distribute brochures inside, and to have employees wear shirts promoting the project (AdoptUSKids, 2011b).
- A study of 113 adoptive parents in East Texas and Louisiana (some from the Bennett Chapel church mentioned earlier) found that they viewed their faith in God as central to their lives and to their choice to adopt. These social work researchers recommended that the message in faith-based recruitment with similar groups may need to be reframed from a marketing-type approach to asking them to search their hearts and discern if this is something God is leading them to do (Belanger *et al*, 2008). It would also be important for child welfare staff who are working with faith-based groups to be culturally competent in respecting their beliefs.

Outcomes

No comprehensive evaluations of targeted recruitment activities with experimental designs could be found. Research on adoption attitudes and behaviour has reported factors linked with adopting among specific groups, many of which were cited earlier in this volume; for example, the Urban Institute found that black parents already adopt foster children at a rate that is double their proportion in the general population (Geen, 2003).

Some studies of specific minority populations investigate attitudes toward adoption, barriers, and types of recruitment practices that could be most influential. For example, Bausch and Serpe (1999) surveyed approximately 600 Mexican Americans about their attitudes towards adoption and identified both structural and cultural obstacles to adopting; structural obstacles were identified by respondents as more important than cultural obstacles. Among respondents who were likely to adopt, factors or techniques that were most likely to influence them were: having friends or relatives who had adopted, more information, support groups for those seeking to adopt, and financial assistance.

Some targeted recruitment programmes have offered data on outcomes.

- **Denver's Village** has been operating for four years. When the project began, children waited an average of 34.6 months after termination of parental rights to achieve permanency. That average has dropped to about 13 months. Additionally, more than 650 children have been adopted over the course of the project, and in its first year, Denver's Village increased the number of resource families from the communities of children in care by 55 per cent (AdoptUSKids, 2011b).

- **The Oklahoma Bridge to the Future project** (2012) established a faith-based recruitment programme for new foster and adoptive families. In 2011, 42 churches from around the state agreed to recruit from their congregations, leading to applications by 110 new families. Nearly 60 per cent of these families completed the approval process, as compared to the usual completion rate of 30 per cent. Another faith-based effort, "Home for the Holidays", was mounted by a large church in Tulsa and then replicated by another in Oklahoma City. This programme sought to find families who were approved as alternative carers to host children from shelter settings over Thanksgiving/Christmas. All eligible children were matched with families, some of whom sought to become licensed.

- **Familias Para Niños** was a collaborative project involving two private adoption agencies seeking to increase the number of Hispanic children adopted in two Texas counties. It placed 124 Hispanic children, nearly double the initial objective of 67 (US DHSS, 2005).

- In 2008 a faith-based organisation, **Focus on the Family**, began a collaborative recruitment effort with seven counties of the Colorado Division of Child Welfare Services. Its first annual event, held in Colorado Springs, was attended by 1,300 people and resulted in 260 families beginning the adoption process. Colorado had 790 waiting children at that time, and by early 2010, this number had been reduced to 365 (*Denver Post*, 2010). The programme now operates in 12 states: www.icareaboutorphans.org/Florida.aspx.

Selected resources

AdoptUSKids (2005) *Finding Common Ground: A guide for child welfare agencies working with communities of faith*. Access at: www.adoptuskids. org/_assets/files/NRCRRFAP/resources/finding-common-ground.pdf

AdoptUSKids (2008) *Nuestra Familia, Nuestra Cultura (our family, our culture): Promoting and supporting Latino families in adoption and foster care*. Access at: www.adoptuskids.org/_assets/files/NRCRRFAP/resources/ nuestra-familia-nuestra-cultura.pdf

AdoptUSKids (2011a) *Overview of Market Segmentation: A tool for targeting recruitment*. National Resource Center for Recruitment and Retention of Adoptive Parents. Access at: www.adoptuskids.org/_assets/files/NRCRRFAP/ resources/overview-of-market-segmentation.pdf

AdoptUSKids (2011b) *National Adoption Month Capacity Building Toolkit*. Sections 2 and 3: Diligent recruitment and Working with diverse populations (pp. 30–60). Access at: www.adoptuskids.org/_assets/files/NRCRRFAP/ resources/national-adoption-month-toolkit-2011.pdf

AdoptUSKids (2012a) *Diligent Recruitment Grantees: Resources developed from grant projects*. Access at: www.adoptuskids.org/about-us/diligent-recruitment-grantees

AdoptUSKids (2012c) *Strategies for Recruiting Lesbian, Gay, Bisexual and Transgender Foster, Adoptive and Kinship Families*. Access at: www.adopt uskids.org/_assets/files/strategies-for-recruiting-LGBT-foster-adoptive-kinship-families.pdf

All Children-All Families Resources (2012) Human Rights Campaign. Access at: www.hrc.org/resources/entry/all-children-all-families-about-the-initiative

Betts B. and Mallon G.P. (2004) *Recruiting, Assessing and Supporting Lesbian and Gay Carers and Adopters*. London: BAAF.

Hill N. (2012) *The Pink Guide to Adoption*, London: BAAF.

Hill N. (2013) *Proud Parents: Lesbian and gay fostering and adoption experiences*, London: BAAF.

Mellish L., Jennings S., Tasker F., Lamb M. and Golombok S. (2013) *Gay, Lesbian and Heterosexual Adoptive Families: Family relationships, child adjustment and adopters' experiences*, London: BAAF.

New Family Social (2012) *Adoption Resources for Recruiting and Supporting LGBT Adoptive and Foster Families in the UK*. Access at: www.newfamily social.co.uk/

Rule G. (2006) *Recruiting Black and Minority Ethnic Adopters/Foster Carers*, London: BAAF.

11 Intensive child-specific adoption recruitment

Description and overview

Child-specific recruitment focuses on finding an adoptive family for a particular child. Media-based child-specific recruitment is the most familiar type, through photo-listing books and websites, newspapers, magazines, newsletters, videos and television appeals. The first adoption photo-listing book was developed over 50 years ago by the Massachusetts Adoption Resource Exchange, and such efforts continued to expand and evolve. Today there are national photo-listing adoption resources in all three countries. There are still conflicting attitudes about the use of media to feature specific children for adoption, and professionals have sought ways to protect children's privacy.

The *National Adoption Register*[9] is a service, operated by BAAF on behalf of the Department for Education in England, that facilitates matches of children and prospective adopters in England. Local authorities must refer children to the Register by three months after their approval for adoption; approved families are referred by agencies or self-referred. Professionals use the database to suggest possible matches. In addition, the Register operates exchange events where children's profiles are presented locally and prospective adopters invited to view profiles and talk with the child's social worker. *Be My Parent*[10] began as a newspaper approximately 30 years ago, with photo-listings of waiting children; it expanded in 2007 to include a website. Some children's profiles are available to the public, but prospective parents must register and subscribe to access details of all children listed and to make enquiries. Some profiles contain video/audio clips and children's artwork. In a survey of local authorities and

---

9   www.adoptionregister.org.uk/
10 www.bemyparent.org.uk/

voluntary agencies, *Be My Parent* and the *Adoption Register* were the third and fourth most common sources for linking children and families, after agencies' own resources and regional consortia of adoption agencies that meet periodically (Dance *et al*, 2010).

The Adoption Council of Canada established a web-based photo-listing service, Canada's Waiting Kids,[11] in 1997. It receives referrals from six Canadian provinces (Alberta, Manitoba, Ontario, Prince Edward Island, Nova Scotia and Saskatchewan). This listing service uses pseudonyms for children's first names and requires prospective adopters to register and receive a password. In order to make enquiries about a specific child, individuals must fill out an application form and be in the adoption process. Council staff follow up when enquiries are referred to workers but families have not heard anything within two weeks. Some individual provinces also have their own adoption listing services, as do some states in the US. These vary in character-istics; for example, Alberta's website contains film clips and is open to the public, whereas British Columbia's Adoption Bulletin has an online profile listing that does not include photos (Sarah Pedersen, personal communication, 28 August 2012).

The US created a national photo-listing website in 1994, which was expanded in 2002 through an agreement with the Adoption Exchange Association and the Collaboration to AdoptUSKids.[12] The website reports that approximately 21,000 children who had been listed now live with permanent families.

Many US states and Canadian provinces have their own adoption registries and photo-listing services, and there are regional ones as well, such as the Northwest Adoption Resource Exchange, facilitating links between children and prospective adoptive parents in four US states. Ontario's Adoption Resource Exchange sponsors province-wide conferences for prospective adoptive parents twice a year where staff of Children's Aid Societies display information on waiting children; they recently added smaller events to draw from specific

---

11 www.canadaswaitingkids.ca/index.html
12 www.adoptuskids.org/

regions of the province. Such exchanges also provide an opportunity for professionals to network with each other, as is the case with adoption consortia between local authorities and voluntary adoption agencies in England.

There are myriad other media-based child-specific recruitment programmes, such as the TV show *Wednesday's Child*, sponsored by the Freddie Mac Foundation (2012) in five large cities across the US and replicated by TV stations in many other cities and in Alberta, Canada. Other news outlets feature photo-listings and profiles, such as "Today's Child", featured once a month in the *Toronto Star*. The *Heart Gallery* (2013) was developed by a professional photographer in New Mexico, who was interested in adopting from foster care and was struck by the "mug shots" presented to her of waiting children. The first showing opened in 2001 in Santa Fe and spread quickly across the US, where there are over 120 Heart Galleries, and also to Canada and other countries. It is a travelling photographic and audio exhibit featuring compelling portraits of waiting children made by professional photographers.

In addition to raising public awareness about waiting children, child-specific recruitment venues allow prospective adopters to take the initiative in identifying the child(ren) whom they would like to adopt – an activity that in the past has been completely under the control of social workers. Adoption professionals use various means to offer approved applicants an opportunity to see and hear from "real" children who are waiting for placement and to get more of a sense of the whole child (Cousins, 2008). A certain amount of chemistry attracts prospective parents to specific children, so providing opportunities for interactions allows adopters to better identify and connect with girls and boys whom they may adopt.

Adoption parties or *activity days* are very effective recruitment opportunities that enable children and adults to engage. The Massachusetts Adoption Resource Exchange (MARE, 2012) reports that 35 per cent of its 173 placements in FY2011 were attributed to adoption parties (one of 12 recruitment sources). A similar effort, operated through the Northwest Adoption Resource Exchange, is an annual Kids' Fest that brings together waiting children and prospective parents in a carnival-type annual event. As a result of MARE's success with adoption parties, England has renewed the use of Adoption Activity Days, which are organised events for waiting children and potential families in a two-year project managed by BAAF (2012a; Hilpern, 2011) and which is now being rolled out across England with funding from the Department for Education.

Finally, exploring the network of kin, fictive kin and other significant adults in the child's current or past life is the most common type of child-specific recruitment (Casey Family Programs, 2003). "Family finding", the systematic exploration of extended family resources based on Campbell's methods, is used both soon after removal within the child's kinship network and after years in care. The same approach is used within a broad network of adults already known to the specific girl or boy in several child-specific recruitment programmes focused on placing older children and teens (North American Council on Adoptable Children, 2009a; Avery, 2010; Eckholm, 2010). Techniques include record mining as well as interviewing former foster carers, former and current caseworkers, teachers, coaches, church members, Boy and Girl Scout leaders – and the wide range of adults with whom every child in care will have had some contact at some time.

A child-specific recruitment model that has been developed in the US and spread to Canada is Wendy's Wonderful Kids (Wendy's Wonderful Kids [WWK], 2013). The Dave Thomas Foundation for Adoption dedicated significant resources to develop, implement and grow a national, evidence-based model of child-focused recruitment, focusing on older and at-risk young people. WWK developed a model that was implemented in seven programme sites in 2004, spreading to over 120 fully funded sites in all 50 states, Washington DC and four Canadian provinces, serving over 7,000 children and young people. Grants from the Dave Thomas Foundation support agencies in hiring full-time, experienced adoption professionals who dedicate 100 per cent of their work to finding families for young people at high risk of ageing out without families. WWK grantees follow a prescribed set of strategies for child-focused recruitment including intensive case file review; monthly contact with children, caseworkers and all relevant stakeholders (guardians ad litem, counsellors, foster parents, etc.); adoption assessment and preparation for the children; due diligence on potential family members or others that may lead to an adoption; and the development of detailed recruitment plans (see Outcomes below for WWK evaluation findings).

Key programme elements

Adoption experts offer general guidelines for media-related, child-specific recruitment activities, including the following.

- **Protect children's privacy by limiting what is disclosed.** Last names and locations, in particular, should never be disclosed. Some sites go further in protecting privacy by requiring those who view profiles to have registered with the sites or to be approved to adopt.
- **Information disclosed should be honest, but balanced and engaging.** It is important not to write anything hurtful that would be damaging to the children should they read the listing now or in the future. The profile needs to be written by someone who really knows and likes the child and serve to personalise him or her through engaging descriptions.
- **Include details about the child's unique qualities and how challenges are manifested and managed.** Canada's Waiting Kids (2012c) offers Guidelines for writing descriptions of children (listed in Selected Resources) and suggests tips such as to include colourful details of their unique qualities; highlight the children's progress and ways to manage challenges; if diagnoses are given, provide examples as to how these manifest themselves; and indicate if financial support is available.
- **Prepare children and their caregivers for any media-based or other child-specific recruitment initiatives**. Make sure the children understand that adoption is the goal and that this activity is to find a family. Children aged 10 or older may help to write their descriptions or pick their photos. Show the children where they will be featured and help them anticipate possible results, including how to handle their feelings. The children may have misinformation,

could fear rejection, or could have a range of other understandable fears or concerns. Share successful adoption stories and, if possible, provide connections with other foster/adopted children as a good source of support.

- **Utilise photos** in photo-listings or media events that are of professional quality, in colour, and show positive attributes.
- **Produce high-quality material about the children**, whether through words, film clips, displaying children's artwork or writing, or other means to help them "come alive".
- **Feature the children in a wide variety of ways**.
- **Set up a system for responding promptly to enquiries** from prospective adoptive parents. A study in England reported that over half of the 442 respondents who enquired about featured children found it to be a negative experience because the social workers they contacted did not return calls and sometimes seemed rude (*Be My Parent*, 2004). It was quite distressing for respondents to continue to see children listed when they had expressed interest and received no acknowledgement (O'Reilly, 2007).

Exploring the network of current and past relationships is a common approach of child-specific recruitment, particularly for older children and teens. Some of the foundational strategies in this work are listed below.

- **Have staff and recruiters who believe that young people can be adopted** and who are committed to this goal.
- **Identify adults known to the children who might be interested in becoming permanent resources for them or in helping to find one**. Mine the case record and interview children to identify important relationships in their past and current lives. Contacts that may prove valuable may include previous carers, respite workers, teachers, school staff, church members, Scout leaders, friends' parents and others. (Friends and family of these people can help by word of mouth.) Also, birth family members who may have had problems in the past may now be in a better place to become permanent resources for young people.

- **Empower young people to be involved in permanency work.** Involve young people in sensitive and careful examinations of their understandings and concerns about adoption and guardianship. For instance, it is more effective to move away from the formulaic question "Do you want to be adopted?" (to which the answer often is "No") to a conversation about "How do we work together to get you a lifelong connection with loving adults?" Sometimes young people do not know the facts about adoption and guardianship; they may have fears of rejection or of never being able to see their birth family again. They may need help to recognise the value of ongoing family support in young adulthood and to allow themselves to be more open to this possibility (National Resource Center for Foster Care and Permanency Planning and Casey Family Services, 2004).
- **Maintain regular contact with young people and all other adults involved** in permanency work on their behalf. Work with these individuals to develop a detailed recruitment plan.
- **General recruitment for those young people without identified resources.** While most adoptions of older children and teens come through foster carers or relatives, homes can be found through outreach methods as well, including telling the young person's story and photo-listings through initiatives such as AdoptUSKids, the *Heart Gallery* of America, *Wednesday's Child*, and *Be My Parent* in the UK.

Lessons learned

Evaluations of some child-specific recruitment programmes identify strategies that are productive in finding families for hard-to-place young people. For example, an agency in New York, You Gotta Believe, piloted a federally funded project from 2004 to 2008 to serve teenagers who were at risk of exiting care to homelessness. The 199 young people referred were on average 15.7 years old and had been in care for more than seven years; 95 per cent resided in residential treatment or group home settings. Recruitment involved diligent work with each teenager to identify significant people from existing or past relationships (kin, fictive kin, friends, teachers, acquaintances). Staff contacted each person on behalf of the young person and encouraged identified resources to attend a team meeting (led by the young person and a staff member) to assist with finding a family for the teenager. The focus was on setting goals and working out strategies for achieving permanency prior to the young person's emancipation. When no possible permanency resources could be identified, young people were quickly engaged in activities that would expose them to prospective adoptive parents, including serving on training panels, working in offices where prospective parents came to learn about available children, and participating in events and other gatherings for current and prospective adoptive families (Avery, 2010).

The agency held heavily advertised training courses around New York, and prospective permanency resources, i.e., those people offering permanence or assisting in finding a permanent family were specifically encouraged to attend. Over the course of the project, nearly 50 per cent of the young people were placed in adoptive homes. One of the most interesting findings of the evaluation was that most of the adults who entered the training were not known to a specific teenager, but were open to the possibility of adopting an older child. These participants were the *least* likely to adopt (or to achieve each step toward adoption, from completing training, to completing a home study, to having a teenager placed with them). Only four per cent in this category had a teenager placed in their homes by the study's conclusion. The adults most likely to finish the process were those already known to the teenager; 53 per cent in this category who attended training ultimately had a young person placed with them. Furthermore, of those in this group who completed all steps through the home study, 99 per cent received a placement. Avery (2010) underscores the power of the combination of teenager-specific recruitment with skilled, experienced and dedicated staff members, along with focused and flexible parent training.

The evaluation of the WWK programme identified key practices that were important to the success of this recruitment model, including recruiters establishing one-on-one relationships with the children they are seeking to place, diligent search for potential families, and aggressive follow-up with identified contacts. It also is important to clarify who is responsible for preparing children for adoption and for those professionals to meet regularly with the children to develop rapport and trust (Malm *et al*, 2011a). The WWK programme is in the process of developing a manualised curriculum on this recruitment model.

Outcomes

It is hard to gauge the actual effectiveness of media-based, child-specific recruitment methods like photo-listing services or television appeals. For example, evaluations of AdoptUSKids reported a 300 per cent increase in traffic to the website over its first four years of operation, reaching 268,000 a month in autumn 2006. Professionals and registered families have an opportunity to provide feedback and have reported high levels of satisfaction with the site. An evaluation in autumn 2006 reported that 42 per cent of the almost 17,000 children who had been photo-listed had been placed (Freundlich *et al*, 2007). Also, Canada's Waiting Kids reported that 85 per cent of children referred to that site go on to find a permanent family (Pedersen, personal communication, 28 August 2012). So we know people visit sites and adopt children, but what is hard to determine is whether the photo-listing itself or another activity was the actual reason for a given adoption.

The Canadian province of Alberta established a photo-listing service in 2003 and reported in an evaluation after its first year that there was a 63 per cent increase in applications received and screened and a 29 per cent increase in applications approved. Among applications approved during the year, 20 per cent were due to the web page. The evaluators interviewed a random sample of 12 children who were photo-listed, all aged seven and older, to assess their thoughts and feelings about the process. Nearly all of them expressed completely positive feelings – hopeful, happy and excited – and one child reported "feeling famous". Two children expressed mixed feelings, with one stating that only parents who were going to adopt children should see the photos and profiles, and another expressing concern about being seen by other children at school. All of the children interviewed believed that putting their photo profiles on the web page was a good idea (Alberta Children's Services, 2004).

One perspective is offered by the Massachusetts Adoption Resource Exchange statistics (2012) on the 173 placements with which it assisted over a year's time. Among 12 recruitment sources listed, half related to photo-listing online or in a book and other media-based activities, such as *Wednesday's Child* and the *Heart Gallery*. A little over one-quarter of the total placements were attributed to six such recruitment sources, with the state adoption exchange being responsible for the greatest number of these. The same evaluation attributed 35 per cent of the adoptions that the exchange assisted with that year to adoption parties.

Wendy's Wonderful Kids' national evaluation is the first randomised control trial of an adoption recruitment effort. Of the 121 individual WWK sites, 20 underwent a randomised control trial; results show that the children in the experimental group were 1.7 times more likely to be adopted, with the greatest positive impact on children who were older or who had mental health disorders (Malm *et al*, 2011a).

As of September 2013, 9,783 children had been served by WWK adoption professionals: 6,499 had a match identified; 3,757 had a finalised adoption; and 631 were in their pre-adoptive placements awaiting finalisation (WWK, 2013). Most importantly, of the children successfully served, 45 per cent were age 12 or older at the time of referral (69% age 9 or older); 48 per cent had at least one identified disability; 27 per cent experienced six or more placements; 50 per cent had been in the system for more than four years (10% for more than 10 years); and 21 per cent had a prior failed or disrupted adoption. This programme underscores the reality that innovative child-specific recruitment strategies result in higher rates of adoption for children who have been in care for many years without finding permanent families.

Selected resources

AdoptUSKids (2006) *Answering the Call: Lasting impressions, A guide for photolisting children.* Access at: www.adoptuskids.org/_assets/files/NRCR RFAP/resources/lasting-impressions.pdf

BAAF (2012) *Picture the Child: Filming children for family-finding* (training DVD). www.youtube.com/playlist?list=PLA0117AEF8714E85A

Canada's Waiting Kids (2012c) Description writing guidelines. Access at: www.canadaswaitingkids.ca/pdf/guidelines.pdf

Grant M. (2010) *Seeing the Difference? Using video clips to help find families for children: Findings from the BAAF Video Research Project.* London: BAAF.

Mallon G.P. (2004) *Facilitating Permanency for Youth: A toolbox for youth permanency.* Washington, DC: CWLA.

PART V

PRE-ADOPTIVE CASEWORK PROCESSES

12 Concurrent planning

Description and overview

Concurrent planning (CP) involves working towards family reunification while simultaneously developing an alternative permanency plan. CP was first developed in the early 1980s by Linda Katz and others at Lutheran Social Services in Seattle, Washington and was based on the earlier works of Heymann and colleagues in Chicago, which emphasised focusing on permanency from intake forward. CP was specifically designed for the growing child welfare population of very young children from families with chronic pathology, often involving substance abuse. An analysis of foster care data from 11 US states, 1983–1998, showed that children entering care under one year of age had the longest lengths of stay of all age groups (Wulczyn *et al*, 2000).

CP combines 'vigorous family outreach, expedited timelines, and potentially permanent family foster care placements to improve the odds of timely permanency for young children' (Katz, 1999, p. 72). It involves providing intensive support for a time-limited period to the birth/first parents and other family members to resolve the problems that led to the child's removal, and working determinedly with allied professionals also involved in the family's treatment and court personnel to remove barriers to timely permanency through either reunification or an alternative plan such as adoption.

The initial CP pilot in Washington state focused on children under age eight and used two workers per case. After this pilot, CP quickly spread to other US states and counties, to Canadian provinces such as British Columbia, Alberta and Ontario, and to parts of England. The UK government has taken a renewed interest in concurrent planning, which has been written into adoption statutory guidance issued early in 2011 as an expectation of all local authorities.

CP was originally developed in small private agencies and targeted families assessed as having below-average likelihood of reunification, not all child welfare families. It has been implemented in different ways and with different populations across different locations. In the US, the Adoption and Safe Families Act of 1997 widely sanctioned the use of CP by shortening the timelines for achieving permanency and specifying that reasonable efforts to place a child for adoption or with a guardian *may be* made concurrently with reasonable efforts to reunify.

Today, all US states report in Child and Family State Reviews conducted by the federal government that CP is being implemented to varying degrees (Child Welfare Information Gateway [CWIG], 2012a). Most states have passed statutes allowing concurrent planning, and some require it. Statutes in at least five states (California, Idaho, Oregon, Texas, Utah) specify that the case plan will describe both the services to assist with reunification and the simultaneous efforts toward an alternative permanency goal. Two states (Mississippi and Oklahoma) require CP from the time the child first enters care, and others require it at a specific time (from 60 days to six months after care entry) or under specific circumstances, such as a six-month assessment indicating that reunification is unlikely (CWIG, 2009).

Key programme elements

Concurrent planning includes nine core components (National Resource Center for Permanency and Family Connections, 2010). Some of these components are in themselves best practice, and are also described individually in this volume. These components are:

- **Differential assessment and prognostic case review:** An early, comprehensive family assessment explores the problems that brought the child into care, the underlying history and needs of the family, family support networks, possible permanency resources within the extended family, and other factors. The original CP model involved differential assessment of the likelihood of reunification and concurrent planning for those with poor prognosis indicators but at least some strengths on which to build. Poor prognosis indicators include aspects of parental functioning:

previously killed or seriously harmed another child; repeatedly harmed a child; no effort to change over time and support system is a harmful one (drug culture); significant, protracted mental health issues; and rights to another child terminated.

- **Full disclosure:** Candid and respectful discussion occurs both up front and on an ongoing basis with parents, other family members and team members regarding permanency goals and timeframes; all of the family's options, including voluntary relinquishment; rights and responsibilities; needed changes and expectations; and so forth.
- **Family search and engagement:** Early identification is made of possible resource families among the child's maternal and paternal relatives (diligent search and family finding).
- **Family group conferencing:** This entails shared planning and decision making with families and team members using approaches such as family group decision-making, family group conferencing and team decision-making.
- **Visiting between family and child or young person:** Supervised visitation is scheduled in advance in a neutral setting.
- **Setting clear timelines for permanency decisions:** Clear and firm timelines for permanency decision-making and reunification efforts are outlined in policy and practice.
- **Transparent written agreements and documentation:** Initial written agreement includes steps that must occur for the child to return home, services to be provided, and so forth – and all inform-ation related to the case should be documented in detail.
- **Committed collaboration:** Collaboration between various parts of the team – including birth families, foster carers, child welfare system, courts and service providers – is important.
- **Specific recruitment, training and retention of dual-licensed approved resource families who are approved for foster care and adoption:** Resource families need initial and ongoing training and support.

Lessons learned

The original CP model required intensive, front-loaded casework by high-functioning, skilled workers with support from administrators, supervisors, allied professionals and court personnel, as well as an adequate supply of resource families. Full implementation of this model in large public child welfare systems has proven to be very complex and to require systemic changes. There are many qualitative evaluations of concurrent planning efforts that have identified both barriers and essential elements for successful implementation (Katz, 1999; Monck *et al*, 2004; Gerstenzang and Freundlich, 2005; D'Andrade *et al*, 2006; Wigfall *et al*, 2006; Kenrick, 2010).

- There must be an **organisational foundation for CP, with clear acceptance of its mission, goals, policies and practices** from administration level to supervisors and line workers. This foundation requires initial and ongoing training, as well as clear articulation in policy and supervision of practice expectations, steps and timelines. When the full framework is not in place to support CP, implementation is likely to be shallow and inconsistent. For example, in California, a 1997 statute required that the case plan describe the services to assist in reunification and those to be provided concurrently to achieve legal permanency if reunification failed (CWIG, 2009). Researchers studying CP's implementation in six California counties through review of 885 cases and interviews found that, even when administrators described CP as fully implemented, it was common that no clear concurrent plan had been documented and essential elements of CP had not occurred. For example, only 103 children of 410 cases open for eight months were with foster carers who intended to adopt, and only 12 of these were placed there in the first six months (D'Andrade *et al*, 2006; D'Andrade, 2009).
- **Effective CP efforts require additional resources and supports** – either two workers per case or one worker with a reduced caseload, additional efforts to recruit foster-adopt carers, and supportive services for both birth/first parents and carers (D'Andrade and

Berrick, 2006). When adequate support and training for workers do not exist, there may be a tendency to minimise reunification efforts.

- There **needs to be a sufficient number of resource/foster-adopt families** available to provide concurrent placements. Since 1999, Coram, a voluntary adoption agency in England, has had a concurrent planning programme for infants under 24 months with a very low likelihood of reunification. Coram focuses on recruiting child-centred carers who are prepared to take a risk on their own behalf in order to ensure that babies will have a smooth passage through care and back home or to adoption. Their central recruitment message is that vulnerable babies need to be protected from disruptions in care by special carers who can focus on the children's needs.

- **Resource families may experience additional stresses** related to expectations to work closely with birth families and the ambivalent nature of their foster-adopt role, so they need additional training and support (Frame *et al*, 2006). Direct interaction with birth parents is also beneficial to carers, allowing them direct knowledge with which to assist the children in identity development and to promote openness if they do adopt (Kenrick, 2010).

- In systems that require transfer of the case from a child welfare worker to an adoption worker prior to moving toward an adoption goal, the **adoption and child welfare units and social workers need to be well integrated** in order to work together collaboratively.

- **Birth parents need to receive necessary services in a timely manner** due to tight timeframes; services include accurate and thorough initial assessments, active engagement, and addressing barriers to accessing services, such as waiting lists, transportation and other factors (Frame *et al*, 2006).

- **Judicial support and involvement** are critically important to timely permanency. A number of projects, such as Colorado's and Kentucky's, have involved simultaneous court improvement components to streamline procedures and avoid delays (CWIG, 2005). For example, Kentucky's project emphasised one child/one legal voice, defined as a dedicated project attorney and a guardian ad litem throughout the legal process (Martin *et al*, 2002).

Outcomes

It is hard to generalise from the research on concurrent planning since various locations have used some elements of CP and not others, and the elements utilised have been implemented inconsistently in some areas. Some of the more rigorous evaluations document that CP does result in improved outcomes, and some state or county systems offer data before and after CP implementation, indicating improved outcomes.

Increasing timely permanency

- **Colorado:** In 1994, state legislation required all children aged six and younger and their siblings to be in permanent placements within 12 months of entering foster care, and directed the courts to work with child welfare agencies to achieve this goal. A study of this Expedited Permanency Planning from 1995 to 1998 found the rate of permanency attainment within a year for the treatment groups (n = 130) was 84 to 85 per cent in the two pilot counties as compared with 22 and 32 per cent in the comparison groups (n = 105), a statistically significant difference. By 2001, this model was implemented throughout the state. For the 1,149 children served by the programme in 2003, 82 per cent attained permanency within a year (Potter and Klein-Rothschild, 2002; CWIG, 2005).
- **England:** A CP pilot project began in 1998 in several agencies, including in Manchester, London and Brighton; 24 infants in three CP sites spent a mean of 7.2 months in non-permanent care, and the 44 children served by two traditional teams had 19 and 16.5 months in care. Infants in the CP programme were adopted within 13 months of coming into care, as compared with a mean of 26.5 months for infants coming into care across England (Monck *et al*, 2004). The Coram agency continued its CP programme, completing an evaluation in 2012 on infants entering from 2000 to

2011. Of the 54 children adopted through the programme, the average time from care entry to adoption was 14 months, as compared to a national average of two years and three months for infants entering care in 2011. None adopted in the CP project experienced disruptions (Laws *et al*, 2012).

- **North Dakota:** After implementing CP state-wide in 1999, average time in care from that year to 2003 was reduced from 17 months to 9.7 months (CWIG, 2012a).
- **Kentucky:** A federally funded demonstration CP project served 114 children from two areas. Compared to the 1,328 other fostered children in those areas, those receiving CP had a length of stay of 11.6 versus 31.8 months (urban) and 16.9 versus 24.7 months (rural); both were statistically significant (Martin *et al*, 2002).

Fewer moves in care

- **England:** Children in the CP programme had significantly fewer moves before achieving permanency (42% of CP children had one move only, and 58% had two or more, compared with only 9% served by traditional teams having only one move).
- **Kentucky:** Most children in a CP project experienced fewer permanent changes, compared to the state's general foster care population (Martin *et al*, 2002).

Increased use of relative placements

- **North Dakota:** After implementing CP state-wide in 1999, 50 per cent more children were placed with relatives in 2003 (CWIG, 2012a).
- **Kentucky:** The evaluation reports increased use of kinship placements for the children in the CP project.
- Predictors of timely permanency attainment in the context of CP identified by researchers include the following: case worker consistency, fewer placements, substance abuse in family, more days of parental visitation, and clear identification of concurrent plan in the written service plan with parental signatures (Potter and Klein-Rothschild, 2002). The California evaluation found that discussion

of voluntary relinquishment was positively associated with adoption, and full disclosure reduced the likelihood of reunification (D'Andrade, 2009).

Selected resources

Child Welfare Information Gateway (2012a) *Concurrent Planning: What the evidence shows*, Washington, DC: US Department of Health and Human Services. Access at: www.childwelfare.gov/pubs/issue_briefs/concurrent_evidence/concurrent_evidence.pdf

Idaho Department of Health and Welfare (2008) *Standard: Concurrent planning*. Access at: www.healthandwelfare.idaho.gov/portals/0/Children/MoreInformation/Concurrent%20Planning.pdf

Lutheran Community Services, Northwest. Concurrent planning guidebooks (3) and video series (6). Seattle, WA: Order at: www.lcsnw.org/concurrentplanning/index.html.

National Resource Center for Permanency and Family Connections (NRCPFC) (2010) A web-based concurrent planning toolkit. Access at: www.nrcpfc.org/cpt/introduction.htm

13 Minimising the trauma of removal and moves in care

Description and overview

The removal of children from their original homes is typically very traumatic; they continue to grieve the loss of immediate and extended family, friends, school, community and culture. Child welfare policies and practice can diminish the impact of the initial removal, as well as promote the well-being of children when later transitions occur.

Initial removal

Attachment theory predicts that separation of a child from a parent or primary carer is severely threatening, even when the parent's care is damaging or very inadequate. Sudden removal is particularly stressful, in that children's circumstances change dramatically, challenging their perceptions of the world and of their parents' ability to protect them. Children typically feel abandoned, worthless, helpless and guilty (Folman, 1998; Center for Improvement of Child and Family Services, 2009; Winter, 2010). How removal and the period just after are handled can facilitate or greatly impede children's adjustment in placement and beyond.

There have been few studies of the impact of children's initial removal from their families and entry into care, despite the prevalence of this experience. The Center for Improvement of Child and Family Services (2009) conducted interviews and focus groups with 37 stake-holders in the various systems involved with children during and just after their removal and first placement, including with case workers, tribal workers (those working with indigenous peoples), supervisors, police, foster carers, birth parents, school personnel, medical personnel, mental health providers, juvenile court staff and fostered children. Stakeholders reported that the potential for trauma for a child in the investigation and removal process is exacerbated by: 1) suddenness of removal; 2) parental distress; 3) the child's previous understanding of the police and child welfare agencies (may have been taught to distrust police or heard "horror stories" about foster care); 4) lack of trust in or feelings of betrayal by those they "told"; 5) the child's sense of confusion and loss of all that is familiar, including home, friends, possessions, routines, school, community, culture and possibly language; 6) lack of information or understanding of what is happening and will happen; 7) the child's fear or guilt (sense of fault, inability to protect others); 8) repeated emphasis on family deficits when child is interviewed and having to repeat the story over and over; and, most importantly, 9) loss or disruption of attachment relationships.

Very few studies examine the impact of first removal from the child's perspective. In her study of the removal recollections of 90 children, ages 8–14, Folman (1998) found that children typically did not feel rescued or protected but, rather, felt like they had been kidnapped. This research supports many of the conclusions listed by stakeholders above. Virtually all the children reported profound and sometimes overwhelming feelings of fear, confusion and helplessness. The consistent message in children's narratives was that the intervention itself was traumatic, a finding supported by Winter's (2010) study of children aged 4–7.

The nature of removal contributed to its negative impact on children in Folman's study. Most of the removals (94%) occurred without preparation or warning, often in the context of great parental distress or hostility to those removing the child. Most (61%) involved the police, and the vast majority of children (94%) were taken to the child welfare agency or to a children's shelter rather than directly to a foster home. Many (48%) were separated from one or more siblings. Children reported they were given very little information (93%) and were too frightened to ask questions. As one child put it, 'I was so scared. I was afraid that I wasn't gonna make it. I was gonna be helpless' (p. 26). The few who were given information reported that it was false (e.g., 'You'll see your mother tomorrow') or superficial ('You're going to stay with a nice family who will take better care of you than your family did.'). Such bromides did not lessen fears but did

'(1) confirm for the children that the new adults in their lives, like the ones they left behind, cannot be trusted and (2) invalidate their feelings of pain, loss and terror' (p. 22). The children continued to have fears of sudden loss of their parents or siblings.

A study in England by Morgan (2010) asked children about what could be done to make moving into foster care easier for them, and the most common response given was "knowing what was happening". Although only a few children in this study had emergency placements, over half of them had not known they were entering care until it happened. Morgan concluded that children wanted to know why they were in care, what would happen to them, and all about the foster family, including information on other children and pets; they also wanted to see pictures of the family, neighbourhood and their room.

Subsequent moves in care

Another chapter in this compendium reviews the impact of placement instability on children and strategies for reducing it. Whatever the cause, many children will have multiple moves in care, which are often abrupt and disruptive. Sometimes such changes are the result of positive events – moving to a less restrictive setting, being reunited with siblings, or moving to an adoptive placement. No matter what the reason, many transitions can be managed in ways that reduce their negative impact.

Few studies examine the perspectives of children and young people on the impact of being moved while in foster care (Unrau, 2007). Festinger's (1983) landmark study of 277 young people who had been in care was one of the first to capture the effects of this experience. Among other concerns, young people discussed the difficulty of moves within the system, which were often highly disruptive.

A much smaller but more recent retrospective study examined the perceptions of moves in care among 22 adults (Unrau et al, 2008). The dominant themes in the interviews were loss and emotional detachment. Respondents described not only the loss of relationships, belongings and familiar settings, but also loss of control of their own lives and destinies. Moves challenged their self-esteem and sense of being normal, but a few found some benefits of moves: a chance to "start over" and escape from difficult placements. Some respondents were able to interpret their moves in care as evidence of personal strength or the ability to bounce back from adversity and challenge; however, 'despite possessing some qualities of resilience, all participants in the study had mostly negative memories of placement moves and were able to identify how those moves negatively impacted the quality of their lives many years after having left care' (p. 1264).

One model programme with a purposeful focus on minimising the trauma of moves in care is in Polk County, Iowa, where case workers hold a pre-removal conference with parents and plan for ways to make the transition easier for their children (*Chicago Tribune*, 2010) (see Outcomes).

Key programme elements

The few studies on initial removal provide insights into how trauma-informed practice can reduce the profound and terrifying impact of forced removal from family.

- **Prepare the child for separation and reduce the level of surprise.** Many removals of children are not emergencies, and could occur without the drama and suddenness that exacerbate their fears (Folman, 1998; Center for Improvement of Child and Family Services [CICFS], 2009). Workers can explain to children what foster care is (including that it is temporary) and provide specific information about the setting into which they will be placed. Folman (1998) suggested having small picture albums or profiles for each foster family, including pictures of the house, all family members and pets, and the neighbourhood, which might be shared in advance with children prior to their arrival. Also, when possible, children should meet the foster carers prior to removal. If that is not feasible, workers should describe the family and home and show pictures of the setting. Of course, they should also determine if the children have any questions and anticipate any that they may be too frightened to ask.

  Even if circumstances require unplanned removal, children can see their parents later at the agency and be assured that they will be in regular contact. Parents can be helped to give their children helpful messages that ease the transition. Bogolub (2008), in a small study of children placed with preparation beforehand rather than abrupt removal, reported that children did not evince trauma when discussing removal, although they reported anxiety about the families they were going to and insecurity about when they would next see their parents.

- **Collaborate with other agencies that are involved, especially law enforcement.** All those involved need to approach removal from a trauma-informed perspective. Separate the child from scenes of arrest, interrogation or parental resistance.
- **Involve parents in preparing their children**, including helping with packing and including mementos that serve as symbolic connections, such as pictures of the parents. Let the parents say goodbye. Answer the parents' questions.
- **Have consistency in support.** Children benefit when the same case worker explains the removal, transports them to the place they will reside, and checks on them afterward.
- **Keep children, parents and other attachment figures connected and keep them in familiar environments if possible.** Folman (1998) and Bogolub (2008) reported that children's biggest fear was not seeing their parents or siblings again. Bogolub found that no matter what birth parents had done, all respondents missed them, longed for them and thought about them frequently. Trauma is reduced when workers do the following.
  - Place children with relatives or others they know and trust, when at all possible.
  - Keep siblings together if at all possible.
  - Arrange contact for children and parents and/or siblings soon after placement, and let the children know when they will see their parents again before leaving.
  - Arrange regular contact and stick to it. (Child participants in Bogolub's study recommended that they receive many more visits than they did.)

- Place children in communities and with families of similar language and culture.
- Keep children in the same schools and activities (CICFS, 2009).

- **Validate the children's feelings and provide continuing interpretation of their experience.** Folman (1998) notes that, 'failing to validate the children's perceptions and feelings teaches them that they cannot trust their own perceptions and feelings. Many have already learned this in their birth families. For example, their mothers tell the caseworker that she does not leave them alone, when they know she does.' Her respondents frequently noted that workers told them everything was going to be OK, when obviously to the child it was not. Workers need to be attuned to children's often inchoate fears and be a reliable and supportive source of information and compassion.
- **Mentoring by other children in care:** Folman's participants suggested that having other foster children to talk to could reduce the anxiety of newly placed children. She recommends that children already in care be assigned to be buddies with newly placed children to answer questions and mentor them through the transition. She notes that this will benefit the mentors as well.

The Center for Improvement of Child and Family Services has developed a tip sheet for parents, foster carers, and law enforcement, medical and educational personnel. The tips briefly instruct readers about the traumatic nature of initial removal and steps they can take to reduce its impact (see Selected Resources).

Reducing trauma of later moves in care

Despite the recognised difficulty faced by children who move within the foster care system, there is little commonly accessible literature about how to reduce its negative impact. This section draws on the work on initial removal, as well as the limited literature on subsequent removal, to suggest ways to make moves less difficult.

- **Carefully plan moves or transitions in care.** Planned transitions do less harm to children than do abrupt or unexpected moves (Fahlberg, 1994, 2012). There needs to be sufficient time to prepare the children for a move. Unrau and Putney's guidance (see Selected Resources) suggest a minimum of two weeks between the decision to move children and the actual move.

- **Honestly and fully inform children and young people of what is happening and why.** Children benefit from developmentally appropriate explanations of changes in care. When the children's behaviour is the primary reason for the move, they need to be helped to see that their actions contributed to the change, but also that they deserve to be in a setting where others are able to meet their needs.

- **Schedule pre-placement contacts that allow parties to address concerns and hopes about the change.** The younger the children, the more critical it is that there be direct, supportive contact between past and future carers (Fahlberg, 1994, 2012). Adults with relationships with the children can be involved in both planning and the actual move, and previous carers need to explain the children's needs, habits and preferences to the new carers.

- **Plan for good goodbyes.** Children need personal, tangible messages that the carer cares about them, will remember them, and wishes them well. In addition to verbalising these things, pictures of the carers and children, as well as a letter from the carers expressing these sentiments, help ease the transition (Johnson and Howard, 2008). Even if the move is preceded by anger or rejection on the part of the carers, they must be helped to (eventually) communicate to the children that they are wished well. Children also need the opportunity to say goodbye to foster siblings, teachers, friends and others important to them. They also need to know that birth family members know where they are going and will have contact as soon as possible after the move.

- **Involve trusted people in the children's lives in exploring their feelings and concerns about moving.** Case workers, therapists, extended family members and others can explore the children's feelings and concerns about moving. Children need to be given multiple opportunities to express how they feel about moving and to have questions answered.

- Whenever it is in their best interests, children's emotional connections to previous foster carers or foster siblings should be maintained, even if they cannot remain in that placement.
- Fully inform the new foster carers about the children's needs and prepare them to expect acting out or withdrawal as a normal response to upheaval.

Lessons learned

Child welfare pioneer and psychiatrist Vera Fahlberg (1994, 2012) once argued that we should treat children first removed from their families as we would treat those whose parents had just died in a car crash. She understood that removal is a crisis and that children are often in a state of shock when they lose all that is familiar, even if what is familiar may be dangerous. Attachment theory holds that adaptation to loss of attachment figures is enhanced by accurate and full information, acknowledgment of grief and support to grieve, and open communication with trustworthy others. It is not the loss *per se* but permission to grieve, clear, honest and open communication, and accurate information that allow children to manage loss and resume normal development (Furman, 1974; Bowlby, 1980; Turner and Avison, 1992; Fahlberg, 1994, 2012). Some children who have experienced traumatic separations continue to have lingering fears of repeated loss many years after they are in a permanent family (Smith and Howard, 1999).

One small example of giving voice to children is found in the province of Alberta's Foster Care Review Report (2008). The report states that when children are moved in care, a Resource Feedback Report is completed. This form records the reasons why children leave their foster homes and their opinions regarding the placements. The goal is to assess foster carers' strengths and areas needing improvement. These forms are completed by the children's case workers and are forwarded to the foster care support workers to identify and address any quality-of-care issues that arise.

Outcomes

The literature does not reveal outcome studies on interventions to reduce trauma associated with initial removal and replacement. Practice can be informed by the limited studies of impact of traumatic removal listed above, and changes that logically reduce the negative effects. Further research is needed to determine the efficacy of such changes.

The Iowa Department of Human Services in Polk County reported that, in the first two years of instituting a pre-removal conference with birth parents to plan for children's initial removal, only one family had tried to run away and no children had suffered severe abuse between the pre-removal conference and removal (*Chicago Tribune*, 2010). This policy is still in place in Polk County four years after it began.

Selected resources

Center for Improvement of Child and Family Services (2009) *Reducing the Trauma of Investigation, Removal, and Initial Out-of-home Placement in Child Abuse Cases: Policy information and discussion guide*, Portland, OR: Portland State University. Access at: http://bit.ly/SPWilE

Infant Parent Institute, *Multiple Transitions: A child's view about foster care and adoption*, Champaign, IL. Access at: www.infant-parent.com/resources/ (This brief video uses children's voices to describe the pain of maltreatment, separation and loss.)

Johnson M. and Howard J. (2008) *Putting the Pieces Together: Lifebook work with children*, Rock Island, IL: Lutheran Social Services of Illinois and the Center for Adoption Studies at Illinois State University. Available from: www.lssi.org/Support/LifebookDVD.aspx (This one-hour video explores the importance of aiding children in making transitions and the roles foster carers, caseworkers and therapists play in maximising children's adjustment in care.)

Unrau Y. and Putney K. (undated) *Moving in Foster Care: A journey of loss and hope* (Provides a brief, graphic overview of what helps children to transition out of and into new placements, with advice for carers whom the child is leaving, the agency and the new carers.) Access at: www.bit.ly/SkpVPy

14 Increasing placement stability

Description and overview

Children who experience multiple moves while in care are at greater risk of experiencing emotional and behavioural difficulty or adoption disruption, or of never being placed for adoption at all. Policy and practice to reduce placement instability may increase the chances of healthy adjustment for children in care and ultimately their ability to successfully join a permanent family.

The odds of children achieving successful permanency of any type increase when their moves in care are reduced. Multiple studies have examined the impact of disruption on children in care. Placement instability is associated with problematic outcomes for children and young people, including increased behavioural and emotional problems (Newton et al, 2000; Rutter and Sroufe, 2000), school difficulties (Rumberger, 2003; Jackson, 2014), dysfunctional attachment (Smith et al, 2001; Wulczyn et al, 2003; Leathers, 2006) and, for males, rates of delinquency and increased risk of incarceration for serious or violent offences during adolescence (Reid-Johnson and Barth, 2000; Ryan and Testa, 2005; Schofield et al, 2014).

Placement changes during the first year in care predict increasing instability for children over time (Webster et al, 2000). Furthermore, multiple moves in care are associated with reduced likelihood of finding permanency through adoption, and increased risk of adoption disruption and unsuccessful reunification (Smith et al, 2001; Chamberlain et al, 2006).

Although disruption in foster care is bad for children, it is common. Studies of disruption in the US find 22 per cent to 70 per cent of foster care placements disrupt in any given year (Pardek, 1984; Staff and Fein, 1995; Berrick et al, 1998; Smith et al, 2001; Chamberlain et al, 2006; Leathers, 2006). The US conducts reviews of states on this and many other measures. The 2007–2008 Child and Family Services

Reviews (CFSRs) found that the majority of states did not meet the standard of 90 per cent placement stability.

The potential therapeutic aspects of care are compromised when children experience multiple moves. Maintaining children in homes where they are safe, nurtured and supported can counteract some of the effects of previous maltreatment (Schofield and Beek, 2005). Children with fewer moves in care develop more secure relationships, have better academic achievement, and experience less trauma and better relationships with adults (Leathers, 2002).

What factors lead to placement instability? The Bremer Project (Jones and Wells, 2008), a comprehensive review of research conducted over 20 years, found the following.

- The first months of placement are the riskiest, with 70 per cent of disruptions occurring in that period (James, 2004; Barber and Delfabbro, 2005).
- Standard foster care (as opposed to kinship and treatment foster care) is linked to greater instability.
- The strongest predictor of disruption is children's behaviour, particularly if it is aggressive or dangerous. Even for children who do not initially exhibit conduct issues, a greater number of placements predicts an increase in both externalising and internalising behaviour problems.
- Foster carers' coping skills, "goodness of fit" between carers and children in temperament, and emotional closeness reduce the risk of placement disruption.
- Foster carers with strong social support have fewer disruptions.
- Case worker stability is associated with placement stability; case worker rapport and time spent with foster carers and children are thought to reduce disruption risk.
- Placement instability predicts later disruption; as the number of previous placements increases, so does the risk for subsequent disruptions.
- Specific interventions with children and foster carers can increase placement stability; foster carers need information and support to meet the emotional and behavioural challenges of many children in care.

Two other studies have found that children's behaviour problems were the reason for removal in a minority of cases in the first year or two after placement, and the majority of moves were system-related (James, 2004; Barber and Delfabbro, 2005). These studies indicate that not all disruption is the same. Some researchers have concluded that a good "final placement" with carers attuned to children's needs promotes well-being even for those who have experienced disruption (Barber and Delfabbro, 2005; Schofield and Beek, 2005; Sinclair *et al*, 2007).

While most children ultimately achieve stability, one study found that 28 per cent were unstable throughout placement (Rubin *et al*, 2007). This study and an earlier one (Newton *et al*, 2000) indicate that placement instability has significant negative impact on behavioural well-being, independent of children's baseline behaviour problems. Children's behaviour is an important predictor of placement disruption, but disruption also increases children's behavioural problems. Even those who entered care with low levels of behavioural or emotional problems exhibited more problematic behaviours as the number of moves grew.

Thus, children may not suffer unduly from planned changes tied to case work goals, particularly early in placement, but they are better served when the first placement is right. Many studies have advanced principles for minimising moves in care and maximising children's placement stability. Targeted, evidence-based interventions, such as those described in the outcomes section, also can reduce placement instability.

Key programme elements

The Bremer Project (Jones and Wells, 2008) and other studies suggest the following practices for promoting placement stability.

- **Maximise the use of kinship placements**, as these tend to be more stable, have a lower risk of removal based on children's behavioural problems, and have a higher likelihood of adoption or guardianship if children cannot be reunified (Iglehart, 1994; James, 2004; Howard, 2006; Winokur *et al*, 2008).

- **Institute policies and practice at various system levels** to emphasise the need to make initial placement decisions that are appropriate to children's needs and likely to remain stable over time. Also, maximise the use of concurrent planning placements.
- **Conduct early assessments of children** to identify their needs and match them with foster carers who can meet them.
- **Consider placing young people** with severe behavioural problems in families without other children.
- **Maximise the recruitment and retention of qualified foster carers** and provide strong social support to them through case worker visits, mentoring and peer support groups.
- **Train foster carers in strategies** for addressing child behavioural problems and provide early intervention to stabilise at-risk placements, particularly during the first six months. Casey Family Programs (2000) recommends that training include behaviour management, addressing attachment and loss, work with birth families, joint training of foster carers and staff, and teamwork and shared decision-making.
- **Employ professional social workers** and provide a range of supports to promote their retention, since case worker stability predicts placement stability.
- For children with significant challenges, **provide specialised placements and evidence-based interventions**, such as Multidimensional Treatment Foster Care or Early Intervention Foster Care, as early as possible and on a continuing basis, as needed.

The Multidimensional Treatment Foster Care Model (MTFC) was originally developed for adolescents and focuses on maintaining young people in family settings rather than in more restrictive group or institutional placements while preparing their carers to provide effective parenting. Its elements include:

- structuring a consistent, reinforcing milieu where children are mentored and supported to develop positive living skills and academic achievement;
- providing structure in daily living with clear expectations, limits

and consequences given in a teaching oriented manner;

- providing close supervision of children's activities and whereabouts;
- supporting teens to develop positive peer relationships and avoid harmful peer associations (Fisher and Chamberlain, 2000).

In the MTFC model, the foster home is the primary clinical environment. Foster carers have access to assistance through a programme supervisor at all times and are encouraged to address behavioural problems early and to seek help often. A treatment team – composed of specialists, including a behaviour support specialist, the young person's therapist, a family therapist, case managers, consulting psychiatrists and clinical supervisors – supports the family.

A variation of MTFC is the Early Intervention Foster Care (EIFC) or Multidimensional Treatment Foster Care for Preschoolers. The latter, based on the principles of MTFC, is a treatment foster care model for three- to six-year-olds with severe behavioural or emotional problems. It, too, uses a team approach to provide training and support to foster carers, family therapy, ready consultation, and specific training to increase children's pro-social behaviour. It uses a developmental framework to tailor intervention to the children's needs.

Lessons learned

- **Policies and practice that support placing children with relatives, as stated above, will ultimately increase placement stability**. A study comparing 505 kin-placed children with 872 in non-kinship foster placements found that children with relatives fared better in terms of permanency, safety and stability. When matched for age, gender, ethnicity and jurisdiction, children in kinship care had significantly fewer placements, were less likely to have new maltreatment allegations, and were less likely to be involved in the juvenile justice system than their peers in regular foster care. They also demonstrated better behavioural and mental health functioning. While less likely to reunify, they were more likely to exit care, particularly to guardianship (Winokur *et al*, 2008).

- **Worker support is also critical to placement stability**. Studies have demonstrated the critical importance of worker constancy in reducing placement disruption, as well as in securing permanent homes for children (Potter and Klein-Rothschild, 2002; James, 2004). For example, in a study of children in care in Wisconsin, those who had one worker over the study period achieved perm-anency 74.5 per cent of the time. As the number of case managers increased, permanency achievement dropped, ranging as low as 0.1 per cent for those with six or seven (Potter and Klein-Rothschild, 2002). Organisational structures that support workers are part-icularly important in the first two years; they include peer support and supportive supervision, reasonable workloads and competitive salaries (Jones and Wells, 2008).

Outcomes

Several studies have sought to determine what interventions with children and foster carers reduce placement disruption. "Wraparound services" are generally conceived of as community-based care for children with serious emotional or behavioural problems, with the goal of keeping them in the community. Individualised service plans are developed by teams that typically include carers, the children if they are old enough, child welfare and mental health professionals, education professionals and others. One evaluation of wraparound services, the Fostering Individualised Assistance Program (FIAP) – a controlled, longitudinal study of fostered young people with behavioural problems using random assignment – found a decrease in disruptions in the treatment group and an increase in the control group (Clark *et al*, 1996). While the strong methodology is promising, the Bremer Report notes that the problem of varying definitions of such services complicates replication.

The strongest interventional model for assuring placement stability is MTFC, which has been positively evaluated in multiple studies beginning in the early 1990s. Results indicate that young people part-icipating in MTFC have lower rates of disruption, fewer behavioural problems and increased foster carer retention compared with regular foster care (Chamberlain *et al*, 1992). Other studies of MTFC have found that young people in the programme have reduced delinquency rates and fewer behavioural problems than peers in the control groups. As noted in the Bremer report, MTFC has also been awarded the highest rating of "1" by the California Evidence-Based Clearinghouse database as the only programme model that has been shown to be a 'well supported, effective practice' in the topic area of placement stability (California Evidence-Based Clearinghouse for Child Welfare, 2011).

Likewise, results from a clinical, randomised study showed that children receiving Early Intervention Foster Care (the MTFC counterpart for younger children) had higher rates of permanency than did children in traditional foster care (90% versus 64%). Even children who had a high number of previous placements showed better stability (Fisher *et al*, 2005). The Bremer Report posits that EIFC holds promise for breaking the cycle of instability that often results from multiple moves in care.

Selected resources

Jones A.S., and Wells S.J. (2008) *PATH/Wisconsin – Bremer Project: Preventing placement disruptions in foster care*, University of Minnesota School of Social Work. Access at: www.state.il.us/DCFS/docs/PhaseIX/Path_Bremer_Report.pdf

National Resource Center for Permanency and Family Connections (2008) *A Web-based Placement Stability Toolkit*. Access at: www.nrcpfc.org/pst/overview.htm (Provides an introduction to the importance of placement stability, an organisational self-study to guide assessment of agency policies and practices, core components of work to promote stability and references.)

Pecora P. (2007) *Why Should the Child Welfare Field Focus on Minimising Placement Change as Part of Permanency Planning for Children? The foster care alumni series*, Seattle, WA: Casey Family Programs. Access at: www.casey.org/Resources/Publications/pdf/MinimizingPlacements.pdf

15 Promoting permanency through life story work

Description and overview

For most children, their family is the keeper of their story. Families literally keep mementos – pictures, school reports, medical records, letters, birth certificates – but they also keep stories about their children's births and infancies, whom they resemble, and what the family traditions and beliefs are. The stories of children in care can become fragmented and tangible elements of personal and family history are often lost.

Life story work (called lifebook work in the US) is a valuable method of helping children who have experienced separation, loss and trauma to reconstruct the pieces of their history and fill in gaps in their understanding. Life story work has long been identified as a valuable tool for therapists and case workers to help children make sense of what has happened to them and to promote a positive sense of self and healthy identity (Fahlberg, 1994, 2012; Henry, 2005). It also provides children with the opportunity to process major life events and to work towards healing from trauma and loss, thus supporting well-being and mental health.

Life story work is based on the premise that children often have gaps in their memory and their understanding of past trauma and loss. It may also include aspects of the children's present – where they live, what they like, their talents, their likes and dislikes. It may also help children to imagine the future through work that addresses their hopes, dreams and plans, and can help prepare for transition to a permanent home.

The underpinnings of life story work lie in attachment and loss theory. Children with breaches in attachment need to develop a coherent personal narrative that incorporates the losses they have experienced (Schofield and Beek, 2006). Life story work serves to encourage introspection and to allow children and young people to construct meaning and explanation of feelings with the assistance of trusted adults (Rose and Philpot, 2005). This exploration helps children make the connections between 'cognition and emotion, thinking and feeling' (Schofield and Beek, 2006, p. 358).

A life story book is both a process and a product. The *product* is a tangible representation of the children's lives: photos, mementos, workbook-like pages where they write their responses to questions like 'Why did I come into care?' or 'If I could ask my birth parents one question, I would ask . . .' and lists of the places they have lived and the reasons for moving from each. There are many pre-packaged life story kits that can aid in the process (see Selected Resources). The *process* is the therapeutic review of aspects of children's histories by caring adults. Through life story work development, carers, case workers and therapists can gauge children's progress in understanding what has happened, in developing stronger relationships, and in identifying ongoing questions, misperceptions or concerns that may prevent children from adjusting to family life.

Therapeutic life story work is an intervention that focuses primarily on processing loss and trauma experiences and facilitating continuity in identity. Developing a coherent life narrative is an aspect of understanding and healing the impact of trauma, loss, and other difficult life experiences. The physical life story book provides the basic tools for understanding what has occurred, and the process of creating, discussing and revising it enables children to begin to make sense of the loss and trauma that they have endured. Furthermore, life story work can demonstrate children's resilience and strength (Johnson and Howard, 2008). Ultimately, children and young people can develop coherent personal narratives that facilitate their adjustment.

Life story work can assist adoptive families as well – promoting open communication between children and parents about complicated issues in the children's history and their understanding of their past. Furthermore, adoptive parents sometimes need help in finding ways to honour children's previous attachments and to address their own fears or feelings about children's dual connections (Smith and Howard, 1999; Hart and Luckock, 2004, 2006).

Adoption professionals in England place considerable emphasis on the use of life story work and life story books in preparing children for adoption and in communicating their history to prospective adoptive parents. *In My Shoes*, an interactive computer programme, is one model used in England to enable workers and children to explore important events and relationships, as well as children's feelings and wishes (see Calam and colleagues in Selected Resources). The professional sits alongside the child and assists, guides and interacts through a series of modules that invite the child to identify experiences and choose emotions. A two-day training course is offered in the use of this programme.

In the US, child welfare systems vary in the extent to which they recommend or mandate the development of life story work with children; ideally, it is begun when children enter care and marks their journey through placement. If children are reunified, life story work enables them and their parents to have a record of their experiences, and if they transition to adoption, provides the pieces of their life history to assist them and their adoptive parents into the future (Johnson and Howard, 2008).

Key programme elements

Life story books are tangible representations of the children's past. They are typically notebooks or journals that contain visual proof of the children's existence, of their place in their original families and a record of the transitions they have experienced. Those children who are moving to adoption may have pages that incorporate information and representation of the adoptive family and their place within it.

- Life story work is generally conducted in multiple sessions over time.
- Life story work is driven by the child's perceptions, co-constructed with the worker.
- Life story work is typically chronological.
- Typical elements include:
  - birth or hospital certificates and details of the child's birth;
  - photographs of the child as an infant and younger child,

including with parents, siblings and other family members, godparents, etc. (many children in care lack information about their fathers and the paternal extended family; life story books are incomplete if such information is not sought out and included);

- photographs of all people who are emotionally significant to the child – extended family members, previous carers, important teachers, mentors, coaches and the like;
- representation through pictures or drawings of each living arrangement and previous carer – often they include timelines or fold-out pages that allow the range of living experiences to be represented;
- medical records, including evidence of adequate parental care as well as of maltreatment;
- school pictures and records;
- records and mementos from social groups or organisations such as Girl Scouts;
- pages that illustrate activities, interests and talents.

• Beyond visual representation and chronology, life story books provide the *context for losses and transitions in the child's life*. Pages allow children to present their understanding of these changes. For example, the book may include a page titled 'How I came into care', where children write down their interpretation of events or another one titled 'Where I went and how I felt'. Such pages allow workers to explore the children's perceptions, identify missing pieces and help them attach feelings to their experiences.

• Another important piece of the life story book is *messages from each carer*, who shares memories of time with the child and conveys messages that the child was cared about, will be remembered and is wished well. Important attachment figures should be helped to convey their wish that the child find happiness in another family. Messages from birth parents whose rights have been terminated are particularly important.

• Decisions about children are often made by strangers. It is important that the life story book includes the *names and roles of people such as judges, therapists, case workers and foster carers*.

- In addition to evidence of the children's history, life story books incorporate *explanations or informed guesses about complicated issues*. These include developmentally-appropriate explanations of maltreatment or other problems that led to foster placement or re-placement.
- Life story work is open-ended. As children's perceptions change or further transitions occur, it can be amended to reflect these changes (Rose and Philpot, 2005).

Lessons learned

Life story work should be begun as soon as children enter placement (Johnson and Howard, 2008; Fahlberg, 1994, 2012). It is much easier to collect pictures, information and mementos from birth families, foster families and schools at that time, rather than later reconstructing them. Some entities have made this policy. For example, Lutheran Social Services of Illinois, a private child welfare agency, requires that all children entering foster care have life story books that are worked on with them throughout their placements. The agency has life story work specialists who work with case workers and therapists, and often with individual children themselves, to assure that they all have life story books.

Life story books often involve investigative work by the adults constructing them with the children. Techniques should include scouring case records, collecting stories from the birth parents, interviewing the children's previous child welfare workers and carers, and collecting information from the files of siblings. Involving children as active participants, rather than as passive recipients of information, provides the most benefits (Baynes, 2008). Giving voice to the children's views can be a partial remedy to the loss of power and control that typically comes from removal from original family and can be exacerbated by moves in care.

Life story work should be revisited and revised throughout the course of children's placements. It also needs to be recast over time so that it can "grow with the child". Explanations of past maltreatment, moves in care, parental mental illness and the like should become more detailed and complex as children age (Baynes, 2008; Johnson and Howard, 2008; Fahlberg, 1994, 2012).

This effort requires skill and training. Polly Baynes (2008), an experienced life story worker, calls it 'one of the most skilled and emotionally draining tasks a worker can undertake' (p. 43). While beginning, workers can gather the elements of children's histories that serve as the foundation of life story books; complicated issues or traumatic events may need to be addressed with a therapist.

Henry (2005) identifies critical skills the worker must use to prepare children for permanency, which fit with the skills used in life story work: engaging the children, listening to their words, speaking the truth, validating their life stories, creating a safe space, going back in time, and recognising pain as part of the process.

Life story work needs to be paced according to the children's capacity to undertake it. It may help to move from loaded content to less complex content (such as plans for the future) when the going gets tough. A 'Not now but later' page allows children to revisit issues later. It also supplies clues to subsequent workers or to parents as they explore the life story book with children (Howard, 2010). Life story information needs to be presented (and re-presented) in ways that are developmentally appropriate.

Life story books should include the meaning of events as the children see them. It is important that workers not contradict children's presentation of events. Doing so reinforces that others are trying to control their story and that yet another adult is not listening. However, life story books may include careful reframing of events by workers to offer alternative explanations that children can consider over time. Baynes (2008) gives an example of how a child's interpretation can be presented along with other views:

> *Raoul thinks that he was a naughty little boy who made his birth mother cross. The family support worker says that Raoul was a lovely little boy who enjoyed playing in the park and only had tantrums when he was upset or frustrated, like most little children. The judge says that Raoul's birth mother took too many drugs and didn't always notice when he needed her to*

cuddle him or play with him. Raoul's birth mother says that no one looked after her properly when she was little, and she just didn't know what to do when he had tantrums. (p. 47)

Because life story books are about helping children derive meaning from often complicated histories, workers need to provide full and honest information (Fahlberg, 1994, 2012; Henry, 2005; Baynes, 2008; Johnson and Howard, 2008).

Outcomes

Despite the recognition of the importance of life story work in the child welfare field, there is little empirical research on its impact as an intervention. One small study, using matched pairs of eight foster children who received life story work and eight others who did not, showed a significant treatment effect on placement stability for the life story group. (The intervention involved 30- to 45-minute sessions with experienced therapists.) In addition, case studies presented on four children showed a marked decline in ratings of behavioural symptoms for all of them. The researchers held that life story work was particularly effective in breaking through children's defences against thinking or talking about difficult experiences and in facilitating communication about them (Kliman and Zelman, 1996).

Rushton and colleagues (1998) examined whether high-quality direct work with children, including life story work, was associated with reducing behavioural problems once children were placed. Some children benefited from such preparation, but those who were overactive or not amenable to the therapy demonstrated little benefit once placed.

Research is needed that is explicit in its definition of life story work, which ties expected outcomes to theory and measures changes in children's behaviour, attitude and understanding. However, the life story work process itself is hard to articulate and measure. Furthermore, it is an encapsulation of the therapeutic process of helping children consider and process loss and trauma. As Baynes (2008) notes, 'Life story work sits somewhat uncomfortably in the world of evidence-based practice and measurable outcomes' (p. 47).

Selected resources

Betts B. and Ahmad A. (2003) *My Life Story*. Access at: www.bridgetbetts.co. uk/publication3.htm

Calam R., Cox A., Glasgow D., Jimmieson P. and Groth Larsen S. (2005) *In My Shoes: A computer assisted interview for communicating with children and vulnerable adults*, User Guide, York: Child and Family Training.

Casey Family Services (2009) *Bibliography, A Casey Family Services compilation: Lifebooks for children and youth in foster care*. Access at: www. caseyfamilyservices.org/userfiles/pdf/bib-2009-lifebooks.pdf

Hammond S.P and Cooper N.J. (2013) *Digital Life Story Work: Using technology to help young people make sense of their experience*, London: BAAF.

Harrison J. (1988) 'Making life books with foster and adoptive children', in Schaefer C.E. (ed.), *Innovative Interventions in Child and Adolescent Therapy* (pp. 377–399), New York: John Wiley & Sons.

Howard J.A. (2010) *Lifebook Principles. Components of the Lifebook. Lifebook checklist. Sample Lifebook pages*, Normal, IL: The Center for Adoption Studies at Illinois State University. Access at: http://adoptionresearch.illinoisstate. edu/publications-reports/

Iowa Foster and Adoptive Parent Association (undated) *IFAPA Lifebook pages*. (Over 70 downloadable lifebook pages free for use.) Access at: www.ifapa.org/resources/IFAPA_Lifebook_Pages.asp

Johnson M. and Howard J. (2008) *Putting the Pieces Together: Lifebook work with children* (DVD), Rock Island, IL: Lutheran Social Services of Illinois. Access at: www.lssi.org/Support/LifebookDVD.aspx

Lacher D., Nichols T. and May J. (2005) *Connecting with Kids through Stories: Using narratives to facilitate attachment in adopted children*, London: Jessica Kingsley Publishers.

Rose R. and Philpot T. (2005) *The Child's Own Story: Life story work with traumatized children*. Philadelphia: Jessica Kingsley Publishers.

Ryan T. and Walker, R. (2007) *Life Story Work: A practical guide to helping children understand their past* (2nd edn.), London: BAAF.

Shah S. and Argent H. (2006) *Life Story Work: What it is and what it means*. London: BAAF. Access at: www.baaf.org.uk/res/pubs/books/book_lwhat. shtml

16 Involving children and adolescents in permanency work

Description and overview

For children and teens removed from their original homes and placed in foster care – typically following confusing and traumatic experiences – their sense of security and who they are in the world is profoundly challenged, contributing to feelings of powerlessness and lack of agency. There are many decisions made on their behalf that are life changing, and the number of adults who have responsibility for them evolves from just their parents to up to a dozen or so people, many of whom are strangers. Children's right to be heard is codified in the United Nations Convention on the Rights of the Child (UNCRC) and in child welfare laws, such as England's Children Act 1989, varying from professionals' responsibility to take children's wishes and feelings into account and make decisions in their best interests to granting young people the legal right to consent (or withhold consent) to an adoption (Schofield, 2005).

Law and policy across the US and Canada give children the right to consent to their adoptions at specific ages. Most Canadian provinces and territories have established 12 as the age of consent for adoption, but the age is seven in Ontario and 14 in Quebec. (In Quebec, children aged 10–13 must be consulted regarding adoption, but full consent is not mandatory until age 14.) In the US, nearly all states and the District of Columbia (DC) require that older children and young people give consent to their adoptions. Approximately 25 states and DC set the age of consent at 14, 18 states at age 12, and six states at age 10. In 16 states, the court can decide to dispense with such consent if it is deemed in the child's best interests (Child Welfare Information Gateway, 2010b).

The vast majority of children adopted from care in England are young; for example, in recent statistics, 76 per cent were aged four or younger, and only 2.6 per cent were 10 or older (Department for

Education [DfE], 2012a). Child welfare statutes and statutory guidance on care planning place an emphasis on consulting children and considering their wishes and feelings in decision-making. The statutory guidelines are founded on the UNCRC and the European Convention on Human Rights, and strongly require ascertaining and giving due consideration to children's wishes and feelings, stating that when children feel they are active participants, understand what is happening and are listened to, they are likely to feel less fearful. Involving children in the process also recognises their difficulties, develops their strengths and promotes resilience. The Children Act guidance and regulations also state:

> *The child's views as expressed should always be discussed, recorded and given due consideration before a placement decision is made, at every review meeting and at case conferences. The possibilities and options identified should be explained, discussed and, if necessary, reassessed in the light of the child's views . . . All children need to be given information and appropriate explanations so that they are in a position to develop their own views and make informed choices . . . Where a child has difficulty in expressing his/her wishes and feelings about any decisions being made about him/her, consideration must be given to securing the support of an advocate.* (DfE, 2010b, pp. 4–5)

A recent report in England reviewed studies of children's perspectives and found that they wanted more choice in final decisions about where they would live, that many did not feel confident in giving their views in review meetings where decisions were made, and that they felt big decisions about their lives occurred outside of meetings (Minnis and Walker, 2012). Acknowledging children's feelings of loss and limited power, and fully involving them in decisions and plans about their futures, can increase the odds that children will agree to and engage in permanency work and promote their adjustment to transitions. Older children and teens in care often accept the idea, in principle, that a permanent family is a good thing to have; yet they are often sceptical about their own ability to achieve permanency through adoption. Doubts about their "adoptability" as well as concerns about losing access or being disloyal to original family members often enter into their decision to say "no" when asked if they wish to be adopted. Sometimes workers have taken a child's "no" to adoption as a permanent barrier; however, as discussed below, this response needs to be explored and revisited.

Studies have examined fostered children and adolescents' perspectives on the meaning of permanency, finding that many experienced emotional pain as a result of repeatedly losing important relationships (Samuels, 2008, 2009). Indeed, the emotional trauma that children experience at separation from their parents is often compounded by separation from siblings, grandparents and other key figures. This trauma can be exacerbated by the subsequent loss of relationships with foster carers, foster siblings, friends and even teachers, case workers or mentors. Is it any wonder that they are less than eager to give another "permanent" relationship a try? For these reasons, involving children and adolescents in permanency work is critically important.

Schofield (2005, p. 30) notes that empowering children is:

> ... not simply about offering them the right to contribute their views on placement choices or levels of birth family contact. It is about understanding children's point of view as well as their developmental needs ... and seeing the world through their eyes. It is about working with them to anticipate, plan for and create a pathway that will bring them their best chance of stability, happiness and personal fulfilment in family and community life.

This level of engagement takes into account children's developmental capacities; strives to elicit their thoughts and feelings; and seeks to have them fully represented in decision-making – either indirectly for young children or directly when they are older. Regularly scheduled six-monthly case reviews often provide opportunities to explore a young person's perceptions of needs and desires and can incorporate anything from a desire to take art lessons or wanting more time with siblings to participation in permanency planning efforts.

Experts in the field have observed that participation in, and preparation of children for, permanency often is not systematic and may not give voice to children's fears, wishes and understandings (Freundlich and Avery, 2005; Henry, 2005; Hanna, 2008; AdoptUSKids, 2013b). Despite support for inclusion of children and adolescents in the decisions that affect them, it has been uncommon for them to be participants in the meetings and discussions where decisions are made (Kendrick and Mapstone, 1991; Freundlich and Avery, 2005), although participation by older children is more common (Grimshaw and Sinclair, 1997; Thomas and O'Kane, 1999).

Key programme elements

- **Assessing attitudes toward permanency:** The first step to engaging young people in permanency work is to examine their attitudes about having a permanent family. Studies reveal that workers do not sufficiently examine young people's attitudes towards permanency – sometimes discouraging them from considering adoption, engaging only in superficial discussion or failing to explore permanency at all (Freundlich and Avery, 2005).

  A tool that can be used to explore young people's feelings about adoption is the Openness to Permanency Scale (LaNoue and Nienhuis, 2006). This 22-item instrument identifies issues related to divided loyalty, self-esteem and self-worth. Young people respond on a scale from "not true at all" to "exactly true" on items such as:

  - *It bothers me that I may disappoint my birth parents if I agree to be adopted.*
  - *I have the courage I need to become part of a new family.*
  - *It would be too hard to fit into a permanent family at my age.*
  - *The right adoptive family could accept my past, even the bad things that happened in my family.*

  This is not a normed instrument resulting in a score, but rather a means to explore young people's attitudes. The replies serve as a basis for exploring feelings and fears. Use of the scale at several points in the worker/young person relationship can also identify shifts in attitudes over time. In Bethany Christian Services' *It's Up to Me/ReConnect* programme, for which the scale was developed, it is administered at intake, six months, one year and termination. It is also used for discussion purposes between the young person, case manager, adoptive parent(s), and/or birth family.

- **Exploring the meaning of permanency fully:** Involving children and young people means fully exploring what they understand permanency to be, answering their questions and listening and responding to them honestly. Children and young people may hold that they do not want to be adopted. Their discomfort or ambivalence at one point should not be regarded as a "no" forever. Part of their reluctance may come from misunderstanding what adoption means. The concept of permanent relationships for life, rather than adoption *per se*, should be emphasised. The PowerPoint presentation, *Unpacking the "No" of Permanency for Adolescents: Planning for youth transitioning from foster care to adulthood,* explores ways to genuinely assess obstacles to older children and adolescents' adoption and to move them to permanency (see Mallon, 2011 in Selected Resources). Such authentic exploration can replace formulaic investigations stemming from the question, 'Do you want to be adopted?,' which too quickly accept young people's negative statements. It is critical to explore what they understand permanency to be, and what they fear and hope for. Exploring their feelings about permanency is a process, not a one-time conversation (Howard and Berzin, 2011).

  Workers need to help young people explore what they want and need in terms of stability, security, nurture, support and guidance through relationships with dependable adults for the course of their lifetimes. Various agencies have developed curricula for helping groups of older children and young people to explore their feelings and fears related to permanency with a new family, and to recognise that this does not equate to giving up connections to important people in their lives. For example, see 'Resources for working with youth' under 'Youth permanency grantee resources' on the National Resource Center for Adoption's website (see Selected Resources).

- **Addressing concerns about contact with original family:** Many young people for whom adoption is the plan have not been asked about their wishes for ongoing connection with birth parents, siblings or other important figures in their lives. Samuels's (2009) qualitative study of young people who had left foster care without permanency found they had negative attitudes about adoption, including that they were betraying their birth family and that adoption would mean a permanent breach. Exploration with young people about who is important to them is critical. Exploration of how connections with these people can be continued or enhanced may help adolescents to be more open to the idea of a permanent home. Even when termination of parental rights has occurred, workers need to explore how to preserve children's wishes for ongoing connections.

- **Expanding the definition of permanency:** Permanence for young people in care who cannot return home has traditionally been framed as "being adopted". Guardianship is another permanency option in the UK, Canada and the US, with subsidised guardianship programmes growing in the US. Unlike adoption, guardianship does not require the termination of parental rights, and children often have ongoing relationships with their biological parents and siblings (Testa, 2008). Given that ongoing connection with original family is a fundamental desire for most young people in care, and the fears young people have that adoption means permanent loss of original family, exploring guardianship or other stable, legally recognised, long-term care options may allow more of them to commit to permanence.

- **Fully preparing children and adolescents for adoptive placement:** Preparing children for adoptive placement is as important as preparing the adoptive parents. This process and some helpful resources were discussed briefly under "Promoting permanency through life story work", and others are listed under Selected Resources. A study of over 200 children adopted from care in England asked them a number of questions about their adoption experiences, including what they had wanted to know when they were being adopted (Morgan, 2006). Their top responses were: about the process, when they could see birth family, what the adoptive parents were like, why they had to be adopted and what it means for them, what would happen if something goes wrong, how long it would take to complete, where they would live, what would being adopted feel like, whether they would be fully a part of the family, and whether they would be safe. For new placements, of course, they need to get to know the family and to have support to explore their feelings and needs throughout the process. This might include anticipating future needs and developing anticipatory guidance for addressing them (National Resource Center for Adoption, 2012). BAAF publishes a guide for children and adolescents, *Adoption: What it is and what it means* (Shah, 2012), to help answer their questions. It also advises them that they have the right to an independent advocate and tells them whom to contact to ask about this.

Lessons learned

- **Professionals seeking to facilitate the participation of children and adolescents in decision-making about their own lives must consider a range of developmental abilities – children's affect, understanding, autonomy, sense of belonging and sense of self**. Adults must also use the model of responsible parents who respect their children; consult on their views; and maximise their decision-making to the extent possible, while helping them understand the reasons for decisions – especially those that differ from the children's expressed desires – and not making the children feel that the total burden of decision-making has fallen upon them (Schofield, 2005).
- **When adults make efforts to empower young people and fully involve them in permanency efforts, they will respond**. In the Casey Family Services' publication, *A Call to Action: An integrated approach to youth permanency and preparation for adulthood*, the authors call for permanency work to include active partnership with young people, acknowledging them as the central players in their own integrated planning for permanency. They emphasise the importance of a collaborative case work process that prepares young people to be active members of the permanency team and

involves them meaningfully in planning (Frey *et al*, 2005).

- **Young people differ in their attitudes about adoption and their willingness to pursue it**. In a study of 54 adolescents involved in a camp-based programme focused on finding adoptive homes, Diehl and colleagues (2006) found statistically significant relationships between demographic factors and attitudes toward adoption. Males were more positive toward adoption than were females, Caucasian adolescents were more positive than minority ethnic peers, and younger teenagers were more open than older ones. A "one size fits all" approach to helping young people consider adoption as an option is thus unlikely to be effective.

- **Adopted young people can be effective mentors and educators – helping other young people to risk pursuing adoption**. Often, young people adopted at older ages can be the best ambassadors for the advantages of permanent homes. Connecting ambivalent young people with others adopted at older ages provides the chance to explore honestly the pros and cons of adoption (Mallon, 2005).

- **Protecting relationships with original family members is a key to helping young people consider and accept permanency**. The power of family is strong. Many young people who "lose" their original families through legal termination of parental rights maintain a deep desire for ongoing connection or reconnection. Indeed, many adolescents who leave foster care without permanency reconnect with family after discharge, despite the court's finding that those families were unsafe or unfit (Collins *et al*, 2008). Young people may benefit from knowing that formal post-adoption contact agreements can be structured. An important part of fully involving young people in planning their permanency is to carefully explore with whom they desire ongoing or re-activated connections, the nature of such connections and the setting of boundaries in such relationships.

Outcomes

There is very limited research on involving young people in permanency decisions, although the practice is encouraged widely in the child welfare field. A Georgia permanency initiative found that child engagement in permanency work was a key factor in achieving permanency. Young people who had not been engaged in permanency planning were 87 per cent less likely to achieve permanency during the project (O'Brien *et al*, 2012). Also, Louisell's (2004) review of nine model programmes directed at increasing permanency among young people (including return home) found that their involvement was identified by several programmes as a critical component, although this factor was not specifically tested as a predictor of permanency. The Northwest Institute for Children and Families' "Connected and Cared For" programme had a 95 per cent participation rate for young people in family group conferences and made their participation a condition from the beginning of the intervention.

The following study was not limited to children being considered for permanency, but it does suggest strategies that would increase participation by children and young people in making plans about their lives. The study of 225 foster children, aged 8–12, in the UK examined their participation in decisions about their care (Thomas and O'Kane, 1999). The research indicated that most children were attending reviews and planning meetings. Inclusion in meetings was tied to three factors:

- **Age:** the older the children, the more likely they were to be invited to the meeting and to participate. For example, 84 per cent of children aged 12 or over were invited to participate versus 37 per cent of children eight or under.
- **Stability:** children were more likely to be invited to meetings when their situations were stable. Sixty-eight per cent were included when the meeting was about maintaining the status quo. Forty-seven per cent were invited when major decisions about their situations were made.
- **Documentation:** as the study was underway, Looking after Children (LAC) review forms were provided by the Department of Health. Sixty-three per cent of children were invited to meetings when the forms were used, compared to only 38 per cent when they were not.

Most children who were invited to attend meetings did so. Variation in attendance was associated with age, i.e., over half (51%) of eight- to 10-year-olds attended, compared to 81 per cent of 11- to 12-year-olds, and with relationships between the family and the agency, as rated by social workers – that is, 46 per cent of children attended when the relationship was conflictual or mixed, while 70 per cent attended when it was perceived as based on partnership. In addition, 'Social workers and caregivers who positively valued children's participation were more successful in involving them effectively' (p. 223). In qualitative interviews, most children felt that all children should be invited and given the choice about whether to attend. Most of the children interviewed (53%) had attended their last meeting.

Although most children attended meetings, there were limitations related to their understanding of the purpose and involvement. Just 32 per cent had been asked who they thought should attend, and fewer than a quarter had been given a choice about time or place (23% and 24%). Social workers reported that in 25 per cent of cases, children had been asked to help set the agenda and had an opportunity to discuss the outcome.

Another study examined the results of intervention that fully involved young people in making decisions about their future. Powers and colleagues (2012) examined the impact of an intervention that enhanced self-determination among fostered adolescents in special education, a group at high risk for difficulty in the period after emancipation. Sixty-nine young people between 16.5 and 17.5 years of age were randomly assigned to the *Take Charge* programme (a structured, ongoing coaching and monitoring intervention) or the regular independent living programme. Those in *Take Charge*, where self-direction with support was the emphasis, found moderate to large effects on self-determination, quality of life and the use of transition services. They also had higher rates of high school completion and employment. These differences were demonstrated both at the close of intervention and at the one-year follow-up. While the focus of the project was not permanency, the findings point to the importance of fully involving young people in the programmes designed to benefit them.

Selected resources

AdoptUSKids (2013b) *Increasing Your Agency's Capacity to Respond to Prospective Parents and Prepare Older Youth for Adoption: Going beyond recruitment for 14–16 year olds*. Access at: www.bit.ly/13vo8eE

Child Welfare Information Gateway (2012b) *Helping Your Foster Child Transition to Your Adopted Child*, Washington, DC: US Children's Bureau. Access at: www.childwelfare.gov/pubs/f_transition.cfm

Mallon G.P. (2005) *Toolkit No. 3: Facilitating Permanency for Youth*, Washington DC: CWLA Press. Access at: www.cwla.org/pubs

Mallon G.P. (2011) *Unpacking the No of Permanency for Older Adolescents* (PowerPoint Presentation), Hunter College, NY: National Resource Center for Permanency and Family Connections. Access at: www.hunter.cuny.edu/socwork/nrcfcpp/info_services/download/Florida.unpacking.11.08.pdf

National Resource Center for Adoption (2010) *Youth Permanency Grantee Resources: Resources for working with youth*. Access at: www.nrcadoption.org/resources/ypc/grantee-resources/

National Resource Center for Adoption (2012) *Adoption Competency Curriculum: Child/youth assessment and preparation* (Participants' handouts). Access at: www.nrcadoption.org/pdfs/acc/PH%20-%20Child%20Assessment%20and%20Preparation%203-10.pdf

National Resource Center for Permanency and Family Connections; Virginia Department of Social Services (2013) *Ten Things that Youth Want Child Welfare Professionals to Know: Engaging youth in foster care*, available at: www.nrcpfc.org/is/downloads/ten%20Tips_Engagement%2011.13.13.pdf; and *Ten Things that Youth Want Child Welfare Professionals to Know: Talking to youth in foster care about permanency*, available at: www.nrcpfc.org/is/downloads/Ten%20Tips–Permanency%2011.13.13.pdf

Romaine M., Turley T. and Tuckey N. (2007) *Preparing Children for Permanence: A guide to undertaking direct work for social workers, foster carers and adoptive parents*, London: BAAF.

Schofield G. (2005) 'The voice of the child in family placement decision-making: a developmental model', *Adoption & Fostering*, 29:1, pp. 29–44.

Shah S. (2012) *Adoption: What it is and what it means: A guide for children and young people*, London: BAAF.

17 Sound parental assessment and an effective home study process

Description and overview

A comprehensive assessment of potential adoptive parents conducted by a qualified social worker in the applicants' jurisdictional residence, referred to as a home study, is required in all US states, Canadian provinces, and throughout the UK. It results in a written, comprehensive assessment to evaluate the safety, suitability and subsequent approval of the prospective parents. It is also instrumental in matching a child with an adoptive family. The home study process is critical and is at the centre of ensuring that placements are in the best interests of children. The focus is on assuring that children will be safe and their well-being will flourish in their adoptive families, thus leading to successful placements.

There are three main purposes of the home study process (Child Welfare Information Gateway [CWIG], 2010a). The first is an opportunity for mutual learning; it should both educate and prepare parents for the realities of adoption, and offer them the opportunity to assess themselves in relation to their readiness and capacities to parent children with a range of special needs. It also gives both the parents and the agency time to become familiar with each other. Throughout the process, prospective parents and the agency should be mutually assessing the fit of adoption for the applicants. Secondly, substantial information is collected to help match children with parents who can reasonably meet their needs. Finally, it is conducted to evaluate the fitness of applicants to parent.

There are several general components and accompanying documents that are similar across jurisdictions for the evaluation of prospective adoptive parents, though agency practices vary (Geen *et al*, 2004). While both foster and adoptive parents undergo home studies, there is variation across jurisdictions as to whether a universal assessment, which would grant a dual approval as both an adoptive or foster parent, or whether differential assessment specific to either foster care or adoption is used. To date, in the US and Canada, there is no universal, uniform, standardised home study in use across all jurisdictions, and there is limited research on the best method to accurately assess family functioning during the home study process (Crea et al, 2007). In England and Wales, a specified template (Prospective Adopter's Report – PAR) is used for adoptive home studies, thus making placements across jurisdictions somewhat easier. A study of voluntary agencies and local authorities reported that it takes, on average, 62 hours to complete this report (Dance et al, 2010). A working group was established to consider revising the PAR, and a streamlined assessment form was piloted prior to the introduction of a revised two-part assessment process. (This form can be viewed online by BAAF members and is available from BAAF on a licence agreement.)

In an effort to update home study methodologies and address issues of concern in the US, the SAFE (Structured Analysis Family Evaluation) home study method was developed, with the following purposes: to consider the necessary strengths and skills required to parent children in the public child welfare system; to create both a comprehensive and uniform instrument to gather prospective family information and in-depth psychosocial evaluations; and to reduce variability and address topics difficult to discuss openly (Crea et al, 2011). SAFE is the first standardised home study process to be widely implemented in the US and Canada (Crea et al, 2007; Cleary and White, 2008; Crea, 2009). Currently, approximately half of US states and six Canadian provinces (Alberta, British Columbia, Manitoba, Nova Scotia, Ontario and Prince Edward Island) use the SAFE methodology for assessing foster, adoptive and kinship-care families.

England offers a unique appeals procedure for prospective adoptive parents and foster carers to apply for a review of any decision made by the agency in relation to their application for approval. The Independent Review Mechanism (IRM) is government funded and operated by BAAF. If accepted, the case is heard by the IRM panel; it makes a recommendation to the adoption agency, which then decides whether or not to change its decision. In 42 per cent of the adoption cases heard over the 2012–13 year, the prospective adopter was ultimately approved (DfE, 2013a).

Key programme elements

The home study process consists of a comprehensive assessment method that includes application, screening, in-depth multiple assessments of family strengths, resources, parenting skills, readiness to parent a child, criminal background checks and training. As a mutual assessment process, the home study is designed to help people decide if adoption is right for them and to help them understand which needs of available children they could meet. Depending on both agency resources and training requirements, the home study process can last from two to 10 months (CWIG, 2010a). In England, the assessment must be completed within six months. This experience should facilitate decision-making about a family's suitability and ability to care for a child, as well as about potential resources or services they may need.

The main components include:

- **Adoption preparation training:** This is a comprehensive education programme for adoptive applicants to address a broad range of topics – from issues of attachment and loss, impact of abuse and neglect, child development, behavioural problems and management, and birth family connections (Child Welfare League of America [CWLA], 2000).
- **Individual and joint interviews with prospective adopters and other significant family members:** The intention is to develop a relationship between the assessor and the applicants to facilitate exploration of a broad range of topics, including but not limited to approaches to parenting, stress and coping capacity, motivation for adoption, issues related to loss or infertility, and child characteristics that would be a good fit for the applicants.
- **Home visits:** Visiting the applicant's residence offers an opportunity to assess whether it meets safety and any other specified

standards as well as whether there is adequate space for a child to live there.

- **Health reviews and documentation:** A current physical exam is required, along with appropriate documentation from a medical professional that indicates state of health, typical life expectancy, and physical and mental capacity to care for a child.

- **Financial information:** Income verification is required and applicants must submit requested and appropriate documentation (e.g., payslips, income tax forms). Additionally, information about savings, health and life insurance policies, investments and debt is also collected.

- **Criminal background checks:** Applicants submit to criminal clearance checks and, in some jurisdictions, registry checks for child abuse and neglect, adult abuse and sex offender charges, aswell as driving, juvenile and employment records (Gilmore *et al*, 2004).

- **Autobiographical information and marriage/civil partnership certificates, if applicable:** Applicants are asked to write an auto-biography so that the worker can learn more about them as individuals and as a couple, including their strengths and weak-nesses. It also offers an opportunity for applicants to consider their goals and parenting plans, and to reflect on being an adoptive family.

- **Personal references:** Applicants are asked to supply several of these, including names, addresses and contact information. Referees are typically asked to provide information about the applicants to better understand their relationships, families and supports.

- **Education and employment:** Information is captured about current educational levels and achievements, plans for further education, employment status and history, and current employ-ment.

- **Psychosocial assessment:** This is an evaluation that includes the physical and emotional health of the applicants and assessments of their connections to necessary services and the community.

Lessons learned

The home study process requires considerable time and effort to ensure that prospective parents have the opportunity to learn about caring for a child with special needs, explore their own concerns and needs, and identify available services to help address child and family needs (Rosenthal *et al*, 1996). For these and other reasons, it is important to put applicants at ease and help them to be candid. It is almost universal that prospective adopters begin the process with anxiety related to being judged inadequate and some resentment at the intrusiveness involved; therefore, it is essential to begin with a discussion of the purposes of the home study, common feelings of applicants, and the importance of mutual exploration of their capacities and needs so that their child will fit well into their family. Various tools have been developed for assisting mutual exploration of how applicants' own experiences will affect their parenting style and expectations, as well as assessing their support networks; for example, see Gray's (2007) 'Assessing attachment readiness and capabilities' (under Selected Resources) and those in England's PAR form.

The parental assessment conveyed in the written home study needs to provide sufficient information about parenting capacities and expectations for workers to be able to make decisions related to the family's compatibility with specific children. This is still an area where much work is needed. While home studies are adequate in gathering general information, their ability to capture critically important and sensitive information is still lacking (Crea *et al*, 2011). Gathering information about a prospective family's ability to meet the needs of a specific child often requires additional strategies beyond reading the home study evaluation because of high variability of home study practice and the general nature of information collected. Additional strategies can include gathering information from people who have engaged with the family and/or provided services, and the inclusion of specific information about parents' preparedness and expectations. When there are potential risk factors that might compromise parenting ability, such as a history of substance abuse or mental health concerns, an in-depth exploration of these issues is important, in addition to gathering information from their doctor or therapist (Noordegraff *et al*, 2009).

Cousins (2003) critiques the utilisation of home study checklists that ask prospective parents to rate their level of ability to accept children with specific types of special needs, particularly as a categorical matching tool. She recognises that during the home study process, applicants are under great stress and are asked to imagine a hypothetical child with a specific condition and project how well they would be able to parent such a child. Often these are applicants who have infertility issues and have never parented a child. She notes that it can be an excruciating process for applicants, with some feeling guilt at excluding any categories of children. Cousins asserts that such an imperfect tool and process should not later totally circumscribe the applicants' ability to be linked with real children in need of homes.

Outcomes

Researchers have established a significant connection between adoption disruption, parenting stress and inaccurate or incomplete information about the child (Barth and Berry, 1988; Rosenthal, 1993; McGlone *et al*, 2002). This process begins during the home study, when it is critical to examine applicants' comfort and experience with children and assess how realistic their expectations are about children's behaviour and development in the context of any special needs (Crea *et al*, 2007).

There has been limited research to explore agency home study practices or the best ways to evaluate a family's functioning during the home study process (Crea *et al*, 2007). Research suggests that the practice of parental screening and assessment can vary in both timing and intensity (Geen *et al*, 2004), even when the general components are covered. Furthermore, variations in home study practice across sites can impact on the facilitation of interjurisdictional adoptions as a result of inconsistency, lack of trust among parties about quality, and reliance on another agency's assessment (Freundlich *et al*, 2004).

Research examining workers' experiences with the implementation of SAFE (Crea *et al*, 2009a, b) indicates that it more effectively identifies most issues of concern when compared with conventional methods. While less experienced workers favoured the structure of SAFE, more experienced workers were somewhat less positive about the approach and indicated that quality interviewing techniques are fundamental to understanding a family. Generally, participants expressed the view that SAFE was a useful method for evaluating prospective resource families across a variety of situations and that it encouraged open communication with families. SAFE's requirement that applicants review and sign the home study means that they are aware of all of its contents and can have input on all issues.

Selected resources

Beesley P. (2010) *Making Good Assessments: A practical resource guide*, London: BAAF.

Child Welfare Information Gateway (2010a) *The Adoption Home Study Process*. Access at: www.childwelfare.gov/pubs/f_homstu.cfm

Consortium SAFE (2011) SAFE home study (Structured Analysis Family Evaluation). Access at: www.safehomestudy.org

Cousins J. (2010) *Pushing the Boundaries of Assessment*, London: BAAF.

Dibben E. (2013) *Undertaking an Adoption Assessment in England*, London: BAAF.

Gray D. (2007) 'Assessing attachment readiness and capabilities in prospective adoptive parents.' Excerpted from Chapter 9, *Nurturing Adoptions: Creating resilience after neglect and trauma*, Indianapolis, IN: Perspectives Press.

National Resource Center for Permanency and Family Connections (2012) *LGBT Prospective Foster and Adoptive Families: The homestudy assessment process*. Access at: www.nrcpfc.org/downloads/wu/Brief2_TheHomestudy AssessmentProcessWithLGBTProspectiveFosterAndAdoptiveFamilies.pdf

18 Effective adoptive parent preparation

Description and overview

Adoptive parent preparation (APP) involves the provision of professional services and supports to help parents develop the knowledge, expectations and skills necessary to understand and meet the unique needs of their adopted children. Although APP has long been part of adoption practice, it has only been in the past few decades, in conjunction with the rise of adoptions from care and international placements, that its importance has been recognised by policy-makers, placement professionals, post-adoption providers and researchers.

Research has shown that many children adopted from care have one or more special needs involving physical, emotional, social or behavioural issues that can pose increased parenting challenges for adoptive families (Barth and Berry, 1988; McRoy, 1999). These developmental difficulties – usually stemming from genetic and prenatal complications, as well as from early life adversities such as neglect and abuse – can undermine parents' commitment to children, decrease their satisfaction with the adoption decision, and increase the risk of placement disruption or dissolution (Barth and Berry, 1988; Smith, 2010). Yet when parents are provided appropriate pre- and post-adoption services, their ability to meet their children's needs is greatly enhanced, increasing positive outcomes for all family members and stabilising placements (Barth and Berry, 1988; Groza and Rosenberg, 1998; Smith and Howard, 1999; Sar, 2000; Farber *et al*, 2003; Puddy and Jackson, 2003; Hart and Luckock, 2004; Brodzinsky, 2008; Smith, 2010).

Despite the recognition of the importance of APP, research suggests that prospective parents often do not receive sufficient information, training and support to understand and manage their children's needs (Peterson and Freundlich, 2000). In fact, Wind and colleagues (2005) reported that of the 1,219 survey respondents in the

California Long-Range Adoption Study, more than half did not receive information about their child's behaviour or services related to their children's past, including information about early family history, social case history or educational history; nor did they have the opportunity to talk with former carers or birth family members. Although the respondents in this study had adopted their children two decades previously, the types of preparation and support deficiencies identified continue to be recognised today as challenging practice issues by most adoption professionals, as well as by parents adopting from the care system.

Throughout the US, Canada and England, parent preparation is required for adoptions from care. Two curricula that are used to provide required training in the US and Canada are PRIDE (Parent Resources for Information, Development and Education) and MAPP (Model Approach to Partnership in Parenting) – both consisting of approximately 10 weeks of three-hour sessions. Research exploring parents' reactions to this training has found that the most common complaint was too much focus on the difficulties of the children and too little information about services and support; moreover, when the latter was provided, it was mostly at the end of training. Participants wanted more information on the adoption process (the timing of steps and how matching decisions are made) as well as more discussion about managing relationships with birth parents after adoption (Geen et al, 2004). BAAF's adopter preparation course (Fursland, 2006a) is widely used in England and consists of a training programme as well as a workbook for participants. This is currently being revised in light of the government's new two-stage assessment process (see Fursland in Selected Resources).

Prospective parents need to receive individual (in addition to group) preparation related to understanding the history and needs of their particular children and the implications of this information for the children's ongoing development; they also should be apprised of the types of services and support that may assist them in parenting. In England, many agencies use "child appreciation days" to bring together professionals and others, such as foster carers who know the child, to exchange in-depth information about the child prior to placement so that adopters are properly prepared (Sayers and Roach, 2011). As an example, the details of the use of this practice in one local authority are outlined in a manual available on the internet (Walsall Council, 2012).

In addition to pre-adoption preparation, there are numerous training opportunities that parents can access before placement and throughout the child's development. Some of these are designed as an early intervention to provide the tools parents need to facilitate positive adjustment, such as the *SafeBase* programme developed by After Adoption (2012) in England or two manualised, 10-session parent training interventions developed and piloted by Rushton and colleagues (2010), also in England. In the US, Adoption Learning Partners (2013) offers an array of online courses for pre-adoptive and adoptive parents that can be taken as preparation prior to adoption or as the family's needs emerge over time.

Key programme elements

Adoption professionals (Brodzinsky, 2008; Cousins, 2008; Smith, 2010) have identified a number of core principles underlying effective adoptive parent preparation (APP):

- **APP requires well-trained professionals**. They should be knowledgeable about: adoption and foster care and their impact on children, adoptive parents and birth parents; child development and family dynamics; biological, experiential, social and cultural factors affecting child development and adoptive family life; the impact of trauma and loss on children; mental health issues in adoption and foster care; how ethnicity, culture, gender and sexual orientation influence adoption practice and family life; and intervention strategies and community resources supporting adoptive families. Adoption professionals should regularly update their training in these and related areas through various means, including continuing education courses and certification programmes, online courses and webinars, training videos and professional supervision.
- **APP should be an ongoing process that is mandatory for all families**. Agencies making adoptive placements, especially of

children with special needs, have a professional and ethical responsibility to ensure that their clients receive the necessary training and support to successfully parent their children. If they are unable to provide the full scope of this education and support themselves, they must ensure that their clients receive it elsewhere. Furthermore, since the needs of children, parents and the family change over time, education and support must be available and accessible following adoption finalisation. Agencies must ensure that their clients are aware of community resources that provide post-adoption services (Smith, 2010).

- **Effective APP is based upon a multi-method, multi-source approach to training**. Combining individual case preparation and group interventions with adoption readings and online courses, such as those offered by Adoption Learning Partners (2013), among others, provides a rich array of training and educational experiences. Adoptive parents benefit not only from working with adoption professionals, but also from having the opportunity to interact with those who have already "walked in their shoes" (e.g., experienced adoptive parents).

- **Promote a receptive atmosphere for APP**. Because the transition to adoptive parenthood is often fraught with uncertainty and anxiety (Brodzinsky and Huffman, 1988; Brodzinsky and Pinderhughes, 2002), especially when families are adopting children with special needs, it is important for child welfare workers to do everything possible to help clients feel welcomed, valued, respected and supported. When this occurs, families are likely to make better use of APP.

- **Provide an objective and balanced view of adoption**. APP should provide parents with accurate information about the challenges that neglected, abused or traumatised children and their families face, as well as information about the benefits of adoption for these boys and girls, the strengths of these children, strategies for parenting, examples of successful adoptions, access to experienced and successful adopters, and referrals to appropriate post-adoption services and support. Combining a risk-based and strength- and support-based approach to APP increases the chances of parents developing realistic expectations about their children, thereby promoting more stable and successful placements.

- **Provide full disclosure of information about children.** Effective APP is based on the principle of transparency. To successfully meet their children's needs, adoptive parents must be provided with all available information about their children's history, including the circumstances leading to their entry into care. They also need to be helped to understand the implications of this history for their children's ongoing development, how they might assist the children in healing or developing to their fullest potential, and how to access services or support that might be useful to the family.

- **Support visits between children and pre-adoptive families.** Successful integration of children into adoptive families is enhanced when parents and children get to know one another gradually. Planned visits allow case workers to more effectively prepare children and parents for adoptive placement.

- **Prepare parents to help the child address loss, grief and identity issues.** APP also needs to help parents understand the normative stresses associated with being adopted and raising adopted children. Loss and grief are inherent parts of the adoption experience, and being adopted inevitably colours the child's sense of self and identity (Grotevant, 1997; Brodzinsky, 2011b). Parents need information and strategies for helping their children manage these issues, as well as information about the ways in which adoption may influence parenting at different phases of the family life cycle. For those adopting transracially, special considerations need to be incorporated into APP focusing on supporting ethnic and cultural socialisation (Smith *et al*, 2008).

- **Prepare parents for contact with birth family.** Many children adopted from care are involved in open adoptions. Not only have they had contact with birth relatives during their foster placements, but more of their adoptive parents are engaging with contact following adoption finalisation. Because contact can be challenging for all involved, adoptive parents need guidance to help them understand the best way to manage relationships with the birth family. Furthermore, because the needs and life circumstances of all adoption kinship members change over time, adoptive parents benefit from post-adoption resources to help them with this evolving responsibility.

- **Prepare parents to understand the benefits of post-adoption services.** Families adopting children with special needs more often require post-adoption services (Smith, 2010). But they sometimes view seeking help as a weakness or a sign of failure, and therefore do not utilise available services or postpone using them until problems are quite serious. Because post-adoption service utilisation is a good predictor of placement stability and greater parental satisfaction with adoption (Barth and Berry, 1988; Berry *et al*, 1996), APP needs to reframe help-seeking as normative and as a strength. When APP is effective, families are more likely to utilise post-adoption services (Wind *et al*, 2007).

Lessons learned

There are many barriers to effective APP (Brodzinsky, 2008); some are systemic or organisational, and others involve relational or personal challenges. Insufficient financial and staffing resources limit the development and implementation of APP programmes. So, too, does high staff turnover in the public child welfare system. Inadequate or outdated training of adoption professionals, as well as insufficient guidelines regarding the scope and content of APP, can also compromise efforts to enhance effective adoptive parenting. In addition, information about birth family and pre-placement history is often lacking or incomplete, making it all the more difficult for parents to understand their children's behaviour and provide the necessary support for successful family integration. Finally, even when professionals are well trained and relevant information and services are available, adoptive parents sometimes do not utilise services or are not receptive to the information provided because of their own personal vulnerabilities, insecurities or unrealistic expectations.

APP is also influenced by kinship status, type of adoption and children's pre-adoptive risk history. Research has found that families adopting biological relatives were less likely to receive general preparation about adoption or information about the child's behavioural past – although, understandably, kinship adopters were more likely to have biological information such as birth history and family background (Wind *et al*, 2005). In addition, investigators found that families involved in open adoptions and those whose children had greater pre-placement risk histories were more likely to receive various types of APP than those in closed placements or whose children were relatively free of adverse histories.

Education, training and support for adoptive families need to be available and accessible throughout the childrearing years. These services and support can take many forms: parenting courses and workshops; online courses; consultations with mental health professionals; books and DVDs on adoption and parenting; adoptive parent support groups; and support from spouses/partners, extended family and friends. Research indicates that the amount and quality of support that adoptive families receive enhances placement stability and positive adjustment for all family members (Barth and Berry, 1988; Groze, 1996; Leung and Erich, 2002; Houston and Kramer, 2008).

Outcomes

APP benefits adoptive families in numerous ways. It reduces placement disruption, affirms parents' adoption decision, promotes more positive views of children, supports more realistic parental expectations, improves parenting skills, strengthens family support networks, and leads to improved functioning on the part of all family members (Barth and Berry, 1988; Groze, 1996; Smith and Howard, 1999; Reilly and Platz, 2004; Wind *et al*, 2007).

What is less clear, however, is the effectiveness of specific APP methods and/or curricula. We do not know, for example, the differential impact of individual and group approaches to parent preparation and education, whether some curricula are more effective than others, or whether certain types of adoptive families are more likely to benefit from specific methods or educational content. These issues, with a few exceptions, have not been adequately examined by child welfare researchers.

Christenson and McMurtry (2007) tested the effectiveness of the PRIDE curriculum with 228 prospective foster/adoptive parents in Idaho using a pre-post survey design. Both kinship and non-kinship participants were included. Key survey questions focused on PRIDE training curriculum competency categories. Pre- and post-test comparisons indicated that the PRIDE programme appropriately increased competency for non-relative foster/adoptive parents; the effectiveness of the programme for kinship respondents, however, was less apparent. Even after going through the PRIDE training, kinship respondents reported having difficulty in a number of key areas targeted by the curriculum (e.g., parenting children with special needs, discipline, supporting visits of children with birth families, feeling like they were members of the professional child welfare team). The researchers suggested that the PRIDE curriculum may not adequately meet all the needs of kinship care providers.

On a smaller, but more empirically rigorous scale, Rushton and colleagues (2010) examined the effectiveness of a training programme targeting parents soon after adoption and used a randomised controlled design, a methodology quite unusual in child welfare intervention research. Adoptive parents of children between the ages of three and seven years, who had been placed with their families between three and 18 months previously, were randomly assigned to one of three groups, each of which lasted 10 weeks: cognitive-behavioural training; educational, insight-oriented training; or a control group. Parenting and child adjustment information was collected at three points: beginning of the study, end of intervention (or at 12 weeks for control group) and six months later.

Results showed that parenting interventions (cognitive-behavioural and educational approaches combined) led to an increase in the level of parenting satisfaction compared with control group members. The targeted interventions did not, however, produce changes in children's behaviour. The researchers suggested that the six-month period of the study may have been too brief to allow affirmative changes in parents' beliefs and attitudes to become integrated into the type of parenting practices that could ultimately impact positively on children's behaviour. But they also emphasised that increased satisfaction with parenting, in the face of ongoing child difficulties, was a positive sign that boded well for placement stability.

Selected resources

Fursland E. (2006a) *Preparing to Adopt: A training pack for preparation groups*, London: BAAF.

Fursland E. (2006b) *Preparing to Adopt: Applicant's workbook*, London: BAAF.

Fursland E., Dibben E. and Probert N. (2014, forthcoming) *Preparing to Adopt*, London: BAAF.

Brodzinsky D. (2008) *Adoptive Parent Preparation Project. Phase I: Meeting the mental health and developmental needs of adopted children*, New York: Donaldson Adoption Institute. Access at: www.adoptioninstitute.org/publications/2008_02_Parent_Preparation.pdf

19 Maintaining a level of openness in the child's best interests

Description and overview

Openness in adoption has evolved over the past 50 years in response to recognition of the negative impact of secrecy and the need for most adopted people to have access to information and birth family in order to integrate their own histories into their identity and come to terms with what has happened to them. Adoptions exist along a continuum of structural openness, from completely closed or confidential with no contact between the birth and adoptive families and no identifying information, to completely open involving ongoing contact between birth and adoptive families, including the child. Mediated adoptions, involving the exchange of letters and pictures through an agency intermediary, are in the middle of this continuum. While we typically think of openness in relation to contact with birth parents, this phenomenon applies to many other significant relationships in children's lives – with siblings, grandparents and other relatives, and previous carers. Children adopted from care typically have developed beneficial attachment relationships with a range of people, and abruptly severing these relationships may not be in their best interests. Children have strong attachments to siblings and may also have siblings with whom they have minimal attachments at the time of adoption, but these relationships have the potential to add considerable richness to their lives as they grow up and become adults.

Communicative openness (defined as free expression and discussion) within adoptive families is a key factor in adoption adjustment, no matter what level of structural openness exists. When adopted young people seek information about their histories or struggle with feelings related to adoption, it is paramount that they feel able to talk freely with their parents and feel heard and understood. A higher level of communicative openness is associated with more positive adjustment for adopted children and teenagers: higher self-esteem, fewer behavioural problems, more trust for their parents, fewer feelings of alienation, and more positive feelings about adoption (Kohler *et al*, 2002; Brodzinsky, 2006; Rueter and Koerner, 2008; Neil, 2009). Several studies have found that adoptive parents in open adoptions have higher levels of communicative openness in talking with their children about adoption than do those without direct contact (Brodzinsky, 2006; Neil, 2009; Grotevant *et al*, 2011).

Most of the research on openness has focused on infant adoptions, so much still needs to be learned about this practice as it pertains to children adopted from care at different ages and from varying circumstances. Silverstein and Roszia (1999) assert that the goals of openness in adoptions from care are to minimise loss and to maintain connections. Openness gives children the information they need to understand the reasons for their adoption, supports their active movement through the grief process, and promotes continuity in children's lives and identity development. Primary concerns some professionals have about contact in these adoptions are that it may confuse the child or interfere with settling into the adoptive family; it might undermine adoptive parents' sense of entitlement; it may increase harm to children who have been maltreated; and it may discourage some adults from adopting (Neil, 2002, 2009).

In England, the Adoption and Children Act 2002 requires adoption agencies to assess and plan for any contact children will have with their birth families or others, including siblings, and to offer all parties support in maintaining contact. Mediated or "letterbox" contact is the most common plan in adoptions from care in England, particularly for younger children, although direct contact is the plan for a minority of children. In Neil and Howe's (2004) longitudinal study of contact after adoption for a cohort of 168 children adopted by age four (primarily from care), a worker survey revealed that almost 90 per cent of the children had some form of contact plan, which was face-to-face for 17 per cent of the sample. (Direct contact involved birth parents in only 45 per cent of cases where it was the plan.) The most important factor in determining the type of contact planned was the adoption agency placing the child.

In some Canadian provinces, children are assessed prior to adoption from care as to the type of contact with birth relatives that is in their best interests after adoption, and post-adoption contact arrangements are planned accordingly. In Ontario, for example, openness can be supported either through an agreement with adoptive parents and birth relatives or through court-ordered access for children to their birth families (Ontario Ministry of Children and Youth Services, 2009).

In the US, some level of openness exists in almost all infant adoptions (Siegel and Smith, 2012), but it is not systematically explored and planned in child welfare adoptions. Despite the lack of a systematic policy or approach across jurisdictions, however, contact does occur in a substantial minority of these adoptions. The National Survey of Adoptive Parents (Vandivere *et al*, 2009) reported that 39 per cent of foster care adoptions by non-relatives involved some post-adoption contact (direct or indirect) between children and their birth relatives, and in an Illinois study of over 1,300 child welfare adoptions, direct contact between children and birth parents was reported by 14 per cent of stranger or matched, 23 per cent of foster, and 80 per cent of relative adopters (Howard and Smith, 2003). For kin adopters, the norm was not frequent contact – 60 per cent reported a frequency from "never" to "a few times a year".

The US Children's Bureau funded nine five-year demonstration projects to design models of open adoption to facilitate permanency in foster care for children aged over 12; a range of resources developed through these grant projects can be downloaded on the website of the National Resource Center for Adoption (2012). These include a Family Connections video that can be viewed online and ordered for a nominal fee and myriad curricula and tools for working with birth families, resource families, young people, courts and social workers around issues of permanency for older children and young people and the importance of maintaining connections.

The internet and social media have profoundly changed the extent of openness in adoption and the methods through which families have contact. They have also created new issues – both benefits and risks – that need to be better understood and addressed. A recent study by Donaldson Adoption Institute (Whitesel and Howard, 2013) surveyed over 2,000 members of the adoption triad, with adoptive parents being the most common respondents (over 1,200). Those adoptive parents who had contact with birth family members reported that almost 80 per cent had email contact and over 60 per cent had contact through Facebook and social media. The majority of children having birth family contact also used these two types of communication. Many of those involved appreciated the "contact with distance" that the internet provides, and few respondents reported that these had led to unwelcome intrusions. Some respondents in all categories also reported that such contact could impact on the privacy of participants, particularly the adopted child, given that the average Facebook user has over 200 friends, and when parents post pictures or share sensitive information, it is shared broadly.

Professionals need to assist families in understanding the benefits and challenges of openness, including the impact of the internet and social media. BAAF offers two resources for adoptive parents and professionals which are included in Selected Resources and authored by Fursland; there is also a guide for young people.

Key programme elements

Interview studies of parties involved in contact arrangements offer the following suggestions for practice (Neil, 2002, 2004a, b; Logan and Smith, 2004; Selwyn, 2004; Logan 2010).

- **Assessment of the children's attachment histories and relation-ships, and the capacities of birth and prospective adoptive families to manage contact effectively, are foundational to developing contact plans**. These should include exploring the children's feelings and wishes regarding contact; the relationships that have been positive sources of nurture and identity for them; the extent of trauma or maltreatment they have experienced and safety considerations; how they interacted with birth relatives during previous visits; and the birth relatives' and prospective adopters' ability to focus on the children's best interests. Adams's volume (see Selected Resources) offers a range of factors to assess, including the children's understanding of reasons why birth parents cannot care for them and the birth parents giving children permission to settle into the new family.

- **Preparation for contact is important for both pre-adoptive parents and birth relatives**. This needs to move beyond education about the benefits of contact to anticipating and preparing parents for potential social and emotional challenges. It is also important to encourage the parties to express their concerns so that these can be discussed. Involving adoptive parents and birth relatives with experience in maintaining contact is ideal. Preparation of birth relatives needs to include their expectations of the roles they can play in the children's lives.
- **Prospective adopters need to be included in planning the parameters of contact as early as possible**. Research on openness in infant adoptions found that self-determination is an important element of successful contact arrangements, and parents who felt pressured to enter into such agreements were less likely to be satisfied or maintain them (Berry *et al*, 1998); the same is true with adoptions from care (Neil 2002, 2004b). Logan and Smith (2004) reported that, 'A high proportion of adoptive families who were excluded from discussions about contact and/or who felt they had been forced to accept problematic arrangements, were facing difficulties in managing contact' (p. 120).
- **It is helpful for workers to facilitate meetings between pre-adoptive and birth relatives to discuss details of contact planning**. Research indicates that adoptive parents who meet with birth parents prior to adoptive placement are more comfortable with contact and have more positive perceptions of them (Berry, 1993). Such contact not only allows discussion of contact arrangements, but also helps to build rapport and trust.
- **Agency systems for managing mediated contact need to be clear and efficient**. Indirect contact (like direct) is not always easy; parties may need support to communicate effectively.
- **Children's physical and emotional well-being should be paramount in developing contact arrangements**. Children who have suffered severe maltreatment may be re-traumatised by contact, and in such circumstances all contact with the abusive individuals should stop, at least for a time (Howe and Steele, 2004).
- **Contact arrangements need to be flexible and dynamic**. Negotiating contact arrangements should not be viewed as a one-time

event. It is important to acknowledge up front that arrangements may need to evolve over time as the child develops and families' circumstances change.

- **Ongoing support, guidance and mediation need to be made available** to both adoptive parents and birth relatives on an ongoing basis, as well as to carers involved in maintaining connections with siblings.

Lessons learned

- **From the child's perspective, it is paramount to consult with them regarding contact.** A study in England (Morgan, 2006) of 208 adopted children found that well over half had some type of contact with their families but two-thirds reported that they had no say in whether or not they had contact. Eighty-five per cent of them thought it was important to be given news about their birth families but believed that each child should have a choice about whether they wanted to receive such news. Children also suggested that any reduction in contact with their birth families should be made gradually.
- **Contact needs to be individually crafted in relation to many factors.** It is critical that contact arrangements are built on a thorough assessment of the children's relationships, birth family and prospective adopters. Furthermore, children's wishes and the quality and safety of contact have to be considered. Research in England reports that too often this has not occurred, and a significant number of children (21%) in Selwyn's (2004) study had been abused during unsupervised contacts while in care or in adoptive placements. Those who study openness stress that contact in itself is not necessarily positive, but it has the potential to maintain or repair relationships and to benefit children's identity development and sense of emotional security when arrangements are safe and supported by all parties (Neil and Howe, 2004; Selwyn, 2004). Professionals need to consider 'for which children, in which circumstances and by which means, contact should be promoted or ended' (Selwyn, 2004, p. 162). All of these plans need to fit within and promote children's ability to: 1) establish a secure attachment

to their new adoptive parents; 2) minimise and resolve separation, loss and feelings of rejection related to other significant attachments; and 3) develop a coherent sense of self and positive identity that incorporates knowledge of their origins, past history and a sense of mastery.

Research on children in foster care generally has established that continued contact with birth parents has a positive impact on their mental health, and frequent contact is associated with fewer externalising behavioural problems (McWey *et al*, 2010). Another study of 12- and 13-year-old foster children (in care an average of 3.8 years) found that young people had difficulty maintaining strong relationships with both their birth mothers and foster families (Leathers, 2003). About half of the children had visited their birth mothers during the previous six months, averaging 13 visits, but those who visited frequently had stronger maternal allegiance and were more likely to have relatively weak relationships with their foster families. Having strong relationships with both was related to greater loyalty conflict. This underscores the need to assist children in developing strong bonds with adoptive families, addressing loyalty conflicts or other complicated feelings, and integrating birth relatives into children's current lives in a manner that supports them.

In a study of adoption disruption, relatively few children were rated as strongly attached to their birth mothers, but these children were more likely to experience disruption (Smith and Howard, 1991). Such children will likely need "disengagement" work to provide them with an opportunity to acknowledge the transition, come to terms with the reality that they will not be returning to live with their birth family, and develop a sense of belonging in their adoptive family.

- **Research on openness finds that the frequency and type of contact change over time as these relationships evolve.** There needs to be some fluidity in renegotiating details of contact arrangements. For example, one study (Logan and Smith, 2004) reported that visits at Christmas or on children's birthdays made these occasions unduly tense for some children or parents, so that modification of the dates or circumstances of visits might be considered. Sometimes contact can stimulate children's feelings of grief or raise questions related to their past or concerns about the well-being of siblings or other relatives. Neil (2004b) reported that children who felt some anxiety were more likely to be those who were older at placement and had more difficult histories. Parents may not understand that children need time to process these feelings. If very challenging situations arise, it is important for them to be able to contact a professional and explore potential solutions. Modifying the parameters of contact for the time being usually is preferable to severing it altogether.

- **Indirect contact also can be complex.** Neil (2004a) interviewed adoptive parents, children and birth relatives with both indirect and direct contact, finding that while workers often assumed indirect contact to be straightforward and easy, there were many **challenges to maintaining indirect contact**. These included a lack of clarity as to the rules and processes of letter exchange and general ambivalence about what to write in letters, failure of birth relatives to respond in some cases, and excluding the children from contact. Not surprisingly, adoptive parents who had more communicative openness with their children about adoption were more likely to involve the children in indirect contact. Another challenge was that some agencies failed to forward letters in a timely manner, and screening procedures appropriate to the case were important in some situations. Neil concluded that in many cases, agency involvement was required to get contact started and keep it going.

Outcomes

- **The body of research that exists on openness in infant adoptions consistently documents benefits for all parties.** Birth mothers with ongoing contact report less regret, grief and worry, as well as more peace of mind, than do those who do not have contact (Cushman *et al*, 1997; Henney *et al*, 2007). Adoptive parents as a group report positive experiences and high levels of comfort with contact. For example, at the second wave of a major longitudinal study, 94 per cent of adoptive mothers whose adolescents had open adoptions were satisfied with the level of openness (Grotevant *et al*, 2005). Greater openness is linked with reduced fear of and greater empathy towards birth parents, more open communication with their children about adoption, and other benefits in their relationships with their adopted children (Berry *et al*, 1998; Grotevant and McRoy, 1998; Grotevant *et al*, 2005; Siegel, 2008).

- **Adolescents with ongoing contact are more satisfied with their level of openness** and identify a range of benefits, including coming to terms with the reasons for their adoption, physical touchstones to identify where personal traits came from, information that aids in identity formation, positive feelings towards birth mother, a better understanding of the meaning of adoption, and more active communication about adoption with their adoptive parents (Wrobel *et al*, 1996, 1998; Berge *et al*, 2006; Grotevant *et al*, 2007).

Less research is available on *contact in adoptions of children from care*. Most of the research that does exist in this realm is from England and generally consists of descriptive studies with samples of around 100 families. Several follow-up studies of contact after adoption support the following findings.

- **Face-to-face contact with birth parents occurs in only a minority of cases involving foster carer or matched adoptions:** 34 per cent of 104 young children in Neil's (2004b) English study; 31 per cent in the first year after placement in Selwyn's (2004) study in England; 34 per cent in Thoburn's study of older child placements in England; 10–15 per cent at two waves in California Long-Range Adoption Study (Frasch *et al*, 2000); and in 23 per cent of foster and 14 per cent of matched adoptions in an Illinois study (Howard and Smith, 2003). For those where this occurs, it is likely to happen infrequently (from one to a few times a year).

- **The percentage of children maintaining direct contact with birth parents falls off somewhat over time.** In Selwyn's study (2004), it had dropped from 31 per cent to 17 per cent at follow-up over six years later, and in the California study it dropped from 14 per cent to 10.5 per cent. Birth parents were more likely to drop out of contact than were adopters; in Neil's study (2004b), contact with birth parents was maintained in just over half of cases where it was planned, whereas those involving someone other than a birth parent were maintained in 86 per cent of cases.

- **Contact arrangements between children and other birth relatives, such as grandparents or siblings living elsewhere, are more common.** For example, in the Illinois study, 82 per cent of relatives, 48 per cent of foster carers and 34 per cent of matched adopters reported contact with children's siblings living elsewhere (Howard and Smith, 2003).
- **Adoptive parents are more comfortable with children's contact with siblings or other adult relatives such as grandparents** than with birth parents, and are less likely to perceive these contacts as harmful to children. According to Neil (2004b), outcomes of face-to-face contacts with grandparents were particularly positive. This does not mean, however, that there are no challenges to work through related to contact with siblings and other relatives (Howard and Smith, 2003; Logan and Smith, 2004; Neil, 2004b). Howard and Smith (2003) also found that comfort with contact varied by type of adopter, with relatives having the most comfort with contact, followed by foster adopters and matched adopters.
- **The large majority of adopters in direct contact arrangements remained satisfied that contact was in their children's best interests** – 87 per cent in Logan and Smith's (2004) study of 96 children in England. Neil (2004b) reported that the majority of adoptive parents with direct contact arrangements were generally positive about contact, with about 25 per cent reporting a mix of positive and negative reactions, and none reporting severe negative reactions. In the Illinois study, those rating contact as harmful ranged from three to 16 per cent across categories of adopters for siblings and other adult birth relatives and from 12 to 33 per cent for contact with birth parents (Howard and Smith, 2003). Thirteen per cent reported contact as negative in the California study (Frasch *et al*, 2000).
- **Adoptive parents report the following benefits of contact for their children:** access to information about their "roots"; ability to integrate aspects of their histories into their identities as they develop; and more open communication about adoption (Logan and Smith, 2004; Neil, 2009).
- **Face-to-face contact has not been found to undermine the**

adoptive parent–child relationship, but in many respects enhances it. For example, in the California study there was no relationship between level of openness and parent–child closeness or satisfaction (Frasch *et al*, 2000). Some studies report that face-to-face contact enhances adoptive parents' relationships with their children (Fratter, 1996; Logan and Smith, 1999; Sykes, 2000; Neil, 2004b). Identified benefits include access to information about their children's histories and enhanced understanding of them; more open communication with them about adoption; reduced fears and greater empathy for birth relatives; and more positive perceptions of birth parents.

- **Birth relatives' satisfaction with contact is associated with their comfort with their role in the child's life and acceptance of the adoption.** The primary benefit to them is their ability to see the children growing up and know that they are well (Neil, 2003; Logan and Smith, 2004).
- One study following up seven years after placement found that indirect mail contact (the plan for 56%) was likely to be maintained – two-thirds of children adopted by strangers and all of those adopted by foster carers maintained such contact with birth families (Selwyn, 2004).

Selected resources

Adams P. (2012) *Planning for Contact in Permanent Placements*, London: BAAF.

Adoptions Unlimited, Inc. (2008) *Family Connections* (DVD), Chicago, IL: Adoptions Unlimited. May be viewed at: www.nrcadoption.org/videos/family-connections-project/

National Resource Center for Adoption (2010) *Youth Permanency Cluster: Grantee projects and grantee resources*. Access at: www.nrcadoption.org/resources/ypc/grantee-projects/ and www.nrcadoption.org/resources/ypc/grantee-resources/

Neil E. (2002) 'Contact after adoption: the role of agencies in making and supporting plans', *Adoption & Fostering*, 26:1, pp. 25–38.

PART VI

SUPPORTING AND PRESERVING
ADOPTIVE FAMILIES

20 Adoption education and support services

Description and overview

Adoption support and preservation (ASAP) services assist parents and children in achieving a positive adjustment after adoptive placement or completion of the adoption. Normative adoption issues such as loss and identity, as well as children's adverse experiences prior to adoption, continue to impact on their development, and adoptive families often need assistance to adequately address these challenges. The availability of post-adoption services has been linked with parents' greater ability and willingness to adopt children from care, and the lack of these services is a barrier to adoptions from care (McRoy, 2007).

There is a range of ASAP services, including information and referral, parent education, child and parent support, respite care, case management, advocacy, therapeutic intervention, crisis intervention, search and reunion, services to facilitate openness and residential treatment. These services have been developed primarily over the past two decades, and very little research exists on their efficacy; however, studies of adoptive families consistently document their desire for ASAP services (Reilly and Platz, 2004; Festinger, 2006; McRoy, 2007). In the US, a wide array of services is offered in some states and very few in others. In England, local authorities are required to appoint an Adoption Support Services Adviser (ASSA) to provide or broker a variety of post-adoption services; adopters have the right to be assessed for these services, but do not have an automatic right to receive them (Hart and Luckock, 2004; Quinton and Selwyn, 2009). A few of the primary ASAP services are discussed in this compendium, beginning with adoption information and support services.

Other than financial and medical support, the most used and important post-adoption service reported by parents adopting from care is gaining information to better understand their children and adoption, particularly through reading books or articles and attending classes and workshops (Brooks *et al*, 2002). There is an array of resources and services to address this need, including lending libraries, training, internet courses and helplines, among others. For example, one such resource in the US is Adoption Learning Partners (2013), which offers various web-based courses and webinars for adoptive parents and professionals. Adoptive parents often utilise support services with a very similar motivation: to better understand their situations and how to effectively help their children. An example of a state-run information and support programme is New Jersey's NJARCH (2012), a web-based adoption resource clearinghouse that provides telephone- and web-based services, a warmline, information and referral (I and R), chat rooms, a lending library and other educational opportunities.

The most common types of support services for adoptive families are parent support groups and mentoring programmes, which may be sponsored and funded directly through child welfare systems or developed as grassroots organisations by parents. Some US states, for example, Minnesota and Kentucky, contract with experienced adoptive parents in each region of the state to provide peer support through a network of support groups and/or mentoring programmes. Other states have post-adoption resource centres in each of their regions that offer I and R, support groups and training, or they contract with private agencies to offer adoption support services in their geographic areas (Smith, 2010). Jockey International funds a programme through the North American Council on Adoptable Children (NACAC) – called Community Champions Network – to develop peer-to-peer support systems in locations around the US and Canada (NACAC, 2009b). To date, they have begun support programmes in 13 areas in the US and three Canadian provinces (New Brunswick, Nova Scotia and Ontario). The website, Canada's Waiting Kids (2012b), maintains a listing of adoption support groups across the country. Respite programmes are very important to sustain families parenting children with complex needs, but are probably the service that is most difficult to access (AdoptUSKids and NACAC, 2008; Smith, 2010).

Social activities enabling adoptive families to come together and develop ongoing relationships are another form of support. There are also phone lines and web-based service systems offering support to parents. Adoption UK (2013) is a national charity run by adoptive parents that provides information, advice, support and training to adoptive families or those interested in adopting in England, Wales, Northern Ireland and Scotland. They offer a helpline, local support groups, a magazine, a lending library and an online community offering support 24/7. A 10-minute video on their website, *Call for Help*, features their family support buddies programme; it offers six 45-minute phone sessions to new adopters. In addition, they offer a family support consultants programme for families experiencing crises.

Services for adopted young people include support groups, mentoring programmes and adoption camps, but there are far fewer publicly supported programmes for adopted young people than for parents. Some areas facilitate simultaneous support groups for children and parents. Examples of weekend or camp opportunities for adopted young people include Alabama's summer camp for 150 adopted children and their siblings. Georgia offers a programme called Adopted Teen Empowerment and Mentoring (ATEAM) that meets monthly on Saturdays for seven hours in each of the 12 regions of the state and offers two weekend retreats each year for up to 360 young people (Smith, 2010). A unique programme in Minnesota was launched in 2010 but recently lost its funding. This organisation, called Adoptees Have Answers and run by and for adopted persons, provided opportunities for adopted individuals to connect, including a virtual community of discussion boards and networking opportunities, a webinar series featuring many adoptee presenters, support groups, and other events/activities.

Key programme elements

- **Prepare parents to know about and understand the benefits of ASAP services and to reframe help-seeking as a strength** rather than a sign of parental inadequacy. Educate them about the types of services they are most likely to need and how to access them.

- **Inform all families about available information and support services** both prior to adoption and at regular intervals. Lack of information about available services is a primary barrier to families receiving needed help (Festinger, 2006; Fuller *et al*, 2006). Professionals need to inform families about all available ASAP services; they need to believe in the efficacy of parent-run groups and be willing to advertise these broadly to families.
- **Offer a continuum of services that families can access as needed.** Several studies indicate that service needs may emerge and resurface at different points in the family life cycle, and services need to be available as needed (Howard, 1999; Atkinson and Gonet, 2007; Smith and Child Welfare Information Gateway [CWIG], 2012c).
- **Do not require adoptive families to come through the child protection services system** in order to access the continuum of adoption support and preservation services. Lower cost services, such as support groups and educational programmes, can be made available to any type of adoptive family. And, wherever possible, more costly therapeutic services can be available to families adopting outside the care system on a sliding scale fee.
- For support groups, it is important to **have an experienced adoptive parent(s) in a leadership role**, either as the primary leader or in partnership with a professional. NACAC discusses the dynamics of parent- versus agency-run groups and suggests a third type – parent-run/agency-supported groups (NACAC, 2002a). If the leader does not have experience in leading such groups, acquiring **training and a mentor or supervisor is invaluable**.
- For parent support groups, **open-ended groups** that provide participants with the opportunity to attend for a period, stop and return when the need arises are ideal. For training or topical groups for parents or children, a closed series of time-limited groups can work well.
- **Getting support groups started requires planning, outreach and patience.** Tips include holding the meeting in a comfortable place at a time convenient for parents, providing food, making child care

available or accessible, and providing some time for parents to interact informally and get to know each other.

- **Managing meetings requires knowledge of group dynamics and skill in drawing out discussion and managing conflict.** Some important aspects of leading meetings include helping the group to establish its goals and ground rules, drawing out quiet members and managing those who tend to dominate, focusing discussion when it gets off track, identifying key points of the discussion, and providing structure and focus to ongoing programming (NACAC, 2002b).

- **Support programmes for children and young people can take many forms.** Most such groups are time limited, although others may be more open and ongoing, particularly those that meet in conjunction with parent support groups. Adequate staffing of children's groups is critically important, and other professionals, interns, experienced volunteers and adoptive parents can be used to assist. Some parent groups have adoptive parents rotate responsibility for leading children's group activities.

- **Adopted teenagers benefit from youth education and advocacy groups.** For example, Lutheran Social Services of New England offers several groups for teenagers to complete an educational project to teach others about adoption. One group made a series of DVDs and presentations in schools, addressing questions that fellow students often ask about adoption, and another group for transracially adopted girls worked with young adult adoptees to develop an educational show for a local public access television channel. Advocacy groups involve teenagers and young adults in education and advocacy related to adoption; these provide many benefits to the young people in normalising their experience. Mounting such a programme requires a training component for young people and a very committed parent or staff member to keep it going (Stevens, 2004).

Lessons learned

Sometimes adoptive parents are reluctant to contact their adoption agency when they are struggling. They may have negative feelings toward the agency or a worker or may fear being judged as inadequate parents, particularly if they are fostering or want to adopt again. In an Ontario study of barriers to post-placement services, workers reported that many parents were unwilling to disclose challenges and felt pressure to be model parents; workers saw the provision of peer support by other adoptive parents as an ideal solution (McKay and Ross, 2011). Peer support provides opportunities to freely express frustrations and other feelings without being judged (Chamberlain and Horne, 2003).

Adoptive parents may feel reluctant to take the plunge and attend support groups or seek out other types of support services. Outreach that provides a personal contact often serves as a bridge to engaging families. For example, a Wisconsin programme operated out of five regional post-adoption resource centres (PARC) has a "welcome wagon"-type programme that visits newly approved adoptive families to inform them of the services of PARC and, with funding from a foundation, brings backpacks with gifts for all children in the families. A Colorado county has a post-adoption worker who visits each new adoptive family to invite them to contact her if they have needs. Some programmes have found that hosting single educational events for parents on popular topics, such as advocating for your child at school, or inviting them to bring their adopted children to a child-focused event, can reduce parental resistance to engaging in an ongoing support group. Pennsylvania's Statewide Adoption and Permanency Network (SWAN, 2012) has a DVD on its post-permanency services that depicts adoptive parents talking about the benefits of support groups and other services. This is shown to parents in pre-adoption preparation and other venues to facilitate their understanding of the benefits of these services and to feel comfortable about accessing them.

"Healthy Marriage" demonstration projects in the US, funded by the Children's Bureau, underscore the value of providing services to strengthen the marriages of adoptive couples. Some of these programmes have developed training curricula, including Adoption Resources of Wisconsin and Michigan State University (Smith, 2010).

Outcomes

Research on the effectiveness of post-adoption services is in its nascent stage, and the studies that do exist on the effectiveness of services generally have methodological flaws (Barth and Miller, 2000; Smith, 2010). The overall body of adoption research generally has linked receiving post-adoption services with more positive outcomes; conversely, having unmet service needs is linked with lower perceived parent–child relationship quality and more negative impact of the adoption on the family and marital relationship (Reilly and Platz, 2004). In many studies, adoptive parents report their need for post-adoption services, ranging from occasional support to intensive interventions (CWIG, 2012c). Overall, 30–38 per cent of parents expressed their need for a support group for themselves across three studies (McDonald *et al*, 2001; Reilly and Platz, 2003; Festinger, 2006). Studies on families who have adopted from care indicate that:

- **The amount and quality of support that adoptive families receive contributes to permanency and positive adjustment** (Barth and Berry, 1988, Groze, 1996; Leung and Erich, 2002; Houston and Kramer, 2008).
- **Parent support groups receive the highest rating of helpfulness in many studies**. A California study found a higher percentage of child welfare adoptive parents rated support groups as more helpful than any other post-adoption service (Brooks *et al*, 2002). Several other studies report that support groups are rated at or near the top in helpfulness by parents using them (Smith and Howard, 1999; Reilly and Platz, 2003; Atkinson and Gonet, 2007).
- **Utilisation of support groups is associated with greater parenting satisfaction** (Reilly and Platz, 2003; Gibbs *et al*, 2005). These groups can be a powerful source of information, social support, and validation for parents and children who may not be connected to

other adoptive families. Being able to share frustrations, joys and feelings that have gone unexpressed or unheard with others coming from similar situations can be very healing and can normalise perceptions of their situations.

- **Providing supportive services early in the placement is linked to more positive outcomes**. A longitudinal study of the contribution of agency and non-agency supportive resources to the well-being of child welfare adoptive families found that those who received more services prior to finalisation were more stable and experienced less conflict three years later (Houston and Kramer, 2008). That was the case even though the families' contact and satisfaction with these formal and informal resources declined from the pre-adoption period to three years later.

- **An evaluation of a network of adoption support groups finds that parents were highly satisfied with the service, and many believed it stabilised their adoptions**. Adoption Support for Kentucky (ASK) is a network of 32 support groups. Based on six focus groups and a state-wide survey of participants (n = 251), an evaluation indicated that parents attended primarily for emotional support and information. They were highly satisfied with the service and many reported that the programme had stabilised their families and prevented adoption breakdown (Bryan *et al*, 2010).

- **Parents report a range of positive outcomes from participation in support groups**. The most common outcomes reported by over 90 per cent of adoptive parents about their support group participation in an Illinois evaluation were: realise other adoptive families have the same problems (98%); learn from other parents (94%); understand my child better (91%); and understand my child's need to grieve (91%) (Smith and Howard, 1999).

- **Support groups or other activities for adopted children are normalising experiences for them**. In one evaluation of their participation in a support group, adopted children were most likely to report that they fit in with this group more than with others, and they liked spending time with other adopted kids (Smith and Howard, 1999).

- **Couples attending a marriage education programme made significant gains.** An evaluation of a marriage education programme in Wisconsin for couples with adopted children with special needs found that the 112 parents receiving this 36-hour intervention made significant gains on measures of forgiveness, marital satisfaction and depression. The evaluation used a comparison group with wait-listed couples and also evaluated them when they went through the intervention. The total group maintained significant gains at the 3.5-month follow-up period (Baskin *et al*, 2011).

Selected resources

Adoption Learning Partners (2013) Online courses and webinars. Access at: www.adoptionlearningpartners.org/

Adoption UK (2012) Family support service. *Call for Help.* 10-minute video available online at: www.adoptionuk.org/one-one-support/family-support-service/

AdoptUSKids and NACAC (2008b) *Taking a Break: Creating foster, adoptive and kinship respite care in your community*, Baltimore, MD: AdoptUSKids. Access at: www.adoptuskids.org/_assets/files/NRCRRFAP/resources/taking-a-break-respite-guide.pdf

Child Welfare Information Gateway (2012c) *Providing Postadoption Services: A bulletin for professionals*, Washington, DC: US Department of Health and Human Services. Access at: www.childwelfare.gov/pubs/f_postadoptbulletin/index.cfm

North American Council on Adoptable Children (2002) *Starting and Nurturing Adoptive Parent Groups: A guide for leaders*, St Paul, MN: NACAC. Access at: www.nacac.org/parentgroups/starting.pdf

North American Council on Adoptable Children (2009) *Developing a Parent-to-parent Support Network*, St Paul, MN: NACAC. Access at: www.nacac.org/adoptalk/parent2parentnetwork.pdf

Smith S. L. (2010) *Keeping the Promise: The critical needs for post-adoption services to enable children and families to succeed*, New York: Donaldson Adoption Institute. Access at: www.adoptioninstitute.org/publications/2010_10_20_KeepingThePromise.pdf

21 Therapeutic interventions to enhance adoption adjustment

Description and overview

Research indicates that adoptive families use clinical services at three to five times the rate reported by birth families, and those adopting from care have the highest rate of seeking a range of counselling and mental health services (Brooks *et al*, 2002; Howard *et al*, 2004; Vandivere *et al*, 2009). Adoptive parents in several studies have rated counselling at the top of the list of services that they had trouble getting (Rosenthal *et al*, 1996; Howard and Smith, 2003; Reilly and Platz, 2003). Often they report that counsellors in mental health and family services agencies do not adequately understand adoption, trauma and other challenges affecting their children, and that it is hard to find specialised services for children with conduct disorders, attachment difficulties or other conditions such as foetal alcohol spectrum disorders (Festinger, 2006; Selwyn *et al*, 2006b; Smith, 2010).

Studies of children in care consistently find that many (40–80% across studies) have significant mental health needs (Pecora *et al*, 2009). Based on a nationally representative US study, 48 per cent of children in out-of-home care score in the clinical range on the Child Behavior Checklist (Burns *et al*, 2004), but far fewer (21%) receive mental health treatment (National Survey of Child and Adolescent Well-Being, 2005). Moreover, there is evidence that fostered young people receiving mental health services from community providers generally do not show significant gains, and experts recommend the use of "adoption or permanency-competent" providers who can address their specialised needs (Ornelas *et al*, 2007; Love *et al*, 2008; Bellamy *et al*, 2010).

Given the traumatic life experiences these children have endured, a substantial proportion of children placed for adoption continue to have ongoing emotional and behavioural problems that may intensify as they age, and at least half of these families will seek counselling services (Reilly and Platz, 2003; Festinger, 2006; Vandivere *et al*, 2009). A study in England reported that 88 per cent of "stranger" adopters found the first year after placement very challenging and sought some type of help, as did 61 per cent of foster carer adopters, noting that sometimes the children's recognition that they would not return home exacerbated their problems (Rees and Selwyn, 2009). Two studies of adoptive families seeking therapeutic counselling indicate that approximately 93–96 per cent of them are concerned about children's emotional and behavioural problems (Lenerz *et al*, 2006; Smith, 2006a).

Therapeutic interventions to enhance adoption adjustment are provided under many auspices and through many types of providers. As discussed above, the potential for these interventions to meet families' needs is related to the provider's knowledge and skill in addressing adoption, trauma, loss, attachment and self-regulation issues, as well as having mastery of some of the evidence-based practices most relevant to this work. There are agencies focused totally on post-adoption work, including the Post-Adoption Centre, After Adoption and Adoption UK (discussed under support services) in England and the Center for Adoption Support and Education in the US. There are state-supported post-adoption programmes in the US that offer a range of counselling services, from short-term crisis-oriented interventions to long-term therapeutic counselling. For example, Tennessee and Illinois offer therapeutic counselling programmes that provide services to families at no cost, with the option of being home-based, and the workers receive training in evidence-informed practices such as Theraplay, Hughes's dyadic developmental psychotherapy (DDP), Parent–Child Interaction Therapy (PCIT), and others (Smith, 2010).

Also, there are adoption agencies in England, Canada and the US that have developed specialised post-adoption therapeutic programmes. One example is the Kinship Center in California, which has a mental health clinic providing adoption-competent services and a programme of adoption/permanency wraparound services to prevent the child being placed back into care or in some other treatment facility. Of course, there are therapists who are "adoption-competent" in private practice or in a range of settings. These are few and far between, however, in that many routine community providers are "adoption blind" (Hart and Luckock, 2004). As reported in an English study on meeting families' needs after adoption, some adopters ultimately rejected services to which they were referred because they felt blamed for difficulties or felt the professional did not understand the complexities of adoption (Rees and Selwyn, 2009).

Key programme elements

Common *goals* of therapeutic interventions to facilitate adoption adjustment (Smith and Howard, 1999; Hart and Luckock, 2004, 2006) include those listed below.

- **Help parents understand children in light of their history**. How past experiences have influenced children's current feelings and behaviours is central to parents' understanding their needs and responding in a healing manner.
- **Strengthen attachments within the adoptive family**. Recognising that new attachments are influenced by the legacy of previous ones, helps parents to understand children's attachment legacy, de-personalise their anger and develop strategies to promote attachment.
- **Enhance therapeutic parenting**. Parents need help to create a healing environment that is attuned to children's needs and capacities. They need to promote resilience and manage behaviours in ways that are nurturing and facilitate emotional regulation and reflective thinking. This process requires that parents gain self-awareness and self-care skills.
- **Open family communication**. Communicative openness is critically important in adoptive families, including facilitating communication throughout the family (between spouses/partners, parents and children, with siblings, and with previous attachment figures as appropriate).
- **Address adoption issues and give voice to children's inner**

feelings. Children may be struggling with unresolved loss, trauma or adoption issues, and often have difficulty identifying and expressing their feelings. A range of expressive therapies may help access the inner life of a child. It is important to involve adoptive parents in the therapeutic process and help them to develop strategies for addressing these issues.

- **Address environmental barriers to meeting child/family needs**. Effectively addressing the needs of families requires multi-systemic interventions, including working with multiple constellations of family members, co-ordination and advocacy with systems such as schools and medical or mental health providers, and linking families with a range of resources.

Based on several evaluations of post-adoption programmes, the ideal principles of services have been identified for working with these families. First, there is a *period of active engagement* in which the worker demonstrates to the family that he/she is indeed there for them by really listening in an accepting and non-blaming manner, and validating their feelings and strengths. Family members need to feel truly heard and understood. Also, *a responsive approach to service delivery* is critical, including being accessible and willing to respond to clients' needs, such as seeing them in the evenings or going to their home, as well as returning phone calls and responding to crises promptly and being willing to engage in collateral activities like attending an important school meeting. Therapists need to *join with and support parents in a way that increases parental entitlement* and empowers parents to find solutions to their problems.

When professionals also work individually with children, parents should be kept abreast of the focus of the work and the children's progress, and should learn how they can work on issues at home. Also, parents who are really struggling may have withdrawn from non-essential activities and become somewhat isolated. *Helping parents to focus on taking care of themselves* may involve a range of goals, from working with the couple to increase their support of each other to linking them with outside supports such as respite care or support groups. Ideally, adoptive families need *to find the type of therapy that has the best chance of effectively addressing their challenges at the earliest possible point.* Therapists should strive to *provide services grounded in knowledge and based on best clinical practice, inclusive of evidence-based protocols* (Smith and Howard, 1999; Hart and Luckock, 2004, 2006; Atkinson and Gonet, 2007; Howard *et al*, 2005).

Lessons learned

Prior to the marked increase in child welfare adoptions beginning in the 1980s, it was assumed that existing community services for all families could meet the therapeutic needs of adoptive families. As adoptive parents were unsuccessful in finding effective help for their children, the *need for specialised services* became apparent. It is critically important for service providers to understand the unique aspects of adoption and the developmental impact of inadequate early care and trauma in order to effectively serve these families. This reality necessitates the *creation of specialised adoption therapeutic programmes*, as well as in-depth *adoption competency training of a cadre of mental health professionals* in the community to adequately serve these families.

Several studies of post-adoption therapeutic programmes indicate that most families come to these services many years after children were placed with them, typically when they are approaching or are in early adolescence, and most families have sought counselling previously (Lenerz *et al*, 2006; Smith, 2006b; Atkinson and Gonet, 2007). *Providing early intervention services* to families whose children have significant challenges could give them the skills to reverse destructive patterns before they become further entrenched and would be the ideal approach to meeting their needs. Standardised programmes of early intervention are more prevalent in England and other areas of the UK where, for example, After Adoption offers an intervention called *SafeBase*, utilising Theraplay techniques and involving an observational assessment and later feedback, a four-day parenting programme focused on the impact of trauma and lack of a secure attachment on the child, practical techniques to modify negative behaviours and build positive attachments, and follow-up support

(After Adoption, 2012). (Another early intervention programme in England, called Enhanced Parent Training, is discussed in the Outcomes section below.)

One model that has been used successfully for early intervention with pre-adoptive and adoptive families whose children experienced complex trauma is *Attachment, Self-Regulation and Competency* (*ARC*), recognised by the National Child Traumatic Stress Network as a promising practice. *ARC* focuses on building secure attachments, enhancing self-regulation and increasing competencies across several domains. It includes a range of therapeutic procedures including psycho-education, relationship strengthening, parent training, building regulatory capacities through sensory and body-based strategies, social skills training, other cognitive behavioural training strategies, and psychodynamic techniques (Blaustein and Kinniburgh, 2010). Research on its outcomes is described below.

A conclusion that has been evidenced through evaluations of post-adoption programmes is that being able to receive services for as long as they are needed, rather than for a time-limited period, is linked with more positive outcomes (Gibbs *et al*, 2002; Atkinson and Gonet, 2007). For parent training programmes, it is likely that the success of an early intervention would be enhanced by the opportunity for families to obtain follow-up support and counselling to apply principles or strategies in their own situations and to address the needs of the children and parents. For example, *ARC* was used in an Anchorage, Alaska treatment programme for foster/adoptive children with complex trauma, and those completing the programme had an average of 50 sessions with children and carers.

Outcomes

Evaluations conducted on some post-adoption programmes are useful in describing the needs and characteristics of families seeking services and their perceptions of outcomes; however, our knowledge is very limited as to the efficacy of these services. Only one evaluation (Maine's) used an experimental research design, described below. We do not yet have an evidence-based model of post-adoption services, so more research on therapeutic interventions with these families is critically needed. Several models of intervention, focused on the types of challenges common among young people adopted from care, have begun to build a research base, although none rise to the level of established evidence-based practice. These are described in a report on post-adoption services published by the Donaldson Adoption Institute (Smith, 2010). Below are examples of some of the relevant post-adoption programme evaluations and studies of interventional models.

- **The Maine Adoption Guided Services (MAGS)** model used a randomised experimental design in its evaluation. In partnership with the Maine Department of Human Services and supported by a Title IV-E Waiver, Casey Family Services designed and implemented this family-centred case management and therapeutic model state-wide. Beginning in 2000, families finalising adoptions were randomly assigned to the Guided Services or Standard Services groups. Those in MAGS had access to an adoption guide, an adoption-competent social worker who could be telephoned 24/7 by any member of the adoptive family, and who met with the family at least every six months and typically more. On average, the workers spent 65 hours a year with each family in MAGS. There were no significant baseline differences in characteristics of the children in both groups; however, after two years, children in the MAGS group scored significantly lower on the Child Behavior Checklist. After five years, government costs for children in the Guided Services group were significantly lower than for those in the Standard Services group (Lahti and Detgen, 2004; Lahti, 2006).
- An evaluation of the **Illinois Adoption Preservation Program** (for adoptive families of any type) analysed outcomes for 1,162 children in 912 families served over a two-year period; 80 per cent of children were adopted from care. The possibility of adoption disruption was raised by 30 per cent of parents, and 13 per cent of children were placed outside the home at the end of services (39% with a goal of returning home). A majority (58%) of families returned

evaluations and 92 per cent were satisfied with services. They rated outcomes slightly more positively than did workers. Frequently reported areas of improvement were: feeling supported (92%); knowing where to get help (89%); understanding the child (87%); parenting skills (85%); reduced family stress (79%); and child's behaviour (74%) (Smith, 2006a).

- **Developmental Dyadic Psychotherapy** (DDP), developed by Daniel Hughes (2007), seeks to increase parent–child attachment while helping children make sense of and cope with their painful histories and the related feelings and behaviours. A 2006 review (Craven and Lee, 2006) of the evidence base for 18 therapeutic interventions for foster children classified DDP at a category 3 (supported and acceptable) on a scale ranging from 1 (well-supported, efficacious) to 6 (concerning treatment). Subsequent to this review, additional evaluative research extending follow-up to four years after treatment was published (Becker-Weidman, 2006; Becker-Weidman and Hughes, 2008). In the latter report, the 34 young people in the treatment group demonstrated significant improvements on all scales of the Child Behavior Checklist; these gains were sustained four years after treatment, while the 30 subjects in the comparison group receiving other forms of treatment did not demonstrate sustained gains on any subscales.

- **Early intervention parent training programmes** developed by Rushton and Monck (2009) in England involve two 10-session manualised interventions. One was a cognitive behavioural training based on *The Incredible Years*, an evidence-based intervention, and the other was an educational programme focused on understand-ing negative behaviours as survival strategies (Rushton and Monck, 2009). An evaluation using random assignment to three groups found that, when compared with the standard care group at the six-month follow-up, adopters receiving both parent training programmes were more satisfied with parenting and that negative parenting approaches were reduced; however, no significant improvements in child problems were found (Rushton *et al*, 2010).

- **Attachment, Self-Regulation, and Competency (ARC)** was imple-mented in the ADOPTS post-adoption programme of Bethany

Christian Services beginning in Michigan in 2004 and later at eight other sites. It was used with pre- and post-adoptive children aged eight to 18 and their parents in an 18-week course of treatment, after which families could continue to work on other issues, if desired. The treatment included a six-week group with children and another with parents. The evaluation reported significant improvement across all subscales of the Trauma Symptom Checklist, except the Sexual Concerns subscale, and gains were maintained after a year (Kinniburgh and Blaustein, 2006). A subsequent Alaska project implementing ARC compared children completing a course of treatment with those dropping out, finding a 19-point improvement in Child Behaviour Checklist scores for clients completing ARC treatment, compared to a 2.5-point improvement with clients not completing treatment (Arvidson *et al*, 2011).

Selected resources

Blaustein M. and Kinniburgh K. (2010) *Treating Traumatic Stress in Children and Adolescents: How to foster resilience through attachment, self-regulation, and competency*, New York: Guilford Press.

Hart A. and Luckock B. (2004) *Developing Adoption Support and Therapy: New approaches for practice*, London: Jessica Kingsley Publishers.

Smith S.L. and Howard J.A. (1999) *Promoting Successful Adoptions: Practice with troubled families*, Thousand Oaks, CA: Sage.

Smith S.L. (2010) *Keeping the Promise: The critical needs for post-adoption services to enable children and families to succeed*, New York: Donaldson Adoption Institute. Access at: www.adoptioninstitute.org/publications/2010_10_20_KeepingThePromise.pdf

22 Adoption preservation services to stabilise at-risk adoptions

Description and overview

Many children and their families undergo periods of severe difficulty, both in the months after the initial placement and periodically thereafter. The ongoing developmental impact of loss and trauma continues to result in adjustment challenges for children; likewise, parental factors can interact with children's challenges in ways that intensify family stress. A considerable body of research on adoption disruption has identified factors linked with adoption breakdown in the year or so after placement; however, less is known about ongoing adoption instability. The primary child characteristics consistently documented as being associated with a higher risk of disruption are older age at adoptive placement and a high level of behavioural problems (Barth and Berry, 1988; Smith and Howard, 1991).

Risk factors for adoption instability

Studies have also identified attachment difficulties as a primary risk factor; for example, an English study (Rushton *et al*, 2003) of children placed in middle childhood found that 27 per cent had not yet developed an attached relationship with at least one parent by one year after placement, and these young people were much more likely than others to have serious behaviour problems. When an adoptive mother perceived a lack of attachment by the child, there was an eightfold increase in adoption disruption; however, when the mother felt she was getting something back from the child, she was much more likely to develop an attachment herself and to remain committed in the face of challenges. At the six-year follow-up, about half of those originally placed for adoption were doing well, but 23 per cent of the adoptions had ended and 28 per cent reported that they were continuing with substantial difficulties (Rushton and Dance, 2006). Other research has found that adoptive mothers with a high degree of maternal sensitivity and secure attachment styles are better able to respond to maltreated children's past loss or trauma issues, and these placements are less likely to disrupt (Steele *et al*, 2003; Kaniuk *et al*, 2004).

An Illinois study of over 1,300 child welfare adoptive families, using a Behavior Problem Index (BPI) ranging from 0–28, also found that behavioural problems escalated with the level of attachment difficulty (Howard and Smith, 2003). Parents rated their children's ability to give and receive affection; the majority (58%) were able to give and receive affection "very well" and their BPI scores averaged 8.7. Those rated as "fairly well" (30%) had a mean of 15.3 and those rated as "poorly" or "not at all" (12%) had a mean BPI of 19.0. (A large national study using the BPI found an overall mean of 6.4 and a mean of 14 or higher for children receiving mental health treatment.) The level of children's behavioural problems and the closeness in the parent–child relationship varies with their ages. Brooks and Barth (1999) found that the proportion of adoptive parents who felt somewhat to very warm and close to their children hit a low of 59 per cent between ages 13 and 18, rebounding to 80 per cent after age 19.

Based on the body of research, we can conclude that: 1) the risk of adoption breakdown is highest in the first year; 2) for adoptions that continue, a substantial proportion (greater than 40%) will involve children with significant behavioural and emotional challenges; and 3) a minority of these will have a very high level of behavioural problems and attachment difficulties that can pose a threat to adoption stability. Other factors identified by research as related to disruption risk include more moves in care; history of sexual abuse and sexual acting out; having been singled out from siblings for rejection or other emotional abuse by birth parents; strong attachment to birth mother; matched (stranger) adopters rather than foster or kin; higher education of adoptive parents; unrealistic expectations; and inadequate information disclosure and inadequate parent preparation (Festinger, 1986; Berry and Barth, 1990; Smith and Howard, 1991; McRoy, 1999; Rushton and Dance, 2006; Smith *et al*, 2006).

In addition to disruption or dissolution, a minority of children adopted from care will experience temporary placements such as psychiatric hospitalisation or residential treatment. One study reported that 10 per cent of families had children who had been in a psychiatric hospital since adoption and five per cent in another type of out-of-home placement. In this study, nine per cent reported each of these areas as a needed service, so it is hard to determine the degree of overlap among these ratings (Rosenthal et al, 1996).

Services to stabilise adoptions

A range of programmes and services focus on preserving at-risk adoptions and preventing child placement, both before and after finalisation. In the US, some state-supported specialised adoption therapeutic programmes accept adoptive families that would fall on a continuum of "risk" either pre- or post-adoption or both; for example, Tennessee's Adoption Support and Preservation Program (ASAP) includes in-home therapeutic counselling, monthly support groups and educational opportunities for families. Some of the families served are pre-adoptive (32%), and about 40 per cent are in crisis. ASAP requires that therapists have face-to-face visits with families in crisis within 48 hours of their initial phone calls. Respite is a component of their approach; they help families develop a relief team, and stipends are available to assist in obtaining respite (Smith, 2010).

Other programmes are designed to serve only those families at imminent risk of breakdown, with some focusing only on the pre-adoption period and others taking only post-adoptive families, and some accepting either. The Kinship Center's Adoption Wraparound Program offers intensive services to children at risk of imminent placement into residential care. This programme serves adoptive and guardianship families in many California counties, and their most recent statistics reported that 83 per cent of children remained in their homes at the end of services (Graham Wright, 3 August 2012). The services involve several types of helpers (social worker, family assistant, parent partner, psychologist) assisting all the family members to develop and work with a team in addressing their needs for an 18-month period.

Some state-supported adoption preservation programmes in the US serve any type of adoptive family (Alabama, Illinois, Massachusetts, New Jersey, Pennsylvania, Virginia, Wisconsin); however, most serve only those adopting from that state's child welfare system. Another approach is the ASAP programme in Tennessee, which serves child welfare adoptive families at no cost but also other types of adoptive families on a sliding scale fee. Some have a crisis-oriented approach for a brief period, with the goal of linking families to other services, while others are more long term or have no time limit (Smith, 2010).

Key programme elements

Key aspects are presented of both effective post-placement services to stabilise all new permanent placements and adoption preservation services to stabilise at-risk placements. Even when those adopting are foster carers or relatives, the process can trigger the resurfacing of issues and create volatility or intensification of children's problems. Some children first disclosed or began talking about prior abuse after adoptive placement. *Effective post-placement services* to support optimal adjustment are often not provided, as families feel the need to present a positive front, and workers often feel like observers providing prescribed, minimal check-ups. Optimal post-placement services should include the following (Smith and Howard, 1991; Rycus and Hughes, 1998).

- making frequent contact (weekly if possible) during the first few months of placement, with lessening frequency as adjustments are solidified;
- encouraging parents and children to express feelings and responding with validation and support (ambivalence is a normal part of the adjustment process);
- helping parents understand children's needs and feelings, including those underlying negative behaviours, i.e., fears of closeness, rejection, grief and loss, etc.;
- empowering parents to use therapeutic behaviour management and attachment building techniques;

- spending regular time alone with the children to access their feelings and fears;
- helping children maintain emotional ties to significant persons to the extent possible;
- building sources of ongoing support for children and families, such as mentors or buddy families;
- helping families adapt to changes and establishing realistic expectations.

Adoption preservation services

The approach to intervention will vary by how far the family has gone down the path of disrupting and the extent to which it is in crisis, although not all crises threaten adoption stability. All of the key elements discussed previously under "Therapeutic interventions to enhance adoption adjustment" are applicable to these adoption preservation services, as are practice and research knowledge on crisis intervention and adoption breakdown. Partridge and colleagues (1986) described a *series of stages a family goes through in escalating problems* leading to removal of the child. These stages can occur during the first year after placement or years later.

- *Diminishing pleasure* as negative aspects of adoption begin to outweigh the positive.
- Acting-out behaviours escalate in response to parental doubt or the child's fear of closeness, and parents *come to view the child as the problem* in the family.
- The family shares its concerns with others outside its inner support circle (*going public*), which serves to increase alienation.
- *Turning point* – a critical incident or crisis takes place, and there is no return to a sense of happiness or optimism; i.e., the last straw.
- The parents set a *deadline for improvement* or give the child an *ultimatum*.
- *Final crisis and decision* to end the parent–child relationship comes.

Important aspects of stabilising adoptions that are at risk of disruption or dissolution include the following.

- **Engage with an adoptive family in crisis**. As with any struggling adoptive family, it is important to listen to their story, normalise their situation, reframe the child's behaviours in light of his/her history, recognise the parents' strengths and demonstrated commitment, and instil hope that their situation can improve. When parents come in determined to end the relationship, workers should assess whether the child is at risk of physical or emotional maltreatment, given the parents' frustration or despair. If there is no immediate danger, the worker may contract with parents to invest eight weeks in working to find a solution, after which they will re-evaluate whether they will continue (Smith and Howard, 1999).
- **Develop a short-term plan with the family for immediate relief**. Parents in crisis may be highly emotional and experiencing intense pain, fear and sadness. They may see no or few options to address a serious problem and act impulsively by forcing a premature solution, such as placement of the child outside the home. Workers may need to encourage them to delay making major decisions until they are better able to cope. Brief respite, such as the child spending a few days with relatives or a former foster family or the parents leaving home for a short time, may help them gain a more reality-based perspective (Rycus and Hughes, 1998).
- **Plan for ways to provide ongoing support to the family**. Workers may see families in crisis frequently and for longer sessions, talk by telephone between sessions and link them with other sources of support such as a "buddy" family or adoption support group. Also, developing an ongoing respite team or support system for all family members may be useful.
- **Assess events leading up to the crisis and design an intervention plan with the family**. Based on a thorough understanding of the trigger event and contributing factors, as well as all family members' perspectives, workers can work with them to choose one to three issues or problems to address, and then develop an intervention plan to achieve their objectives (Rycus and Hughes, 1998).
- **Provide advocacy and case co-ordination as needed**. Adoption preservation work often involves extensive collateral work advoca-

ting for needed services, such as a therapeutic school placement or specialised medical or psychiatric treatment, as well as co-ordinating efforts of helpers across several systems who are involved with the family.

- **When a disruption, dissolution or other adoption breakdown occurs, support and therapeutic help should be provided to those involved**. The child and family need to process the event both with each other and separately, and the family needs to be helped to support the child through this transition. For example, when an adoptive placement disrupts in England, a disruption meeting is often held to bring together those affected (Argent and Coleman, 2012).

Lessons learned

Persistent externalising behaviour problems are the most common presenting problem of families who seek adoption preservation services. Frequently, these negative behaviours are maladaptive coping patterns for defending against underlying emotional struggles, and addressing the emotional issues is key to successfully modifying the behaviours (Smith *et al*, 2000). For some children, the emotional demands of attaching to adoptive parents, trusting and yielding control bring a resurgence of issues related to previous trauma and loss; this can intensify behaviour problems and increase attachment-related fears. It is critically important to assess the inner life of the children in order to identify their fears and emotions and to help them heal and find more functional ways to cope. A study of adoption disruption found that workers often met with children only in con-junction with adoptive parents, and some children had severe emotional turmoil that was unexplored until after disruptions occurred (Smith and Howard, 1991, 1994).

When there are difficulties early on, parents often assume that things will get better with time, but they may feel growing disenchant-ment and hopelessness if the problems intensify or do not improve as the years go on. Adoption practice literature reports a number of dynamics commonly seen in families who have children with high levels of behaviour problems that have not improved despite repeated attempts to get help: severe power struggles and parents who become more extreme in their attempts to exert control; the mother taking the brunt of the child's anger; marital tension and disagreement on how to parent; conflict throughout the family, including between siblings; isolation; parental difficulty in connecting or empathising with the child; and parents feeling exhausted, like failures and hopeless. Sometimes families that were very functional at the time of adoption have become dysfunctional, and parents may present as harsh, volatile and unreasonable. In this state, families are very vulnerable to a crisis, and a triggering event can result in their being unable to cope. At the beginning, professionals may need to gauge the parents' emotional state and level of anger towards their children to determine whether to first talk with the entire family together or with its members separately (Smith and Howard, 1999).

A significant minority of parents seeking adoption preservation services many years after adoption may raise the possibility of dissolution (30% in a study of one preservation programme); however, most of them are truly committed to their children and are searching for other solutions (Smith, 2006a).

In their discussion of 'When is a disruption not a disruption?', Argent and Coleman (2012, p. 33) focus on the importance of differentiating between a 'cry for help' from distraught carers who have nearly, but not quite, reached their limits and a 'plea for closure' from parents who cannot continue to care for the child. Sometimes the child's condition is so extreme that he/she requires residential placement. When workers act punitively toward the parents, the possibility of their continuing to be a support to the child is diminished. These English adoption experts recommend an intervention meeting to determine if there is a way to provide for the child and parents' current needs and to leave the door open for continuation or disruption. It is also important to hear and understand the child's wishes and feelings. If disruption is going to occur, it is important to plan for the best way to support the child and parents through this transition.

Argent and Coleman (2012) also advocate convening a disruption meeting to facilitate increased understanding and to be able to make future plans for the child based on this information. They describe a structured process for these meetings and an agenda in their practice guide, *Dealing with Disruption in Fostering and Adoption Placements*.

Outcomes

Evaluations of adoption preservation services have not used experimental designs, so we cannot draw conclusions about their efficacy in preventing adoption breakdown. Generally these evaluations are descriptive, and many involve fewer than 50 families. Most evaluations report the *number of children out of the home at the end of services*, ranging from eight to 13 per cent in two evaluations (Prew *et al*, 1990; Smith, 2006a), to 29 per cent in an Iowa project (Groze *et al*, 1991), to 59 per cent in a four-week Washington project (Barth and Miller, 2000). Being out of the home at the end of services does not always signal an adoption failure since some of these children are receiving needed residential treatment, their parents maintain a strong commitment to them, and they are expected to return home. In one programme evaluation, social workers rated close to half (45%) of the parents of children placed at case closing as displaying an ongoing commitment to their sons and daughters (Smith, 2006a).

- **Brief crisis intervention alone is generally not sufficient to address the needs of post-adoption families**. Based on a review of evaluations of post-adoption preservation programmes conducted in the 1990s, Barth and Miller (2000, p. 450) concluded that ' . . . the disappointing results from the evaluations of brief intensive adoption preservation services models suggests that they do not generally fit the needs of adoptive families (Barth, 1995; Howard and Smith, 1995). A less time-limited and more family-focused approach appears more suitable (Prew *et al*, 1990; Howard and Smith, 1995).' This was the experience of the Illinois adoption preservation programme, which was originally designed as a family preservation model of intensive home-based services for 10 to 12 weeks, with the goal of linking families to existing community services. It was soon discovered that there were few, if any, adoption-competent community services to which to link these families, and they wanted less-intensive services for a longer time period to effectively address chronic difficulties. The timeframe of this programme was extended twice during its first year of operation to 12–18 months.

A subsequent evaluation of Massachusetts' crisis response team programme, which provided an average of eight hours of services within a few weeks, found that even though families gave the providers high ratings, their average rating of their own progress in resolving problems on a scale of 0 = none to 4 = achieved was 1.8 or between minimal (1) and moderate (2) (Hudson *et al*, 2006). Also, a Virginia programme evaluation found that families who received services for a longer period (accessing support groups and counselling services as needed over multiple years) were most likely to rate their progress as substantial, and the evaluators concluded that the most helpful model includes an array of services that allows families to receive help at different times over a period of years (Atkinson and Gonet, 2007). The latter evaluation also reported that the most significant changes described 'were not in the children but in the capacity of parents to understand, love, and cope with their children' (p. 98).

- **Intensive services promote stability in at-risk pre-adoptive families.** A Kansas programme providing intensive preservation services for pre-adoptive families at risk of imminent out-of-home child placement developed an after-care plan and provided four follow-up checks within the first year after case closing. An evaluation of the outcomes of services for 99 families reported that services began, on average, 60 days into the adoptive placements and lasted for a mean of 36 days; it reported that out-of-home placement was prevented for 83 per cent of families served. A regression analysis evaluated factors predicting family intactness at both six and 12 months. At the latter point, service characteristics explained more of the variance in remaining intact than did child and family characteristics; as the number of days of intensive services increased, so did levels of family intactness (Berry *et al*, 2007).

Selected resources

Argent H. and Coleman J. (2012) *Dealing with Disruption*, London: BAAF.

Rycus J.S. and Hughes R.C. (1998) *Field Guide to Child Welfare, Vol. IV: Placement and permanence*, Washington, DC: Child Welfare League of America.

Smith S.L. and Howard J.A. (1999) *Promoting Successful Adoptions: Practice with troubled families*, Thousand Oaks, CA: Sage.

Conclusions and recommendations

While child welfare/child care systems across the United States, England and Canada have made progress in law and practice to move foster children who cannot safely return home to permanent families, we are far from adequately meeting the needs of tens of thousands of children each year. Debates continue over the best pathways to permanence for children in care who cannot safely return home, but one reality remains across the three countries: far too many girls and boys remain in temporary placements and transition to adulthood without an enduring family to sustain them. The knowledge and research synthesised in this volume describe specific practices that are particularly important for providing children with the greatest likelihood of achieving permanency through adoption or guardianship. Based on these practices, a number of recommendations appear self-evident.

1. **In statute and policy, provide clear requirements for achieving permanency for every child in foster care who cannot return home and operationalise this expectation through organisational leadership and culture.**

2. **Facilitate tracking outcomes at every level of the system in order to understand the barriers to permanency and to enforce accountability for achieving it.**

3. **Use aggressive family finding and engagement to maximise the use of relatives as permanency resources for children in care, as this contributes to child well-being.**

4. **Reduce barriers and disincentives to adoption or guardianship by providing adequate and reliable subsidies to those who make the commitment to become legal parents to these children.**

5. **Incorporate sound casework practices that minimise harm: place children initially with families who are likely resources for alternative permanency, support children to understand and cope with traumatic experiences, and minimise the extent of losses they must endure by stabilising placements, requiring life story work, and facilitating the level of openness in the child's best interests.**

6. **Monitor court timeframes in order to avoid unwarranted delays in achieving permanency – delays which themselves lessen a child's chances of adoption.**

7. **Employ a range of recruitment and retention strategies to find permanent families for children and young people in care, including promoting consumer-friendly practices to retain families who do apply to adopt.** (Strategies should include checks within the system to identify children and teens who are lingering in care and to provide expert support and consultation for workers to effectively resolve barriers to permanency.)

8. **Provide a continuum of adoption support and preservation services to stabilise at-risk placements and enable families to successfully parent children to adulthood.**

Adoption provides a lifetime of benefits for children who cannot return to their families of origin, including the emotional security of caring adults and a committed family to ensure that their needs are met. Gaining a family for life not only transforms the futures of children in care, but also brings benefits to child welfare systems, governments and communities. For example, one economist found that every dollar invested in the adoption of a child from care returns about three dollars in public and private benefits (Hansen, 2006). Adoption also delivers societal benefits after these children become adults, such as reduced likelihood of their receiving public assistance, having criminal or substance abuse involvement, or experiencing a range of other difficulties affecting individuals, their families and the communities in which they live.

Child welfare systems across all jurisdictions need to regularly assess their performance in achieving permanency for the young people in their care and to search for ways to better meet their needs, including incorporating practices described in this volume.

References

Ad Council (2012) *Adopting Children from Foster Care*. Access at: www.adcouncil.org/Impact/Case-Studies-Best-Practices/Adopting-Children-from-Foster-Care

Adoption and Safe Families Act of 1997, 42 USC. § 1305 (1997)

Adoption Council of Ontario Youth Network (2011) *Youth Speak Out* (DVD). Available from: www.adoptontario.ca/Public/Default.aspx?I=165 andn=Youth+Network

Adoption Learning Partners (2013) Online courses and webinars. Access at: www.adoptionlearningpartners.org/

Adoption UK (2013) *Family Support Service: Call for help* (video). Available at: www.adoptionuk.org/one-one-support/family-support-service

Adoptions Unlimited, Inc. (2008) *Family Connections* (DVD). Chicago: Adoptions Unlimited. Access at: www.nrcadoption.org/videos/family-connections-project/

AdoptUSKids (2003) *Practitioner's Guide: Getting more parents for children from your recruitment efforts, practitioner's guide*. Baltimore, MD: The Collaboration to AdoptUSKids. Access at: www.adoptuskids.org/_assets/files/NRCRRFAP/resources/practitioners-guide-getting-more-parents-from-your-recruitment-efforts.pdf

AdoptUSKids (2004) *Finding Common Ground: A guide for child welfare agencies working with communities of faith*. Access at: www.adoptuskids.org/_assets/files/NRCRRFAP/resources/finding-common-ground.pdf

AdoptUSKids (2010) *Minority Specializing Agency: Directory*. Access at: www.adoptuskids.org/_assets/files/NRCRRFAP/resources/minority-specializing-agency-directory.pdf

AdoptUSKids (2011a) *Overview of Market Segmentation: A tool for targeting recruitment. Adoptive Parents. National Resource Center for Recruitment and Retention of Adoptive Parents*. Access at: www.adoptuskids.org/_assets/files/NRCRRFAP/resources/overview-of-market-segmentation.pdf

AdoptUSKids (2011b) *National Adoption Month Capacity Building Toolkit. Section 1: Supporting and retaining families* (pp. 1–29). *Sections 2 and 3: Diligent recruitment* and *Working with diverse populations* (pp. 30–60). Access at: www.adoptuskids.org/_assets/files/NRCRRFAP/resources/national-adoption-month-toolkit-2011.pdf

AdoptUSKids (2012a) *Diligent Recruitment Grantees: Resources developed from grant projects.* Access at: www.adoptuskids.org/about-us/diligent-recruitment-grantees

AdoptUSKids (2013a) *Using Customer Service Concepts to Enhance Recruitment and Retention Processes.* National Resource Center for Diligent Recruitment at AdoptUSKids. Access at: www.adoptuskids.org/_assets/files/using-customer-service-concepts-to-enhance-recuitment-and-retention-practices.pdf

AdoptUSKids and NACAC (2008) *Taking a Break: Creating foster, adoptive and kinship respite care in your community.* Access at: www.adoptuskids.org/_assets/files/NRCRRFAP/resources/taking-a-break-respite-guide.pdf

After Adoption (2012) *The SafeBase Parenting Programme.* Access at: www.afteradoption.org.uk/page.asp?section=0001000100010011

Akin B.A. (2011) 'Predictors of foster care exits to permanency: a competing risks analysis of reunification, guardianship, and adoption', *Children and Youth Services Review*, 33, pp. 999–1011.

Alberta Children's Services (2004) *Evaluation of the Adoption Profile Webpage.* Access at: www.assembly.ab.ca/lao/library/egovdocs/alchs/2004/146666.pdf

Alberta Children's Services (2006) *A New Casework Practice Model.* (Child Intervention Planning and Implementation Office Program Quality and Standards Division). Access at: www.child.alberta.ca/home/documents/rpt_06_Casework_Practice_Model.pdf

Alberta Children's Services (2008) *Foster Care Review Report.* Access at: www.cwrp.ca/sites/default/files/publications/en/AB-fostercarereview_report.pdf

Allen T., Malm K., Williams S.C. and Ellis R. (2011) *Piecing Together the Puzzle: Tips and techniques for effective discovery in family finding.* Washington, DC: Child Trends.

American Bar Association (1996) *ABA Standards of Practice for Lawyers who Represent Children in Abuse and Neglect Cases, §§L-1. L. The Court's Role in*

Assuring Reasonable Lawyer Caseloads. L-1. Controlling Lawyer Caseloads. Chicago: American Bar Association. Access at: www.americanbar.org/content/dam/aba/migrated/family/reports/standards_abuseneglect.authcheckdam.pdf

American Bar Association's Center on Children and the Law, National Center for State Courts, and National Council of Juvenile and Family Court Judges (2004) *Building a Better Court: Measuring and improving court performance and judicial workload in child abuse and neglect cases.* Los Altos, CA: The David and Lucile Packard Foundation.

Anderson G. and Whalen P. (2004) *Permanency Planning Mediation Pilot Program Evaluation Final Report.* East Lansing, MI: Michigan State University School of Social Work. Access at: http://courts.michigan.gov/scao/resources/publications/reports/PPMPevaluation2004.pdf

Annie E Casey Foundation (2001) *Innovative Programs: Shortening children's stays in temporary care, Part Two.* Baltimore, MD: Annie E. Casey Foundation. Access at: www.aecf.org/upload/PublicationFiles/innovative%20programs%20part%202.pdf

Annie E Casey Foundation (2012) *Stepping up for Kids: What government and communities should do to support kinship families.* Baltimore, MD: AECF. Access at: www.aecf.org/~/media/Pubs/Initiatives/KIDS%20COUNT/S/SteppingUpforKids2012PolicyReport/SteppingUpForKids PolicyReport2012.pdf

Argent H. and Coleman J. (2012) *Dealing with Disruption.* London: BAAF.

Argys L. and Duncan B. (2008) *Economic Incentive and Foster Child Adoption: Working paper # 08-02.* Denver: University of Colorado. Access at: www.ucdenver.edu/academics/colleges/CLAS/Departments/economics/Documents/Argys_Duncan_08_2.pdf

Arvidson J., Kinniburgh K., Howard K., Spinazzola J., Strothers H., Evans M., Andres B., Cohen C. and Blaustein M.E. (2011) 'Treatment of complex trauma in young children: developmental and cultural considerations in application of the ARC intervention model', *Journal of Child and Adolescent Trauma,* 4:1, pp. 34–51.

Association of Family and Conciliation Courts (2012) *Guidelines for Child Protection Mediation.* Access at: www.afccnet.org/Portals/0/Guidelines%20for%20Child%20Protection%20Mediation.pdf

Atkinson A. and Gonet P. (2007) 'Strengthening adoption practice, listening to adoptive families', *Child Welfare,* 86:2, pp. 87–104.

Avery R. (1999a) *New York's Longest Waiting Children 1998: A study of New York state children in need of adoptive families.* Ithaca, NY: Cornell University.

Avery R. (1999b) 'Identifying obstacles to adoption in New York State's out-of-home care system', *Child Welfare*, 78:5, pp. 653–671.

Avery R. (2000) 'Perceptions and practice: agency efforts for the hardest-to-place children', *Children and Youth Services Review*, 22:6, pp. 399–420.

Avery R. (2010) 'An examination of theory and promising practices for achieving permanency for teens before they age out of foster care', *Children and Youth Services Review*, 32, pp. 399–408.

Bala N. and Birnbaum R. (2010) 'Reforming family justice: one judge for one family', *The Lawyers Weekly*, 9–10. Access at: www.lawyersweeklydigital.com/lawyersweekly/3026?pg=10#pg10

Barber J. and Delfabbro P. (2005) 'Children's adjustment to long-term foster care', *Child and Youth Services Review*, 27, pp. 329–340.

Barth R.P. (1993) 'Fiscal issues and stability in special-needs adoption', *Public Welfare*, 51:3, pp. 21–28.

Barth R.P. (1995) 'Adoption services', in Edwards R.L. (ed.), *Encyclopedia of Social Work* (19th ed., Vol. 1). Washington, DC: NASW Press, pp. 48–59.

Barth R.P. (1997) 'Effects of age and race on the odds of adoption versus remaining in long-term out-of-home care', *Child Welfare*, 76:2, pp. 285–308.

Barth R.P. and Berry M. (1987) 'Outcomes of child welfare services under permanency planning', *Social Services Review*, 61:1, pp. 71–90.

Barth R.P. and Berry M. (1988) *Adoption and Disruption: Rates, risks, and responses.* Hawthorne, NY: Aldine de Gruyter.

Barth R.P., Courtney M., Berrick J.D. and Albert V. (1994) *From Child Abuse to Permanency Planning: Child welfare services, pathways and placements.* Hawthorne, NY: Aldine de Gruyter.

Barth R.P., Gibbs D.A. and Siebenaler K. (2001) *Assessing the Field of Post-Adoption Service: Family needs, program models, and evaluation issues: Literature review.* Washington, DC: Department of Health and Human Services. Access at: www.aspe.hhs.gov/hsp/PASS/lit-rev-01.htm

Barth R.P. and Jonson-Reid M. (2000) 'Outcomes after child welfare services: implications for the design of performance measures', *Children and Youth Services Review*, 22, pp. 763–787.

Barth R.P. and Miller J.M. (2000) 'Building effective post-adoption services: what is the empirical foundation?' *Family Relations*, 49:4, pp. 447–455.

Barth R.P., Wildfire J., Lee C.K. and Gibbs D. (2003) 'Adoption subsidy dynamics', *Adoption Quarterly*, 7:2, pp. 3–27.

Baskin T.W., Rhody M., Schoolmeesters S. and Ellingson C. (2011) 'Supporting special-needs adoptive couples: assessing an intervention to enhance forgiveness, increase marital satisfaction, and prevent depression', *The Counseling Psychologist*, 39:7, pp. 933–955.

Bausch R.S. and Serpe R.T. (1999) 'Recruiting Mexican American adoptive parents', *Child Welfare*, 78:5, pp. 693–716.

Baynes P. (2008) 'Untold stories: a discussion of life story work', *Adoption & Fostering*, 32:2, pp. 43–49.

Becker M.A., Jordan N. and Larsen R. (2007) 'Predictors of successful permanency planning and length of stay in foster care: the role of race, diagnosis and place of residence', *Children and Youth Services Review*, 29, pp. 1102–1113.

Becker-Weidman A. (2006) 'Treatment for children with trauma-attachment disorders: dyadic developmental psychotherapy', *Child and Adolescent Social Work*, 23:2, pp. 147–171.

Becker-Weidman A. and Hughes D. (2008) 'Dyadic developmental psycho-therapy: an evidence-based treatment for children with complex trauma and disorders of attachment', *Child & Family Social Work*, 13:3, pp. 329–337.

Beckett C. (2001) 'The wait gets longer: an analysis of recent information on court delays', *Adoption & Fostering*, 25:4, pp. 55–62.

Belanger K., Copeland S. and Cheung M. (2008) 'The role of faith in adoption: achieving positive adoption outcomes for African American children', *Child Welfare*, 98:2, pp. 99–123.

Bell M., Wilson K. and Crawshaw M. (2002) 'Managing diversity in preparation for adoption', *Adoption & Fostering*, 26:3, pp. 8–19.

Bellamy J.L., Gopalan, G. and Traube D.E. (2010) 'A national study of the impact of outpatient mental health services for children in long-term foster care', *Clinical Child Psychology and Psychiatry*, 15:4, pp. 467–479.

Be My Parent (2004) *Be My Parent Subscriber Survey*. London: BAAF.

Berge J.M., Mendenhall T.J., Wrobel G.M., Grotevant H.D. and McRoy R.G.

(2006) 'Adolescents' feelings about openness in adoption: implications for adoption agencies', *Child Welfare*, 85, pp. 1011–1039.

Berrick J.D. (2009) *Take me Home: Protecting America's vulnerable children and families*. London: Oxford University Press.

Berrick J.D. (2011) 'Trends and issues in the US child welfare system', in Gilbert N., Parton N. and Skivenes M. (eds), *Child Protection Systems: International trends and orientations*. London: Oxford University Press, pp. 17–34.

Berrick J.D., Needell B., Barth R.P. and Johnson-Reid M. (1998) *The Tender Years: Toward developmentally sensitive child welfare services for very young children*. London: Oxford University Press.

Berry M. (1993) 'Adoptive parents' perceptions of and comfort with open adoption', *Child Welfare*, 72, pp. 231–253.

Berry M. and Barth R.P. (1989) 'Behavior problems of children adopted when older', *Children and Youth Services Review*, 11, pp. 221–228.

Berry M. and Barth R.P. (1990) 'A study of disrupted adoptive placements of adolescents', *Child Welfare*, 69, pp. 209–225.

Berry M., Barth R. and Needell B. (1996) 'Preparation, support, and satisfaction of adoptive families in agency and independent adoptions', *Child and Adolescent Social Work*, 13:2, pp. 157–183.

Berry M., Dylla D.J.C., Barth R.P. and Needell B. (1998) 'The role of open adoption in the adjustment of adopted children and their families', *Children and Youth Services Review*, 20:1–2, pp. 151–171.

Berry M., Propp J. and Martens P. (2007) 'The use of intensive family preservation services with adoptive families', *Child & Family Social Work*, 12, pp. 43–53.

Berzin S.C. (2008) 'Difficulties in the transition to adulthood: using propensity scoring to understand what makes foster youth vulnerable', *Social Service Review*, 82, pp. 171–196.

Biehal N., Ellison S., Baker C. and Sinclair I. (2009) *Characteristics, Outcomes and Meanings of Three Types of Permanent Placement – Adoption by strangers, adoption by carers and long-term foster care*. DCSF Research Brief, DCSF-RBX-09-11. London: Department for Children, Schools and Families. Access at: www.york.ac.uk/inst/spru/research/pdf/3types.pdf

Bingham J. (2012) 'Half of councils failing adoption targets, controversial "scorecards" show', *The Telegraph*, 11 May. Access at: www.telegraph.co.uk/news/politics/9259148/Half-of-councils-failing-adoption-targets-controversial-scorecards-show.html

Bissell M. and Mille J. (2007) *Making "Relative Search" Happen: A guide to finding and involving relatives at every stage of the child welfare process.* Silver Spring, MD: ChildFocus.

Blackston E.A., Buck A.J., Hakim S. and Spiegel U. (2008) 'Market segmentation in child adoption', *International Review of Law and Economics*, 28:3, pp. 220–225.

Blaustein M. and Kinniburgh K. (2010) *Treating Traumatic Stress in Children and Adolescents: How to foster resilience through attachment, self-regulation, and competency.* New York: Guilford Press.

Bogolub E. (2008) 'Child protective services investigations and the transition to foster care: children's views', *Families in Society*, 89, pp. 90–99.

Bohman M. and Sigvardsson S. (1990) 'Outcome in adoption: lessons from longitudinal studies', in Brodzinsky D. M. and Schechter M. D. (eds) *The Psychology of Adoption.* New York: Oxford University Press, pp. 93–106.

Bowlby J. (1980) *Attachment and Loss: Loss, sadness and depression: Volume 3.* New York: Basic Books.

Briere J., Kaltman S. and Green B.L. (2008) 'Accumulated childhood trauma and symptom complexity', *Journal of Traumatic Stress*, 21:2, pp. 223–226.

Bringewatt E., Allen T. and Williams S.C. (2013) *Client Voices: Youth, parent, and relative perspectives on family finding.* Bethesda, MD: Child Trends. Access at: www.childtrends.org/wp-content/uploads/2013/05/2013-23ClientVoices.pdf

British Association for Adoption and Fostering (BAAF) (2012a) *Adoption Activity Days.* Access at: www.baaf.org.uk/ourwork/activitydays

British Columbia Government (2012) *Census Statistical Profiles of Aboriginal Peoples: 2006 census.* Victoria, BC: BC Stats. Access at: www.bcstats.gov.bc.ca/StatisticsBySubject/AboriginalPeoples/CensusProfiles.aspx

Brodzinsky D. (2006) 'Family structural openness and communication openness as predictors in the adjustment of adopted children', *Adoption Quarterly*, 9:4, pp. 1–18.

Brodzinsky D. (2008) *Adoptive Parent Preparation Project. Phase I: Meeting the mental health and developmental needs of adopted children.* New York:

Donaldson Adoption Institute. Access at: www.adoptioninstitute.org/research/2008_02_parent_prep.php

Brodzinsky D. (2011a) *Expanding Resources for Children III: Research-based best practices in adoption by gays and lesbians.* New York: Donaldson Adoption Institute.

Brodzinsky D. (2011b) 'Children's understanding of adoption: developmental and clinical implications', *Professional Psychology: Research and Practice*, 42, pp. 200–207.

Brodzinsky D. and Huffman L. (1988) 'Transition to adoptive parenthood', *Marriage and Family Review*, 12, pp. 267–286.

Brodzinsky D. and Pinderhughes E. (2002) 'Parenting and child development in adoptive families', in Bornstein M. (ed.) *Handbook of Parenting. Vol 1: Children and parenting* (2nd ed.). Hillsdale, NJ: Lawrence Erlbaum Associates, pp. 79–311.

Brooks D., Allen J. and Barth R.P. (2002) 'Adoption services use, helpfulness, and need: a comparison of public and private agency and independent adoptive families', *Children and Youth Services Review*, 24, pp. 213–218.

Brooks D. and Barth R.P. (1999) 'Adult transracial and inracial adoptees: effects of race, gender, adoptive family structure, and placement history on adjustment outcomes', *American Journal of Orthopsychiatry*, 69:1, pp. 87–99.

Bryan V., Flaherty C. and Saunders C. (2010) 'Supporting adoptive families: participant perceptions of a statewide peer mentoring and support program', *Journal of Public Child Welfare*, 4:1, pp. 91–112.

Buckles K. (2009) *Do Adoption Subsidies Help At-Risk Children?* University of Kentucky Center for Poverty Research Discussion Paper Series, DP2009-09. Access at: www.ukcpr.org/Publications/DP2009-09.pdf.

Buckles K. (in press) 'Adoption subsidies and placement outcomes for children in foster care', *Journal of Human Resources*.

Bullock R., Courtney M.E., Parker R., Sinclair I. and Thoburn, J. (2006) 'Can the corporate state parent?', *Children and Youth Services Review*, 28, pp. 1344–1358.

Burns B.J., Phillips S.D., Wagner H.R., Barth R.P., Kilko D.J., Campbell Y. and Landsverk J. (2004) 'Mental health need and access to mental health services by youths involved with child welfare: a national survey', *Journal of the American Academy of Child and Adolescent Psychology*, 43, pp. 960–970.

Butler I. and Hickman, C. (2011) *Social Work with Children and Families: Getting into practice*, (3rd edn.). London: Jessica Kingsley Publishers.

California Blue Ribbon Commission on Children in Foster Care (2010) *Building a Brighter Future for California's Children, 17*. Access at: www. courts.ca.gov/documents/brc-progress-0810.pdf

California Evidence-Based Clearinghouse for Child Welfare (2011) *Multidimensional Treatment Foster Care – Adolescents (MTFC-A)*. Access at: www. cebc4cw.org/program/multidimensional-treatment-foster-care-adolescents/

California Judges Association (2012) *FAQ*. San Francisco, CA: California Judges Association. Access at: www.caljudges.org/faq.vp.html

Campbell K. (2007) 'Kevin Campbell: pioneer in finding families for youth in care. Close-up, Casey Family Services', *Voice Magazine*, 8:2, pp. 13–15. Access at: www.caseyfamilyservices.org/images/uploads/connectionscount/ v1-i1-article3-voice_campbell.pdf

Campbell K., Castro S., Houston N., Koenig D., Roberts T. and Rose J. (2003, Fall) 'Lighting the fire of urgency: families lost and found in America's child welfare system', *Permanency Planning Today*. New York: National Resource Center for Foster Care and Permanency Planning, Hunter College School of Social Work.

Canada's Waiting Kids (2012a) *About CWK*. Access at: www.canadas waitingkids.ca/about.html

Canada's Waiting Kids (2012b) *Info and Support Groups*. Access at: www. canadaswaitingkids.ca/support.html#national

Canada's Waiting Kids (2012c) *Description Writing Guidelines*. Access at: www.canadaswaitingkids.ca/pdf/guidelines.pdf

Canadian Forum on Civil Justice (2010) *Inventory of Reforms, New Brunswick Family Court Pilot Project*. Toronto, ON: Osgoode Hall Law School York University. Access at: www.cfcj-fcjc.org/inventory/reform.php?id=121

Casey Family Programs (2000) *Lighting the Way: Attracting and supporting foster families*. Seattle, WA: Casey Family Programs.

Casey Family Programs and National Center for Resource Family Support (2003) *Resources on Individualized and Targeted Recruitment for Adoption*. Washington, DC.

Casey Family Services (2007) *A Call to Action: An integrated approach to youth permanence and preparation for adulthood*. New Haven, CT: Casey

Family Services. Access at: www.caseyfamilyservices.org/userfiles/pdf/pub-2005-call-to-action.pdf

Center for Adoption Research and Massachusetts Adoption Resource Exchange (2006) *Massachusetts Adoption from Foster Care: Knowledge and attitudes survey*. Worcester, MA: Center for Adoption Research.

Center for Improvement of Child and Family Services (CICFS) (2009) *Reducing the Trauma of Investigation, Removal, and Initial Out-of-Home Placement in Child Abuse Cases: Policy information and discussion guide*. Portland, OR: Portland State University.

Center for Policy Research (2005) *Child Advocacy Mediation Project: Jefferson Parish Juvenile Court and Orleans Parish Juvenile Court*. Denver, CO: Centre for Policy Research.

Chamberlain K. and Horne J. (2003) 'Understanding normality in adoptive family life: the role of peer group support', in Argent H. (ed.) *Models of Adoption Support: What works and what doesn't*. London: BAAF, pp. 87–99.

Chamberlain P., Moreland S. and Reid K. (1992) 'Enhanced services and stipends for foster parents: effects on retention rates and outcomes for children', *Child Welfare*, 71:5, pp. 387–401.

Chamberlain P., Price J.M., Reid J.B., Landsverk J., Fisher P.A. and Stoolmiller M. (2006) 'Who disrupts from placement in foster and kinship care?' *Child Abuse Neglect*, 30:4, pp. 409–424.

Chicago Tribune (2010) 'Iowa county tries gentler way to remove kids', 9 August, *Chicago Tribune*.

Child Welfare Information Gateway (2005) *Concurrent Planning: What the evidence shows*. Washington, DC: US Children's Bureau.

Child Welfare Information Gateway (2009) *Concurrent Planning for Permanency for Children: Summary of state laws*. Washington, DC: US Children's Bureau. Access at: www.childwelfare.gov/systemwide/laws_policies/statutes/concurrent.cfm.

Child Welfare Information Gateway (2010a) *The Adoption Home Study Process*. Washington, DC. Access at: www.childwelfare.gov/pubs/f_homstu.cfm.

Child Welfare Information Gateway (CWIG) (2010b) *Consent to Adoption*. Washington, DC: US Department of Health and Human Services.

Child Welfare Information Gateway (2011a) *Major Federal Legislation Concerned with Child Protection, Child Welfare, and Adoption*. Washington,

DC: US Children's Bureau. Access at: www.childwelfare.gov/pubs/otherpubs/majorfedlegis.pdf

Child Welfare Information Gateway (2012a) *Concurrent Planning: What the evidence shows*. Washington, DC: US Children's Bureau. Access at www.childwelfare.gov/pubs/issue_briefs/concurrent_evidence/concurrent_evidence.pdf

Child Welfare Information Gateway (2012c) *Providing Postadoption Services: A bulletin for professionals*. Washington, DC: US Department of Health and Human Services. Access at: www.childwelfare.gov/pubs/f_postadopt bulletin/index.cfm

Child Welfare League of America (2000) *Standards for Excellence in Adoption Services*. Washington, DC: CWLA.

Child Welfare League of Canada (2003) *Children in Care in Canada*. Access at: www.nationalchildrensalliance.com/nca/pubs/2003/Children_in_Care_March_2003.pdf

Children's Rights (2006) *Ending the Foster Care Life Sentence: The critical need for adoption subsidies*. New York: Children's Rights. Access at: www.childrensrights.org/wp-content/uploads/2008/06/ending_the_foster_care_life_sentence_july_2006.pdf.

Children's Rights (2012) *Facts about Foster Care*. Access at: www.childrensrights.org/issues-resources/foster-care/facts-about-foster-care/

Christenson B. and McMurtry J. (2007) 'A comparative evaluation of preservice training of kinship and nonkinship foster/adoptive families', *Child Welfare*, 86, pp. 125–140.

Clark H.B., Lee B., Prange M.E. and McDonald B.A. (1996) 'Children lost within the foster care system: can wraparound service strategies improve placement outcomes?', *Journal of Child and Family Studies*, 5:1, pp. 39–54.

Cleary K. and White A. (2008) *Structured Analysis Family Evaluation (SAFE)*. Access at: www.icpc.aphsa.org/home/Doc/UniformHomeStudies.pdf.

Coakley J.F. and Berrick J.D. (2008) 'Research review: in a rush to permanency: preventing adoption disruption', *Child & Family Social Work*, 13, pp. 101–112.

Collins M.E., Amodeo M. and Clay C. (2007a) *Review of the Literature on Child Welfare Training: Theory, practice, and research*. Access at: www.bu.edu/ssw/files/pdf/BUSSW_CSReport21.pdf

Collins M.E., Amodeo M. and Clay C. (2007b) *Evaluation of Independent Living Training Grantees: Final case study report*. Washington, DC: Children's Bureau, Administration on Children, Youth and Families, U.S. Department of Health and Human Services.

Collins M.E., Paris R. and Ward R.L. (2008) 'The permanence of family ties: implications for youth transitioning from foster care', *American Journal of Orthopsychiatry*, 78, pp. 54–62.

Connell C.M., Katz K., Saunders L. and Tebes J.K. (2006) 'Leaving foster care – the influence of child and case characteristics on foster care exit rates', *Children and Youth Services Review*, 28, pp. 780–798.

Consortium for Children (2012) *Permanency Planning Mediation: General information*. San Rafael, CA: Consortium for Children. Access at: www.consortforkids.org/Permanency-Planning-Mediation/General-Information.aspx

Coppernoll C. (2011) 'Adoptions in Oklahoma increasing at fastest rate in nation', *NewOK*, 20 November.

Courtney M.E. and Dworsky A. (2006) 'Early outcomes for young adults transitioning from out-of-home care in the USA', *Child & Family Social Work*, 11, pp. 209–219.

Courtney M.E., Dworsky A., Lee J.S. and Rapp M. (2010) *Midwest Evaluation of the Adult Functioning of Former Foster Youth: Outcomes at age 23 and 24*. Chicago, IL: Chapin Hall Center for Children, University of Chicago.

Courtney M. and Hook J.L. (2012) 'Timing of exits to legal permanency from out-of-home care: the importance of systems and implication for assessing institutional accountability', *Children and Youth Services Review*, 34, pp. 2263–2272.

Courtney M. and Wong Y. (1996) 'Comparing the timing of exits from substitute care ', *Children and Youth Services Review*, 18, pp. 307–334.

Cousins J. (2003) 'Are we missing the match? Rethinking adopter assessment and child profiling', *Adoption & Fostering*, 27:4, pp. 7–18.

Cousins, J. (2008) *Ten Top Tips for Finding Families*. London: BAAF.

Coyne A. (1990) 'Administrative and policy issues', *Journal of Children in Contemporary Society*, 21:3–4, pp. 93–115.

Craven P.A. and Lee R.E. (2006) 'Therapeutic interventions for foster children: a systematic research synthesis', *Research on Social Work Practice*, 16:3, pp. 287–304.

Crea T. (2009) 'Brief note: intercountry adoptions and domestic home study practices: SAFE and the Hague Adoption Convention', *International Social Work*, 52:5, pp. 673–678.

Crea T., Barth R.P. and Chintapalli L.K. (2007) 'Home study methods for evaluating prospective resource families: history, current challenges, and promising approaches', *Child Welfare*, 86, pp. 141–157.

Crea T., Barth R.P., Chintapalli L.K. and Buchanan R.L. (2009a) 'Structured home study evaluations: perceived benefits of SAFE vs. conventional home studies', *Adoption Quarterly*, 12, pp. 78–99.

Crea T., Barth R.P., Chintapalli L.K. and Buchanan R.L. (2009b) 'The implementation and expansion of SAFE: frontline responses and the transfer of technology to practice', *Children and Youth Services Review*, 31:8, pp. 903–910.

Crea T., Griffin A. and Barth R. (2011) 'The intersection of home study assessments and child specific recruitment: the performance of home studies in practice', *Children and Youth Services Review*, 33, pp. 28–33.

Cushing G. and Greenblatt S.B. (2009) 'Vulnerability to foster care drift after the termination of parental rights', *Research on Social Work Practice*, 19:6, pp. 694–704.

Cushman L.F., Kalmuss D. and Namerow P.B. (1997) 'Openness in adoption: experiences and social psychological outcomes among birth mothers', *Marriage and Family Review*, 2:1, pp. 7–18.

Dalberth B., Gibbs D. and Berkman N. (2005) *Understanding Adoption Subsidies: An analysis of AFCARS data*. Washington, DC: Office of the Assistant Secretary for Planning and Evaluation, US Department of Health and Human Services. Access at: www.aspe.hhs.gov/hsp/05/adoption-subsidies/report.pdf

Dance C., Ouwejan D., Beecham J. and Farmer E. (2010) *Linking and Matching: A survey of adoption agency practice in England and Wales*. London: BAAF.

Dance C. and Rushton A. (2005) 'Predictors of outcome for unrelated adoptive placements made during middle childhood', *Child & Family Social Work*, 10:4, pp. 269–280.

D'Andrade A.C. (2009) 'The differential effects of concurrent planning practice elements on reunification and adoption', *Research on Social Work Practice*, 19:6, pp. 694–704.

D'Andrade A. and Berrick J.D. (2006) 'When policy meets practice: the untested effects of permanency reforms in child welfare', *Journal of Sociology and Social Welfare*, 33:1, pp. 31–52.

D'Andrade A., Frame L. and Duerr Berrick J. (2006) 'Concurrent planning in public child welfare agencies: oxymoron or work in progress?' *Children and Youth Services Review*, 28:1, pp. 78–95.

Day D. (1979) *The Adoption of Black Children*. Lexington, MA: D.C. Heath.

Delaware Family Court (2006) *2006 Annual Report of the Delaware Judiciary, 51*, Wilmington, DE: Delaware Judiciary. Access at: www.courts.delaware.gov/aoc/AnnualReports/FY06/FamilyCourt.pdf

Denby R.W., Alford K.A. and Ayala J. (2011) 'The journey to adopt a child who has special needs: parents' perspectives', *Children and Youth Services Review*, 33:9, pp. 1543–1554.

Denver Post (2010) 'Church and state can work in harmony, *Denver Pact*, 6 March; (2008) 'Adoption effort gets phenomenal results, 26 November. Access at: www.denverpost.com/opinion/ci_14521717; www.denverpost.com/search/ci_11075305

Denver's Village (2012) *Diligent Recruitment Information and Resources*. Access at: www.adoptuskids.org/about-us/diligent-recruitment-grantees/denvers-village

Department for Education (2010a) *A Review of the Comparability of Statistics of Children Looked After by Local Authorities in the Different Countries of the United Kingdom*. London: DfE.

Department for Education (2010b) *The Children Act 1989 Guidance and Regulations, Vol. 2: Care planning, placement and case review*. London: DfE. Access at: www.webarchive.nationalarchives.gov.uk/20130401151715 and www.education.gov.uk/publications/eOrderingDownload/DCSF-00185-2010.pdf

Department for Education (2012a) *Children Looked After in England (including Adoption and Care Leavers) Year Ending 31 March 2012*. London: DfE. Access at: www.gov.uk/government/uploads/system/uploads/attachment_data/file/167451/sfr20-2012v2.pdf.pdf

Department for Education (2012b) *Adoption Scorecards*. London: DfE. Access at: www.education.gov.uk/childrenandyoungpeople/families/adoption/a00208817/adoption-scorecards

Department for Education (2012c) *Statistics – Intercountry adoption*. London: DfE. Access at: www.media.education.gov.uk/assets/files/pdf/i/intercountry%20adoptions%20table%20by%20country%202002%20to%202008.pdf

Department for Education (2012d) *Independent Review Mechanism – England*. Access at: www.independentreviewmechanism.org.uk

Department for Education (2013) Children looked after in England (including adoption and care leavers) year ending 31 March 2013. London: Department for Education. Access at: www.gov.uk/government/publications/children-looked-after-in-england-including-adoption

Department of Family Administration, Administrative Office of the Courts (2007) *Best Practices Manual, 3*. Annapolis, MD: Foster Care Court Improvement Project. Access at: www.cdm16064.contentdm.oclc.org/cdm/singleitem/collection/p266901coll7/id/3066/rec/7

Diehl D.C., Howse R.B. and Trivette C.M. (2006) 'Youth in foster care: developmental assets and attitudes towards adoption and mentoring', *Child & Family Social Work*, 16, pp. 81–92.

Dobbin S., Gatowski S. and Litchfield M. (2001) *The Essex County Child Welfare Mediation Program: Evaluation results and recommendations*. Reno, NV: Permanency Planning for Children Department. National Council of Juvenile and Family Court Judges. Technical Assistance Bulletin, V(4), viii. Access at: www.ncjrs.gov/pdffiles1/Digitization/194265NCJRS.pdf

Eckholm E. (2010) 'A determined quest to bring adoptive ties to foster teenagers', *New York Times*, 30 January. Access at: www.nytimes.com/2010/01/31/us/31adopt.html?pagewanted=all

Edwards L. (2007) 'Achieving timely permanency in child protection courts: the importance of frontloading the court process', *Juvenile and Family Court Journal*, 58:2, pp. 1–37. Access at: www.nccourts.org/Citizens/CPrograms/Improvement/Documents/frontloadingSpring07_Edwards.pdf

Edwards L. (2008) 'Family finding from a judicial perspective', *The Judges' Page* (October newsletter of National CASA Association and National Council of Juvenile and Family Court Judges). Access at: www.bit.ly/Kh2EZT

Eggertson L., MacDonald N., Baldassi C.L., Hébert P.C., Flegel K. and Ramsay J. (2009) 'Every child deserves a home', *Canadian Medical Association Journal*, 181:12, pp. 255–256.

Etter J. (1988) 'Use of mediated agreements in adoptions', *Mediation Quarterly*, 22, pp. 83–89.

Etter J. (1993) 'Levels of cooperation and satisfaction in 56 open adoptions', *Child Welfare*, 72, pp. 257–267.

Fahlberg V.I. (1994) *A Child's Journey Through Placement.* VK edition. London: BAAF.

Fahlberg V.I. (2012) *A Child's Journey Through Placement.* US edition. Philadelphia, PA: Jessica Kingsley Publishers.

Family Helper (2012) 'Canadians go abroad to adopt 1,946 children in 2010'. Access at: www.familyhelper.net/news/111027stats.html

Fanshel D. (1976) 'Status changes of children in foster care: final results of the Columbia University Longitudinal Study', *Child Welfare*, 55, pp. 143–171.

Fanshel D. (1978) 'Children discharged from foster care in New York City: where to – when – at what age?', *Child Welfare*, 57:8, pp. 467–483.

Farber M.L.Z., Timberlake E., Mudd H.P. and Cullen L. (2003) 'Preparing parents for adoption: an agency experience', *Child and Adolescent Social Work*, 20, pp. 175–196.

Farmer E. and Lutman E. (2010) *Case Management and Outcomes for Neglected Children Returned to their Parents: A five year follow-up study.* Bristol: University of Bristol, and London: Department for Education.

Federation of BC Youth in Care Networks (2010) *Belonging 4 Ever: Creating permanency for youth in and from care.* New Westminster, BC: FBCYICN. Access at: www.firstcallbc.org/pdfs/Transitions/2-permanency%20report.pdf

Festinger T. (1972) *Why Some Choose not to Adopt through Agencies.* New York: Metropolitan Applied Research Center.

Festinger T.B. (1983) *No one ever Asked us: A postscript to foster care.* New York: Columbia University Press.

Festinger T. (1986) *Necessary Risk: A study of adoptions and disrupted adoptive placements.* Washington, DC: Child Welfare League of America.

Festinger T. (2002) 'After adoption: dissolution or permanence?' *Child Welfare*, 81:3, pp. 525–533.

Festinger T. (2006) 'Adoption and after: adoptive parents' service needs', in Dore M.M. (ed.) *The Postadoption Experience: Adoptive families' service needs and service outcomes.* Washington, DC: Child Welfare League of America and Casey Family Services, pp. 17–44.

Festinger T. and Maza P. (2009) 'Displacement or post-adoption placement? A research note', *Journal of Public Child Welfare*, 3:3, pp. 275–286.

Festinger T. and Pratt R. (2003) *Retaining Interest: A look at New York City's recruitment of adoptive parents for waiting children*. Unpublished paper.

Fidler B.J., Bala N. and Saini M. (2013) *Children who Resist Post-Separation Parental Contact: A differential approach for legal and mental health professionals*, 262. Preview copy. Access at: www.bit.ly/TsMYuw

Fine D. (2000) *Adoptive Family needs Assessment: Final report*. Salem, OR: Oregon Department of Human Resources State Office of Services to Children and Families.

Fine D., Doran L., Berliner L. and Lieb R. (2006) 'Factors affecting recent adoption support levels in the Washington state adoption support program', in Dore M. M. (ed.), *The Postadoption Experience: Adoptive families' service needs and service outcomes*. Washington, DC: Child Welfare League of America and Casey Family Services, pp. 197–232.

Fisher P.A., Burraston B. and Pears K. (2005) 'The early intervention foster care program: permanency placement outcomes from a randomized trial', *Child Maltreatment*, 10:1, pp. 61–71.

Fisher P.A. and Chamberlain P. (2000) 'Multidimensional treatment foster care: a program for intensive parenting, family support, and skill building', *Journal of Emotional and Behavioral Disorders*, 8:3, pp. 155–164.

Fisher P.A. and Gunnar M.R. (2010) 'Early life stress as a risk factor for disease in adulthood', in Lanius R.A. Vermetten E. and Pain C. (eds), *The Impact of Early Life Trauma on Health and Disease*. Cambridge: Cambridge University Press., pp. 133–141.

Flango C., Flango V. and Rubin H. (1999) *How are Courts Coordinating Family Cases?*. Williamsburg, VA: National Center for State Courts.

Flicker Barbara (2005) *Best Practices in Child Protection Courts*, 14. Washington, DC: American Bar Association. Access at: www.apps. americanbar.org/child/rclji//bestpractices.doc

Folman R. (1998) '"I was tooken": how children experience removal from their parents preliminary to placement into foster care', *Adoption Quarterly*, 2:2, pp. 7–35.

Ford M. and Kroll J. (2005) *A Family for Every Child: Strategies to achieve permanence for older foster children and youth*. North American Council on Adoptable Children. Baltimore, MD. Access at: www.aecf.org/upload/ publicationfiles/ff3622h1188.pdf

Fostering Connections to Success and Increasing Adoptions Act of 2008, Public Law 110-351, US Statutes at Large 122 (2008): 3949.

Frame L., Berrick J.D. and Coakley J.F. (2006) 'Essential elements of implementing a system of concurrent planning', *Child & Family Social Work*, 11, pp. 357–367.

Franke T., Bagdasaryan S. and Furman W. (2009) 'A multivariate analysis of training, education, and readiness for public child welfare practice', *Children and Youth Services Review*, 31, pp. 1330–1336.

Frasch K.M., Brooks D. and Barth R.P. (2000) 'Openness and contact in foster care adoptions: an eight-year follow-up', *Family Relations*, 49, pp. 435–446.

Fratter J. (1996) *Adoption with Contact: Implications for policy and practice.* London: BAAF.

Freddie Mac Foundation (2012) 'Wednesday's Child'. Access at: www. freddiemacfoundation.org/ourwork/founwedn.html

Freundlich M. and Avery R.J. (2005) 'Planning for permanency for youth in congregate care', *Children and Youth Services Review*, 27:2, pp. 115–134.

Freundlich M., Heffernan M. and Jacobs J. (2004) 'Interjurisdictional placement of children in foster care', *Child Welfare*, 83, pp. 5–26.

Freundlich M., Gerstenzang S. and Holtan M. (2007) 'Websites featuring children waiting for adoption: a cross-country review', *Adoption & Fostering*, 31:2, pp. 6–16.

Frey L., Greenblatt S. and Brown J. (2005) *A Call to Action: An integrated approach to youth permanency and preparation for adulthood.* New Haven, CT: Casey Family Services. Access at: www.caseyfamilyservices.org

Fuller T.L., Bruhn C., Cohen L., Lis M., Rolock N. and Sheridan K. (2006) *Supporting Adoptions and Guardianships in Illinois: An analysis of subsidies, services and spending.* Urbana-Champaign, IL: University of Illinois. Access at: www.cfrc.illinois.edu/pubs/rp_200600201_SupportingAdoptionsAnd GuardianshipInIllinoisAnAnalysisOfSubsidiesServicesAndSpending.pdf

Furman E. (1974) *A Child's Parent Dies.* Yale: Yale University Press.

Gates G.J., Badgett M.V. Macomber J.E. and Chambers K. (2007) *Adoption and Foster Care by Gay and Lesbian Parents in the United States.* Technical report issued jointly by the Williams Institute (Los Angeles, CA) and the Urban Institute (Washington, DC).

Gatowski S.I., Dobbin S.A., Litchfield M. and Oetjen J. (2005) *Mediation in*

Child Protection Cases: An evaluation of the Washington, D.C. family court child protection mediation program. Reno, NV: National Council of Juvenile and Family Court Judges.

Geen R. (2003) *Who will Adopt the Foster Care Children Left Behind? The Urban Institute. Caring for Children Brief No. 2.* Access at: www.urban.org/url.cfm?ID=310809

Geen R., Malm K. and Katz J. (2004) 'A study to inform the recruitment and retention of general applicant adoptive parents', *Adoption Quarterly*, 7:4, pp. 1–28.

Generations United (2010) *Factsheet: Grandfamilies-Subsidized guardianship programs.* Access at: www.gu.org/RESOURCES/Publication/tabid/157/ItenID/16/Default.aspx.

Gerstenzang S. and Freundlich M. (2005) 'A critical assessment of concurrent planning in New York State', *Adoption Quarterly*, 8:4, pp. 1–22.

Gibbs D., Barth R.P. and Houts R. (2005) 'Family characteristics and dynamics among families receiving post-adoption services', *Families in Society*, 86, pp. 520–532.

Gibbs D., Siebenaler K. and Barth R.P. (2002) *Assessing the Field of Post-Adoption Services: Family needs, program models, and evaluation issues. Summary report.* Washington, DC: US Department of Health and Human Services, Office of the Assistant Secretary for Planning and Evaluation. Access at: www.aspe.hhs.gov/hsp/post-adoption01/summary/report.pdf

Gilbert N. (1997) *Combating Child Abuse: Comparative perspectives on reporting systems and placement trends.* London: Oxford University Press.

Gilbert N. (2012) 'A comparative study of child welfare systems: abstract orientations and concrete results', *Children and Youth Services Review*, 34:3, pp. 532–536.

Gilbert N., Parton N. and Skivenes M. (2011) *Child Protection Systems: International trends and orientations.* London: Oxford University Press.

Gilles T. and Kroll J. (1991) *Barriers to Same Race Placement.* St Paul, MN: NACAC.

Gilmore U., Oppenheim E. and Pollack D. (2004) 'Delays in the interstate foster and adoption home study process', *UC Davis Journal of Juvenile Law and Policy*, 8:1, pp. 55–94.

Goldstein J., Freud A. and Solnit A.J. (1973) *Beyond the Best Interests of the Child.* New York: The Free Press.

Goldstein J., Freud A. and Solnit A.J. (1979) *Before the Best Interests of the Child*. New York: The Free Press.

Goodman D. (2012) Personal communication with Susan Smith, 12 September.

Gough P., Shlonsky A. and Dudding P. (2009) 'An overview of the child welfare system in Canada', *International Journal of Child Health and Development*, 2:3, pp. 357–372.

Grimshaw R. and Sinclair R. (1997) *Planning to Care: Regulation, procedure, and practice under the Children Act, 1989*. London: National Children's Bureau.

Grotevant H.D. (1997) 'Coming to terms with adoption: the construction of identity from adolescence into adulthood', *Adoption Quarterly*, 1, pp. 3–27.

Grotevant H.D., Dunbar N., Kohler J.K. and Esau A.L. (2007) 'Adoptive identity: how contexts within and beyond the family shape developmental pathways', in Javier R.A., Baden A.L., Biafora R.A. and Comacho-Gingerich A. (eds), *Handbook of Adoption*. Thousand Oaks, CA: Sage, pp. 77–89.

Grotevant H.D. and McRoy R.G. (1998) *Openness in Adoption: Exploring family connections*. London: Sage Publications.

Grotevant H.D., Perry, Y.V. and McRoy, R.G. (2005) 'Openness in adoption: outcomes for adolescents within their adoptive kinship networks', in Brodzinsky D.M. and Palacios J. (eds), *Psychological Issues in Adoption: Research and practice*. Westport, CT: Praeger, pp. 167–180.

Grotevant H.D., Rueter M., Von Korff L. and Gonzalez C. (2011) 'Post-adoption contact, adoption communicative openness, and satisfaction with contact as predictors of externalizing behavior in adolescence and emerging adulthood', *Journal of Child Psychology and Psychiatry*, 52:5, pp. 529–536.

Groza V. and Rosenberg K.F. (1998) *Clinical and Practice Issues in Adoption*. Westport, CT: Bergin and Garvey.

Groze V. (1996) *Successful Adoptive Families: A longitudinal study of special needs adoption*. Westport, CT: Praeger.

Groze V., Young J. and Corcoran-Rumppe K. (1991) *Post Adoption Resources for Training, Networking and Evaluation Services (PARTNERS): Working with special needs adoptive families in stress*. Washington, DC: Four Oaks, Inc., for the Department of Health and Human Services, Adoption Opportunities.

Hafford C. and DeSantis J. (2009) *Evaluation of the Court Teams for*

Maltreated Infants and Toddlers: Final report. Arlington, VA: James Bell Associates. Access at: www.zerotothree.org/maltreatment/safe-babies-court-team/court-team-maltreated-infants-and-toddlers_final-report_jb.pdf

Hanna M.D. (2008) 'Preparing school age children for adoption', *Adoption Quarterly*, 10:2, pp. 1–32.

Hansen B. and Hansen M.E. (2006) 'The economics of adoption of children from foster care', *Child Welfare*, 85:3, pp. 559–583.

Hansen M.E. (2005) *Using Subsidies to Promote the Adoption of Children from Foster Care*. American University Department of Economics Working Paper Series No. 2005–15. Access at: www.american.edu/academic.depts/cas/econ/workingpapers/2005-15.pdf

Hansen M.E. (2006) *The Value of Adoption*. Working Paper Series No. 2006–15. Washington, DC: American University, Department of Economics. Access at: www.w.american.edu/cas/economics/repec/amu/workingpapers/1506.pdf

Hansen M.E. (2007) 'Using subsidies to promote the adoption of children from foster care', *Journal of Family and Economic Issues*, 28:3, pp. 377–393.

Hansen M.E. (2012) Personal communication with Susan Smith, 7 July. Data extracted from the AFCARS Adoption File for FY 2010, version 1. AFCARS data made available by the National Data Archive on Child Abuse and Neglect, Cornell University, Ithaca, NY, and used with permission. Data originally collected by the US Children's Bureau.

Hart A. and Luckock B. (2004) *Developing Adoption Support and Therapy: New approaches for practice*. London: Jessica Kingsley Publishers.

Hart A. and Luckock B. (2006) 'Core principles and therapeutic objectives for therapy with adoptive and permanent foster families', *Adoption & Fostering*, 30:2, pp. 29–42.

Heart Gallery (2013) *Heart Gallery of America Website*. Access at: www.heartgalleryofamerica.org/

Helm A., Peltier J. and Scovotti C. (2006) 'Understanding the antecedents to recruiting foster care and adoptive parents: a comparison of white and African-American families', *Health Marketing Quarterly*, 22:4, pp. 109–129.

Henney S.M., Ayers-Lopez S., McRoy R.G. and Grotevant H.D. (2007) 'Evolution and resolution: birthmothers' experience of grief and loss at different levels of adoption openness', *Journal of Social and Personal Relationships*, 24:6, pp. 875–889.

Henry D.L. (2005) 'The 3-5-7 model: preparing children for permanency', *Children and Youth Services Review*, 27, pp. 197–212.

Herzog E., Sudia C., Harwood J. and Newcomb C. (1971) *Families for Black Children*. Washington, DC: US Government Printing Office.

Hill-Tout J., Pithouse A. and Lowe K. (2003) 'Training foster carers in a preventative approach to children who challenge: mixed messages from research', *Adoption & Fostering*, 27:1, pp. 47–56.

Hilpern K. (2011) 'Adoption parties: are they a solution to the adoption crisis?' *The Guardian*, 30 September. Access at: www.guardian.co.uk/society/2011/oct/01/adoption-parties-solution-to-placement-crisis

Hollingsworth L.D. (2002) 'A content analysis of reasons given by African American adoption-seekers regarding their decision not to adopt', *African American Research Perspectives*, 7:1, pp. 226–236.

Holtan B. (2004) 'Defining permanence for older kids', *Fostering Families Today*, July/August, p. 35.

Houston D.M. and Kramer L. (2008) 'Meeting the long-term needs of families who adopt children out of foster care: a three-year follow-up study', *Child Welfare*, 87:4, pp. 145–170.

Howard J.A. (2006) 'Should one size fit all? An examination of post-adoption functioning and needs of kin, foster, and matched adoptive families', in DeVore M.M. (ed.) *Innovations in Post Sdoption Practice and Policy*. Washington, DC: Child Welfare League of America.

Howard J.A. and Berzin S. (2011) *Never too Old: Achieving permanency and sustaining connections for older youth in foster care*. New York: Donaldson Adoption Institute.

Howard J.A. and Smith S.L. (1995) *Adoption Preservation in Illinois: Results of a four year study*. Normal, IL: Illinois State University.

Howard J.A. and Smith S.L. (2003) *After Adoption: The needs of adopted youth*. Washington, DC: Child Welfare League of America.

Howard J.A., Smith S.L. and Ryan S.D. (2004) 'A comparative study of child welfare adoptions with other types of adopted children and birth children', *Adoption Quarterly*, 7:3, pp. 1–30.

Howard J.A., Smith S.L., Zosky D.L. and Woodman K. (2006) 'A comparison of subsidized guardianship and child welfare adoptive families served by the Illinois adoption and guardianship preservation program', *Journal of Social Service Research*, 32:3, pp. 123–134.

Howe D. and Steele M. (2004) 'Contact in cases in which children have been traumatically abused or neglected by their birth parents', in Neil E. and Howe D. (eds) *Contact in Adoption and Permanent Foster Care: Research, theory and practice.* London: BAAF, pp. 203–23.

Hudson C.G., Cedeno-Zamor P., Springer C., Rosenthal M., Silvia S.C., Alexander S. and Kowal L. (2006) 'The development of postadoption services in Massachusetts', in Dore M.M. (ed.) *The Postadoption Experience: Adoptive families' service needs and service outcomes.* Washington, DC: Child Welfare League of America, pp. 135–157.

Hughes D. (2007) *Attachment-Focused Family Therapy.* New York: W. W. Norton.

HUMA Committee (2012) *Federal Support Measures to Adoptive Parents: Report of the Standing Committee on Human Resources, Skills and Social Development and the Status of Persons with Disabilities.* Ottawa, ON: Parliament of Canada.

Hutchinson D. (2011) *Looked After Children Talking to ChildLine.* London: NSPCC. Access at: www.nspcc.org.uk/Inform/publications/casenotes/clcase noteslookedafterchildren_wdf80622.pdf

Iglehart A. (1994) 'Kinship foster care: placement, service, and outcome issues', *Child Youth Service Review,* 16:1–2, pp. 107–122.

Jackson S. (ed) (2014) *Pathways through Education for Young People in Care,* London: BAAF.

James S. (2004) 'Why do foster care placements disrupt? An investigation of reasons for placement change in foster care', *Social Service Review,* 78, pp. 601–627.

Johnson M. and Howard J. (2008) *Putting the Pieces Together: Lifebook work with children* (DVD). Rock Island, IL: Lutheran Social Services of Illinois.

Jones A.S. and Wells S.J. (2008) *PATH/Wisconsin – Bremer Project. Preventing Placement Disruption in Foster Care.* Minneapolis, MN: University of Minnesota Regents. Access at: www.cehd.umn.edu/ssw/cascw/attributes/PDF/publications/Path_BremerReport.pdf

Jones R., Everson-Hock E.S., Papaioannou D., Guillaume L., Goyder E., Chilcott J., Cooke J., Payne N., Duenas A., Sheppard L.M. and Swann C. (2011) 'Factors associated with outcomes for looked-after children and young people: a correlates review of the literature', *Child: Care, Health and Development,* 37:5, pp. 613–622.

Kaniuk J., Steele M. and Hodges J. (2004) 'Research on a longitudinal research project, exploring the development of attachments between older, hard-to-place children and their adopters over the first two years of placement', *Adoption & Fostering*, 28, pp. 61–67.

Kat L. (1999) 'Concurrent planning: benefits and pitfalls', *Child Welfare*, 78:1, pp. 71–87.

Kendrick A. and Mapstone E. (1991) 'Who decides?: Child care reviews in two Scottish social work departments', *Children & Society*, 5:2, pp. 165–181.

Kenrick J. (2010) 'Concurrent planning (2): "The rollercoaster of uncertainty"', *Adoption & Fostering*, 34:2, pp. 38–48.

Kentucky Court of Justice (2011) *Family Court*. Frankfort, KY: Kentucky Court of Justice. Access at: www.courts.ky.gov/circuitcourt/familycourt/

Kinniburgh K. and Blaustein M. (2006) 'A.R.C.: Attachment, self-regulation and competency. A comprehensive framework for intervention with complexly traumatized youth', Unpublished manuscript.

Kirton D., Beecham J. and Ogilvie K. (2006) 'Adoption by foster carers: a profile of interest and outcomes', *Child & Family Social Work*, 11, pp. 139–146.

Kliman G.W. and Zelman A.B. (1996) 'Use of a personal life history book in the treatment of foster children: an attempt to enhance stability of foster care placements', in Zelman A.B. (ed.) *Early Intervention with High-Risk Children: Freeing prisoners of circumstance*. Northvale, NJ: Jason Aronson, Inc.

Koh E. (2010) 'Permanency outcomes of children in kinship and non-kinship foster care: testing the external validity of kinship effects', *Children and Youth Services Review*, 32:3, pp. 389–398.

Koh E. and Testa M.F. (2008) 'Propensity score matching of children in kinship and nonkinship foster care: do permanency outcomes still differ?' *Social Work Research*, 32:2, pp. 105–116.

Kohler J.K., Grotevant H.D. and McRoy R.G. (2002) 'Adopted adolescents' preoccupation with adoption: impact of adoptive family dynamics', *Journal of Marriage and the Family*, 64, pp. 93–104.

Lahti M. and Detgen A. (2004) *State of Maine IV-E Child Welfare Demonstration Project: Maine adoption guides project, Final evaluation report*. Portland, ME: Muskie School of Public Service, University of Southern Maine. Access at: www.muskie.usm.maine.edu/Publications/ipsi/maine_adopt_guides_05.pdf

Lahti M.F. (2006) 'Maine adoption guides: a study of postlegalization services', in Dore M.M. (ed.) *The Postadoption Experience: Adoptive families' service needs and service outcomes*. Washington, DC: Child Welfare League of America, pp. 111–134.

LaNoue S. and Nienheis P. (2006) *The Openness to Permanency Scale*. Nashville, TN: Bethany Christian Services.

Lansdown R., Burnell A. and Allen M. (2007) 'Is it that they won't do it, or is it that they can't? Executive functioning and children who have been fostered and adopted', *Adoption & Fostering*, 31:2, pp. 44–53.

Lawrence C.R., Carlson E.A. and Egeland B. (2006) 'The impact of foster care on development', *Development and Psychopathology*, 18, pp. 57–76.

Laws S., Wilson R. and Rabindrakumar S. (2012) *Concurrent Planning Study – Interim report*. London: Coram. Access at: www.coram.org.uk/assets/downloads/Coram_Concurrent_Planning_Interim_Report_final.pdf

Leathers S.J. (2002) 'Foster children's behavioral disturbance and detachment from caregivers and community institutions', *Children and Youth Services Review*, 24:4, pp. 239–268.

Leathers S.J. (2003) 'Parental visiting, conflicting allegiances, and emotional and behavioral problems among foster children', *Family Relations*, 52:1, pp. 53–63.

Leathers S.J. (2006) 'Placement disruption and negative placement outcomes among adolescents in long-term foster care: the role of behavior problems', *Child Abuse and Neglect*, 30, pp. 307–324.

LeBeau M. (2013) Personal communication with Susan Smith, 24 April.

Ledesma K. (2012) Personal communication with Susan Smith, 26 October.

Ledesma K., Pettaway S., McRoy R., Madden E. and Cody P.A. (2011) 'Engaging African American communities and organizations to support foster care and adoption for children in the child welfare system', *The Roundtable*, 25:1, pp. 1–3. Southfield, MI: National Resource Center for Adoption.

Lenerz K., Gibbs D. and Barth R.P. (2006) 'Postadoption services: a study of program participants, services, and outcomes', in Dore M.M. (ed.) *The Postadoption Experience: Adoptive families' service needs and service outcomes*. Washington, DC: Child Welfare League of America, pp. 95–110.

Leung P. and Erich S. (2002) 'Family functioning of adoptive children with special needs: implications of familial supports and child characteristics', *Children and Youth Services Review*, 24:11, pp. 799–816.

Lewis E.E., Dozier M., Ackerman J. and Sepulveda-Kozakowski S. (2007) 'The effect of placement instability on adopted children's inhibitory control abilities and oppositional behavior', *Developmental Psychology*, 43:6, pp. 1415–1427.

LGBT Foster Care Project (2012) *The Lesbian, Gay, Bisexual and Transgender Community Center*. Access at: www.gaycenter.org/families/fostercareproject

LGBT Fostering and Adoption Week (2013) *UK website*. Access at: www.lgbtadoptfosterweek.org.uk/

Lloyd E.C. and Barth R.P. (2011) 'Developmental outcomes after five years for foster children returned home, remaining in care, or adopted', *Children and Youth Services Review*, 33, pp. 1383–1391.

Logan J. (2010) 'Preparation and planning for face-to-face contact after adoption: the experience of adoptive parents in a UK study', *Child & Family Social Work*, 15, pp. 315–324.

Logan J. and Smith C. (1999) 'Adoption and direct post-adoption contact', *Adoption & Fostering*, 23:4, pp. 58–59.

Logan J. and Smith C. (2004) 'Direct post-adoption contact: experiences of birth and adoptive families', in Neil E. and Howe D. (eds) *Contact in Adoption and Permanent Foster Care: Research, theory and practice*. London: BAAF.

Louisell M.J. (2004) *Model Programs for Youth Permanency*. Oakland, CA: National Center for Permanent Family Connectedness. Access at: www.senecacenter.org/files/cpyp/Files/ModelPrograms.pdf

Love S., Koob J. and Hill L. (2008) 'The effects of using community mental health practitioners to treat foster children: implications for child welfare planners', *Scientific Review of Mental Health Practice*, 6:1, pp. 31–39.

Lyons J.S. (2009) *Communimetrics: A theory of measurement for human service enterprises*. New York: Springer.

Macomber J.E., Zielewski E.H., Chambers K. and Geen R. (2005) *Foster Care Adoption in the United States: An analysis of interest in adoption and a review of state recruitment strategies*. Washington, DC: Urban Institute. Access at: www.urban.org/publications/411254.html

Mallon G.P. (2005) *Toolkit No. 3: Facilitating permanency for youth*. Washington, DC: CWLA Press. Access at: www.cwla.org/pubs

Mallon G.P. (2011) *Unpacking the No of Permanency for Older Adolescents.* (PowerPoint Presentation). New York: National Resource Center for Permanency and Family Connections. Access at: www.hunter.cuny.edu/socwork/nrcfcpp/info_services/download/Florida.unpacking.11.08.pdf

Malm K. and Allen T. (2011) *Family Finding: Does implementation differ when serving different child welfare populations?* Washington, DC: Child Trends. Access at: www.childtrends.org/Files/Child_Trends-2011_10_17_RB_FamilyFinding.pdf

Malm K., Vandivere S., Allen T., DeVooght K., Ellis R., McKlindon A., Smollar J., Williams E. and Zinn A. (2011a) *Evaluation Report Summary: The Wendy's Wonderful Kids initiative.* Washington, DC: Child Trends. Access at: www.davethomasfoundation.org/wp-content/uploads/2011/10/Evaluation_Report_Summary.pdf

Malm K., Vandivere S. and McKlindon A. (2011b) *Children Adopted from Foster Care: Adoption agreements, adoption subsidies, and other post-adoption supports.* ASPE Research Brief. Washington, DC: Office of the Assistant Secretary for Planning and Evaluation, US Department of Health and Human Services. Access at: www.aspe.hhs.gov/hsp/09/nsap/brief2/rb.shtml

Martin M.H., Barbee A.P., Antle B.F. and Sar B. (2002) 'Expedited permanency planning: evaluation of the Kentucky Adoption Opportunities Project', *Child Welfare*, 81:2, pp. 203–224.

Mason J. and Williams C. (1985) 'The adoption of minority children: issues in developing law and policy', in Segal E. and Hardin M. (eds) *Adoption of Children with Special Needs: Issues in law and policy.* Washington, DC: American Bar Association, pp. 81–93.

Massachusetts Adoption Resource Exchange (2012) *Massachusetts Adoption Resource Exchange Statistics Report FY 2011* (July 1, 2010–June 30, 2011).

Maynard J. (2005) 'Permanency mediation: a path to open adoption for children in out-of-home care', *Child Welfare*, 84:4, pp. 507–526.

Maza P.L. (1999) 'Recent data on the number of adoptions of foster children', *Adoption Quarterly*, 3:2, pp. 71–8.

Maza P. (2006) 'Patterns of relative adoption', *The Roundtable*, 20:1, pp. 7–9.

Maza P.L. (2009) 'A comparative examination of foster youth who did and did not achieve permanency', in Kerman B., Freundlich M. and Maluccio A. N. (eds) *Achieving Permanence for Older Children and Youth in Foster Care.* New York: Columbia University Press, pp. 32–39.

McDonald T., Propp J. and Murphy K. (2001) 'The postadoption experience: child, parent, and family adjustment to adoption', *Child Welfare*, 80:1, pp. 71–94.

McGlone K., Santos L., Kazama L., Fong R. and Mueller C. (2002) 'Psychological stress in adoptive parents of special needs children', *Child Welfare*, 81:2, pp. 151–171.

McKay K. and Ross L.E. (2011) 'Current practices and barriers to the provision of post-placement support: a pilot study from Toronto, Ontario, Canada', *British Journal of Social Work*, 41, pp. 57–73.

McRoy R.G. (1999) *Special Needs Adoptions: Practice issues*. New York: Garland Publishing.

McRoy R.G. (2007) *Barriers and Success Factors in Adoptions from Foster Care: Perspectives of families and staff*. Baltimore, MD: AdoptUSKids, US Children's Bureau. Access at: www.adoptuskids.org/_assets/files/NRCRRFAP/resources/barriers-and-success-factors-family-and-staff-perspectives.pdf

McRoy R.G., Oglesby Z. and Grape H. (1997) 'Achieving same-race adoptive placement for African American children: culturally sensitive practice approaches', *Child Welfare*, 76:1, pp. 85–104.

McWey L.M., Acock A. and Porter B.E. (2010) 'The impact of continued contact with biological parents upon the mental health of children in foster care', *Children and Youth Services Review*, 32, pp. 1338–1345.

Mehaffey T. (2012) 'Task force study examines ways to make Iowa courts more efficient, affordable', *The Gazette*. Access at: www.thegazette.com/2012/03/15/task-force-study-examines-ways-to-make-iowa-courts-more-efficient-affordable

Meredith T., Baldwin K. and Johnson S. (2010) *The Georgia Cold Case Project Executive Summary*. Atlanta, GA: Applied Research Services, Inc. Access at: www.w2.georgiacourts.org/cj4c/files/The%20Georgia%20Cold%20Case%20Project_2010%20Executive%20Summary%282%29.pdf

Minnis M. and Walker F. (2012) *The Experiences of Fostering and Adoption Processes: The views of children and young people: Literature review and gap analysis*. Slough: National Federation for Educational Research.

Monck E., Reynolds J. and Wigfall V. (2004) 'Using concurrent planning to establish permanency for looked after young children', *Child & Family Social Work*, 9:4, pp. 321–331.

Mor Barak M.E., Levin A., Nissly J.A. and Lane C.J. (2006) 'Why do they leave? Modeling child welfare workers' turnover intentions', *Children and Youth Services Review*, 28, pp. 548–577.

Morgan R. (2006) *About Adoption: A children's views report.* Newcastle upon Tyne: Office of the Children's Rights Director, Commission for Social Care Inspection. Access at: www.rights4me.org/~/media/Library%20Documents/Reports/Reports%202006/Report%20About%20Adoption.pdf

Morgan R. (2010) *Before Care: A report of children's views on entering care by the Children's Rights Director for England.* London: Ofsted. Access at: www.ofsted.gov.uk/resources/care

North American Council on Adoptable Children (2002a) *Who should Run a Support Group: Parent-run vs. agency-run groups.* St Paul, MN: NACAC. Access at: www.nacac.org/parentgroups/whoruns.html

North American Council on Adoptable Children (2002b) *Starting and Nurturing Adoptive Parent Groups: A guide for leaders.* St Paul, MN: NACAC. Access at: www.nacac.org/parentgroups/starting.pdf

North American Council on Adoptable Children (2009a) *It's Time to Make Older Child Adoption a Reality.* St Paul, MN: NACAC.

North American Council on Adoptable Children (2009b) *Developing a Parent-to-Parent Support Network.* St Paul, MN: NACAC. Access at: www.nacac.org/adoptalk/parent2parentnetwork.pdf

North American Council on Adoptable Children (2012) *Adoption Subsidy Website: US state profiles and Canada provincial profiles.* St Paul, MN: NACAC. Access at: www.nacac.org/adoptionsubsidy/adoptionsubsidy.html

National Association of Counsel for Children (2001) *NACC Recommendations for Representation of Children in Abuse and Neglect Cases.* Denver, CO: National Association of Counsel for Children. Access at: www.bit.ly/SOR09Q

National Center for Youth Law (2012) *Foster Care Litigation Docket: All cases printout.* Access at: www.youthlaw.org/fileadmin/ncyl/youthlaw/publications/Foster-Care-Lit-Docket-NCYL-20120210.pdf

National Center for State Courts (2006) *Justice for Children. Changing lives by changing systems: A national call to action.* Williamsburg, VA: National Center for State Courts. Access at: www.aecf.org/upload/PublicationFiles/CallToActionInside.pdf

National Conference of State Legislatures (2007) *Delivering on the Promise: Promoting court capacity to improve outcomes for abused and neglected children*. Denver, CO: National Conference of State Legislatures. Access at: www.ncsl.org/Portals/1/documents/cyf/deliveringpromise.pdf

National Council of Juvenile and Family Court Judges (NCJFCJ) (2012) *Project ONE Key Principles, 1.* New Orleans, LA: *NCJFCJ Board of Trustees.* Access at: www.ncjfcj.org/sites/default/files/Project_ONE_Key_Principles_July_2012.pdf

National Data Archive on Child Abuse and Neglect (2012) *Adoption and Foster Care Analysis and Reporting System* (AFCARS). Access at: www.ndacan.cornell.edu/Ndacan/Datasets/Abstracts/DatasetAbstract_AFCARS_General.html

National Resource Center for Adoption (2010) *Youth Permanency Cluster: Grantee projects and grantee resources.* Access at: www.nrcadoption.org/resources/ypc/grantee-projects/ and www.nrcadoption.org/resources/ypc/grantee-resources/

National Resource Center for Adoption (2012) *Adoption Competency Curriculum: Child/youth assessment and preparation; Participants' handouts.* Access at: www.nrcadoption.org/pdfs/acc/PH%20-%20Child%20Assessment%20and%20Preparation%203-10.pdf

National Resource Center for Foster Care and Permanency Planning and Casey Family Services (2004) *Permanence for Young People Framework.* Access at: www.hunter.cuny.edu/socwork/nrcfcpp/downloads/permanency/Permanency_Framework.pdf

National Resource Center for Permanency and Family Connections (NRCPFC) (2010) *A Web-Based Concurrent Planning Toolkit.* Access at: www.nrcpfc.org/cpt/introduction.htm

Needell B. and Gilbert N. (1997) 'Child welfare and the extended family', in Berrick J.D., Barth R.P. and Gilbert N. (eds) *Child Welfare Research Review, Volume II.* New York: Columbia University Press.

Neil E. (2002) 'Contact after adoption: the role of agencies in making and supporting plans', *Adoption & Fostering*, 26:1, pp. 25–38.

Neil E. (2003) 'Accepting the reality of adoption: birth relatives' experiences of face-to-face contact', *Adoption & Fostering*, 27:2, pp. 32–43.

Neil E. (2004a) 'The "contact after adoption" study: indirect contact', in Neil E. and Howe D. (eds.) *Contact in Adoption and Permanent Foster Care: Research, theory and practice.* London: BAAF, pp. 46–64.

Neil E. (2004b) 'The "contact after adoption" study: Face-to-face contact', in Neil E. and Howe D. (eds) *Contact in Adoption and Permanent Foster Care: Research, theory and practice.* London: BAAF, pp. 65–84.

Neil E. (2009) 'Post-adoption contact and openness in adoptive parents' minds: consequences for children's development', *British Journal of Social Work,* 39:1, pp. 5–23.

Neil E. and Howe D. (2004) *Contact in Adoption and Permanent Foster Care: Research, theory and practice.* London: BAAF.

Newton R.R., Litrownik A.J. and Landsverk J.A. (2000) 'Children and youth in foster care: disentangling the relationship between problem behaviors and number of placements', *Child Abuse and Neglect,* 24, pp. 1363–1374.

NJARCH (2012) Website operated by Children's Aid and Family Services, Inc. Access at: www.njarch.org/

Nolan-Haley J.M. (1999) 'Informed consent in mediation: a guiding principle for truly educated decision making', *Notre Dame Law Review,* 74, pp. 775–840.

Noordegraaf M., Ninjnattan C. and Elders E. (2009) 'Assessing parents for adoptive parenthood: institutional reformulations of biographical notes', *Children and Youth Services Review,* 31, pp. 89–96.

Northcutt F.S. and Jeffries W. (2012) 'Family finding and engagement beyond the bench: working across international borders', *Juvenile and Family Court Journal,* 63:1, pp. 31–47.

NSCAW (2005) *National Survey of Child and Adolescent Well-Being. CPS Sample Component: Wave I Data Analysis Report.* April 2005. Access at: www.acf.hhs.gov/programs/opre/abuse_neglect/nscaw/reports/cps_sample/cps_report_revised_090105.pdf

O'Brien K., Davis C.W., Morgan L.J., Rogg C.S. and Houston M. (2012) 'The impact of roundtables on permanency for youth in foster care', *Children and Youth Services Review,* 34:9, pp. 1915–1921.

Office for National Statistics (2010) *Adoptions in England and Wales.* London: ONS. Access at: www.ons.gov.uk/ons/rel/vsob1/adoptions-in-england-and-wales/2010/index.html

Office of Children and Families in the Courts (2009) *Three Month Court Reviews: Permanency practice initiatives.* Harrisburg, PA: Office of Children and Families in the Courts. Access at: www.ocfcpacourts.us/permanency-practice-initiatives/three-month-court-reviews

Office of Juvenile Justice and Delinquency Prevention (2009) *The Toolkit for Court Performance Measures in Child Abuse and Neglect Cases.* Washington, DC: US Department of Justice. Access at: www.ojjdp.gov/publications/courttoolkit.html

Ontario Ministry of Children and Youth Services, Toronto (ON) Ministry (2009) *Raising Expectations: Recommendations of the expert panel on infertility and adoption.* Access at: www.children.gov.on.ca/htdocs/English/documents/infertility/RaisingExpectationsEnglish.pdf

O'Reilly M. (2007) 'Finding families on the web: *Be My Parent* goes online in the UK', *Adoption & Fostering*, 31:2, pp. 17–21.

Ornelas L.A., Silverstein D.N. and Tan S. (2007) 'Effectively addressing mental health issues in permanency-focused child welfare practice', *Child Welfare*, 86:5, pp. 93–112.

Pardek J.T. (1984) 'Multiple placement of children in foster family care: an empirical study', *Children and Youth Services Review*, 18, pp. 589–601.

Partridge S., Hornby H. and McDonald T. (1986) *Learning from Adoption Disruption: Insights for practice.* Portland, ME: University of Southern Maine.

Pecora P.J., Jensen P.S., Romanelli L., Jackson L.J. and Ortiz A. (2009) 'Mental health services for children placed in foster care: an overview of current challenges', *Child Welfare*, 88:1, pp. 5–26.

Pedersen S. (2012) Personal communication with Susan Smith, 28 August.

Pennsylvania Office of Children and Families in the Courts (2009) *Permanency Practice Initiatives: Family finding (and other resources for court and other professionals on same site).* Access at: www.ocfcpacourts.us/permanency-practice-initiatives/family-finding

Performance and Innovation Unit (2000) *Adoption: Prime Minister's Review.* London: Cabinet Office. Access at: www.webarchive.nationalarchives.gov.uk/+/ and www.cabinetoffice.gov.uk/media/cabinetoffice/strategy/assets/adoption.pdf

Perry B. (1998) 'Homeostasis, stress, trauma, and adaptation: a neuro-developmental view of childhood trauma', *Child and Adolescent Psychiatric Clinics of North America*, 7:1, pp. 33–51.

Perry G., Daly M. and Kotler J. (2012) 'Placement stability in kinship and non-kin care: a Canadian study', *Children and Youth Services Review*, 34:2, pp. 460–465.

Peterson L. and Freundlich M. (2000) 'Wrongful adoption', *Children's Voice*, 1, pp. 20–23.

Pew Commission on Children in Foster Care (2004) *Fostering the Future: Safety, permanence and well-being for children in foster care.* Philadelphia, PA: The Pew Charitable Trusts. Access at: www.pewtrusts.org/uploadedFiles/wwwpewtrustsorg/Reports/Foster_care_reform/foster_care_final_051804.pdf

Pew Commission on Children in Foster Care (2009) *Progress on Court Reforms: Implementation of recommendations from the Pew Commission on Children in Foster Care.* Philadelphia, PA: The Pew Charitable Trusts. Access at: www.bit.ly/Q3F.sez

Potter C.C. and Klein-Rothschild S. (2002) 'Getting home on time: predicting timely permanency for young children', *Child Welfare*, 81:2, pp. 123–150.

Powers L.E., Geenen S., Powers J., Pommier-Satya S., Turner A., Dalton L.D., Drummond D. and Swank P. (2012) 'My life: effects of a longitudinal, randomized study of self-determination enhancement on the transition outcomes of youth in foster care and special education', *Children and Youth Services Review*, 34, pp. 2179–2187.

Prew C., Suter S. and Carrington J. (1990) *Post Adoption Family Therapy: A practice manual.* Salem, OR: Children's Services Division.

Puddy R.W. and Jackson Y. (2003) 'The development of parenting skills in foster parent training', *Children and Youth Services Review*, 25, pp. 987–1013.

Quinton D. and Selwyn J. (2009) 'Adoption as a solution to intractable parenting problems: evidence from two English studies', *Children and Youth Services Review*, 31, pp. 1119–1126.

Rees C. and Selwyn J. (2009) 'Non-infant adoption from care: lessons for safeguarding children', *Child: Care, health and development*, 35:4, pp. 561–567.

Reid-Johnson M. and Barth R.P. (2000) 'From placement to prison: the path to adolescent incarceration from child welfare supervised foster or group care', *Children and Youth Services Review*, 7, pp. 493–516.

Reilly T. and Platz L. (2003) 'Characteristics and challenges of families who adopt children with special needs: an empirical study', *Children and Youth Services Review*, 25, pp. 781–803.

Reilly T. and Platz L. (2004) 'Post-adoption service needs of families with special needs children: use, helpfulness, and unmet needs', *Journal of Social Service Research*, 30:4, pp. 51–67.

Reinhart M.K. (2012) 'Arizona's courts overloaded with CPS cases', *Arizona Republic*, 26 May. Access at: www.azcentral.com/arizonarepublic/news/articl es/2012/05/14/20120514arizona-cps-court-system-overloaded.html

Renne J. and Mallon G.P. (2005) 'Facilitating permanency for youth: The overuse of long-term foster care and the appropriate use of another planned permanent living arrangement as options for youth in foster care', in Mallon G.P. and Hess P.M. (eds) *Child Welfare for the Twenty-First Century*. New York: Columbia University Press, pp. 488–503.

Rodriguez P. and Meyer A.S. (1990) 'Minority adoptions and agency practices', *Social Work*, 35:6, pp. 528–531.

Rogg C.S., Davis C.W. and O'Brien K. (2009) *Permanency Roundtable Project: Process evaluation report*. ATLANTA, GA: Georgia Department of Human Services.

Rose R. and Philpot T. (2005) *The Child's Own Story: Life story work with traumatized children*. London: Jessica Kingsley Publishers.

Rosenthal J. (1993) 'Outcomes of adoption of children with special needs', *The Future of Children*, 3:1, pp. 77–88.

Rosenthal J.A. and Groze V.K. (1992) *Special Needs Adoptions: A study of intact families*. Westport, CT: Praeger.

Rosenthal J.A. and Groze V.K. (1994) 'A longitudinal study of special-needs adoptive families', *Child Welfare*, 73:6, pp. 689–706.

Rosenthal J.A., Groze V.K. and Morgan J. (1996) 'Services for families adopting children via public child welfare agencies: use, helpfulness, and need', *Children and Youth Services Review*, 18:1/2, pp. 163–182.

Rowe J. and Lambert L. (1973) *Children who Wait*. London: Association of British Adoption Agencies.

Rubin D.M., Alessandrini E.A., Mandell D.S., Localio A.R. and Hadley T. (2004) 'Placement stability and mental health costs for children in foster care', *Pediatrics*, 113:5, pp. 1336–1341.

Rubin D.M., Downes K.J., O'Reilly A.L.R., Mekonnen R., Luan X. and Localio R. (2008) 'Impact of kinship care on behavioral well-being for children in out-of-home care', *Archives of Pediatrics*, 162:6, pp. 550–556.

Rubin D.M., O'Reilly A.L., Luan X. and Localo A.R. (2007) 'The impact of placement stability on behavioral well-being for children in foster care', *Pediatrics*, 119:2, pp. 336–44.

Rueter M.A. and Koerner A.F. (2008) 'The effect of family communication patterns on adopted adolescent adjustment', *Journal of Marriage and Family*, 70, pp. 715–727.

Rumberger R. (2003) 'The causes and consequences of student mobility', *Journal of Negro Education*, 72, pp. 6–21.

Rushton A. and Dance C. (2006) 'The adoption of children from public care: a prospective study of outcome in adolescence,, *Journal of American Academy of Child and Adolescent Psychiatry*, 45:7, pp. 877–883.

Rushton A., Mayes D., Dance C. and Quinton D. (2003) 'Parenting late-placed children: the development of new relationships and the challenge of behavioral problems', *Clinical Child Psychology and Psychiatry*, 8:3, pp. 389–400.

Rushton A. and Monck E. (2009) *Enhancing Adoptive Parenting: A test of effectiveness*. London: BAAF.

Rushton A., Monck E., Leese M., McCrone P. and Sharac J. (2010) 'Enhancing adoptive parenting: a randomized controlled trial', *Clinical Child Psychology and Psychiatry*, 15:4, pp. 529–542.

Rushton A., Quinton D., Dance C. and Mayes D. (1998) 'Preparation for permanent placement: evaluating direct work with older children', *Adoption & Fostering*, 21:4, pp. 41–48.

Rutter M. and Sroufe L.A. (2000) 'Developmental psychopathology: concepts and challenges', *Development and Psychopathology*, 12, pp. 265–296.

Ryan J.P. and Testa M.F. (2005) 'Child maltreatment and juvenile delinquency: investigating the role of placement instability', *Children and Youth Services Review*, 27, pp. 227–249.

Ryan S.D., Hinterlong J., Hegar R.L. and Johnson L.B. (2010) 'Kin adopting kin: in the best interest of the children?' *Children and Youth Services Review*, 32, pp. 1631–1639.

Rycus J.S. and Hughes R.C. (1998) *Field Guide to Child Welfare, Volume IV: Placement and permanence*. Washington, DC: Child Welfare League of America.

Samuels G.M. (2008) *A Reason, a Season, or a Lifetime: Relational permanence among young adults with foster care backgrounds*. Chicago, IL: Chapin Hall Center for Children at the University of Chicago. Access at: www.chapinhall. org/sites/default/files/old_reports/415.pdf

Samuels G.M. (2009) 'Ambiguous loss of home: the experience of familial (im)permanence among young adults with foster care backgrounds', *Children and Youth Service Review*, 31:12, pp. 1229–1239.

Sar B.K. (2000) 'Preparation for adoptive parenthood with a special-needs child: role of agency preparation tasks', *Adoption Quarterly*, 3, pp. 63–80.

Sayers A. and Roach R. (2011) *Child Appreciation Days*. London: BAAF.

Schofield G. (2005) 'The voice of the child in family placement decision-making: a developmental model', *Adoption & Fostering*, 29:1, pp. 29–44.

Schofield G. and Beek M. (2005) 'Providing a secure base: parenting children in long-term foster family care', *Attachment & Human Development*, 7:1, pp. 3–25.

Schofield G. and Beek M. (2006) *Attachment Handbook for Foster Care and Adoption*. London: BAAF.

Schofield G. and Beek M. (2009) 'Growing up in foster care: providing a secure base through adolescence', *Child & Family Social Work*, 14:3, pp. 255–266.

Schofield G., Beek M. and Ward E. (2012) 'Part of the family: planning for permanence in long-term family foster care', *Children and Youth Services Review*, 34:1, pp. 244–253.

Schofield G., Biggart L., Ward E., Scaife V., Dodsworth J., Haynes A. and Carsson B. (2014) *Looked After Children and Offending: Reducing risk and promoting resilience*, London: BAAF

Schofield G. and Simmonds J. (2009) *The Child Placement Handbook: Research, policy and practice*. London: BAAF.

Schweigert M. (2012) 'In family court, it's 'one judge, one family'', *Lancaster Sunday News*. Access at: www.lancasteronline.com/article/local/607033_In-family-court--it-s--one-judge--one-family-.html

Sedlak A.J. (1991) *Study of Adoption Assistance Impact and Outcomes: Phase II report*. Rockville, MD: Westat.

Selwyn J. (2004) 'Placing older children in new families: changing patterns of contact', in Neil E. and Howe D. (eds.) *Contact in Adoption and Permanent Foster Care: Research, theory and practice*. London: BAAF, pp. 144–64.

Selwyn J. (2012) Personal communication with Susan Smith, 16 October.

Selwyn J., Frazer L. and Quinton D. (2006a) 'Paved with good intentions: the pathway to adoption and the costs of delay', *British Journal of Social Work*, 36, pp. 561–576.

Selwyn J. and Nandy S. (2012) 'Kinship care in the UK: using census data to estimate the extent of formal and informal care by relatives', *Child & Family Social Work*, advance online publication, 1–11.

Selwyn J. and Quinton D. (2004) 'Stability, permanence, outcomes and support: foster care and adoption compared', *Adoption & Fostering*, 28:4, pp. 6–15.

Selwyn J. and Sturgess W. (2002) 'Achieving permanency through adoption: following in US footsteps?', *Adoption & Fostering*, 26:3, pp. 40–49.

Selwyn, J., Sturgess W., Quinton D. and Baxter C. (2006b) *Costs and Outcomes of Non-Infant Adoptions*. London: BAAF.

Seneca Center (2012) *What did CYCP Accomplish?* Access at: www.senecacenter.org/familyconnectedness/about_CPYP

Shirk M. (2006) *Hunting for Grandma: Family finding strategy connects foster kids with relatives and permanent homes. Perspectives on youth.* Access at: www.ussearch.com/others/consumer/reunion/youthtoday.html

Siegel D.H. (2008) 'Open adoption and adolescence', *Families in Society*, 89:3, pp. 366–374.

Siegel D.H. and Smith S.L. (2012) *Openness in Adoption: From secrecy and stigma to knowledge and connections.* New York: Donaldson Adoption Institute. Access at: www.adoptioninstitute.org/research/2012_03_openness.php

Silverstein D.N. and Roszia S.K. (1999) 'Openness: a critical component of special needs adoption', *Child Welfare*, 78:5, pp. 637–651.

Simmel C. (2007) 'Risk and protective factors contributing to the longitudinal psychosocial well-being of adopted foster children', *Journal of Emotional and Behavioral Disorders*, 15:4, pp. 237–249.

Simmel C., Barth R.P. and Brooks D. (2007) 'Adopted foster youths' psychosocial functioning: a longitudinal perspective', *Child & Family Social Work*, 12, pp. 336–348.

Simmel C., Brooks D., Barth R.P. and Hinshaw S.P. (2001) 'Externalizing symptomatology among adoptive youth: prevalence and preadoption risk factors', *Journal of Abnormal Psychology*, 29:1, pp. 57–69.

Simmonds J. (2001) *First Steps in Becoming an Adoptive Parent: An evaluation of NAW 1999*. London: BAAF.

Sinclair I. (2005) *Fostering Now: Messages from research*. London: Jessica Kingsley Publishers.

Sinclair I., Baker C., Lee J. and Gibbs I. (2007) *The Pursuit of Permanence: A study of the English care system*, Quality Matters in Children's Services Series. London: Jessica Kingsley Publishers.

Sinclair I., Wilson K., and Gibbs I. (2000) *Supporting Foster Placements*. Social Work Research and Development Unit, University of York.

Smith B.D. (2003) 'After parental rights are terminated: Factors associated with exiting foster care', *Children and Youth Services Review*, 25:12, pp. 965–985.

Smith D.K., Stormshak E., Chamberlain P. and Bridges-Whaley R. (2001) 'Placement disruption in treatment foster care', *Journal of Emotional and Behavioral Disorders*, 9:3, pp. 200–205.

Smith S.L. (2006a) 'A study of the Illinois adoption/guardianship preservation program', in Dore M.M. (ed.) *The Postadoption Experience: Adoptive families' service needs and service outcomes*. Washington, DC: Child Welfare League of America, pp. 67–94.

Smith S.L. (2006b) 'The nature of effective adoption preservation services: a qualitative study', in Dore M.M. (ed.) *The Postadoption Experience: Adoptive families' service needs and service outcomes*. Washington, DC: Child Welfare League of America, pp. 159–196.

Smith S.L. (2010) *Keeping the Promise: The critical needs for post-adoption services to enable children and families to succeed*. New York: Donaldson Adoption Institute. Access at: www. adoptioninstitute.org/publications /2010_10_20_KeepingThePromise.pdf

Smith S.L. and Howard J.A. (1991) 'A comparative study of successful and disrupted adoptions', *Journal of Social Service Review*, 65, pp. 248–265.

Smith S.L. and Howard J.A. (1994) 'The impact of previous sexual abuse on children's adjustment in adoptive placement', *Social Work*, 39:5, pp. 491–501.

Smith S.L. and Howard J.A. (1999) *Promoting Successful Adoptions: Practice with troubled families*. Thousand Oaks, CA: Sage Publications.

Smith S.L., Howard J.A., Garnier P.C. and Ryan S.D. (2006) 'Where are we now? A post-ASFA examination of adoption disruption', *Adoption Quarterly*, 9:4, pp. 19–44.

Smith S.L., Howard J.A. and Monroe A.D. (2000) 'Issues underlying behavior problems in at-risk adopted children', *Children and Youth Services Review*, 22:7, pp. 539–562.

Smith S., McRoy R.G., Freundlich M. and Kroll J. (2008) *Finding Families for African American Children: The role of race and law in adoption from foster care*. New York: Donaldson Adoption Institute. Access at: www.adoptioninstitute.org.

Smith-McKeever T.C. (2005) 'Child behavioral outcomes in African American adoptive families', *Adoption Quarterly*, 7:4, pp. 29–56.

Snowden J., Leon S.C. and Sieracki J.H. (2008) 'Predictors of adoption out of foster care: a classification tree analysis', *Children and Youth Services Review*, 30, pp. 1318–1327.

Stack K. (2003) *Information Packet: Child welfare mediation*. National Resource. Center for Foster Care & Permanency Planning. Access at: www.hunter.cuny.edu/socwork/nrcfcpp/downloads/child-welfare-mediation.pdf

Staff I. and Fein E. (1995) 'Stability and change: initial findings in a study of treatment foster care placements', *Children and Youth Services Review*, 17:3, pp. 379–389.

Steele M., Hodges J., Kaniuk J., Hillman S. and Henderson K. (2003) 'Attachment representations and adoption: associations between maternal states of mind and emotion narratives in previously maltreated children', *Journal of Child Psychotherapy*, 29:2, pp. 187–205.

Stevens K. (2004) 'Meeting the challenge: youth as advocates', *Common Ground*, 18:2, a newsletter of the New England Association of Child Welfare Commissioners and Directors.

Sturgess W. and Selwyn J. (2007) 'Supporting the placements of children adopted out of care', *Clinical Child Psychology and Psychiatry*, 12, pp. 13–28.

Sullivan A. (1994) 'On transracial adoption', *Children's Voice*, 3:3, pp. 4–6.

Summers A., Wood S. and Russell J. (2011) *Assessing Efficiency and Workload Implications of the King County Mediation Pilot*. Reno, NV: National Council of Juvenile and Family Court Judges. Access at: www.journalofjuvjustice.org/JOJJ0101/article04.htm

Supreme Court of Ohio (1997) *Ohio Family Court Feasibility Study, 8*. Access at: www.supremecourt.ohio.gov/Boards/familyCourts/fcfeas.pdf

SWAN (2012) *SWAN Post-Permanency Services* (DVD) Pittsburgh, PA: Pennsylvania Department of Public Welfare Statewide Adoption and Permanency Network.

Swift K. (2011) 'Canadian child welfare: child protection and the status quo', in Gilbert N., Parton N. and Skivenes M. (eds) *Child Protection Systems: International trends and orientations*. London: Oxford University Press, pp. 36–59.

Sykes M. (2000) 'Adoption with contact: a study of adoptive parents and the impact of continuing contact with families of origin', *Adoption & Fostering*, 24:2, pp. 20–33.

Testa M. (1997) 'Kinship foster care in Illinois', in Berrick J.D., Barth R. and Gilbert N. (eds) *Child Welfare Research Review, Vol. 2*. New York: Columbia University Press, pp. 101–129.

Testa M. (2001) 'Kinship care and permanency', *Journal of Social Service Research*, 28:1, pp. 25–43.

Testa M.F. (2004) 'When children cannot return home: adoption and guardianship', *The Future of Children*, 14:1, pp. 115–129.

Testa M. (2008) *Subsidized Guardianship: Testing the effectiveness of an idea whose time has finally come*. Urbana-Champaign, IL: University of Illinois. Children and Family Research Center.

Testa M., Shook K., Cohen L. and Woods M. (1996) 'Permanency planning options for children in formal kinship care', *Child Welfare*, 75:5, pp. 451–70.

Thoburn J. (2007) *Globalisation and Child Welfare: Some lessons from a cross-national study of children in out-of-home care*. Norwich: University of East Anglia. Access at: www.oned.gouv.fr/recherches/J_Thoburn_rapport.pdf

Thoennes N. (2009) 'What we know now: findings from dependency mediation research', *Family Court Review*, 47:1, pp. 21–37.

Thomas N. (2011) 'Care planning and review for looked after children: fifteen years of slow progress?' *British Journal of Social Work*, 41:2, pp. 387–398.

Thomas N. and O'Kane C. (1999) 'Children's participation in reviews and planning meetings when they are "looked after" in middle childhood', *Child & Family Social Work*, 4, pp. 221–230.

Triseliotis J. (1980) *New Developments in Foster Care and Adoption*. London: Routledge & Kegan Paul.

Triseliotis J. (1983) 'Identity and security in long-term fostering and adoption', *Adoption & Fostering*, 7, pp. 22–31.

Triseliotis J. (2002) 'Long-term foster care or adoption? The evidence examined', *Child & Family Social Work*, 7, pp. 23–33.

Turner R.J. and Avison W.R. (1992) 'Innovations in the measurement of life stress: crisis theory and the significance of event resolution', *Journal of Health and Social Behavior*, 33:1, pp. 36–50.

UK National Archives (2012) *UK Legislation: The Adoption Support Services Regulations, 2005*. Access at: www.legislation.gov.uk/wsi/2005/1512/contents/made

Unrau Y.A. (2007) 'Research on placement moves: seeking the perspective of foster children', *Children and Youth Services Review*, 29, pp. 122–137.

Unrau Y.A., Seita J.R. and Putney K.S. (2008) 'Former foster youth remember multiple placement moves: a journey of loss and hope', *Children and Youth Services Review*, 30:11, pp. 1256–1266.

Urban Institute (2002) *Foster Care Adoption in the United States: A state by state analysis of barriers and promising approaches*. Access at: www.urban.org/uploadedpdf/411108_fostercareadoption.pdf

Urban Systems Research and Engineering (1985) *Evaluation of State Activities with Regard to Adoption Disruption*. Washington, DC: USRandE.

US Children's Bureau (2012) *CFSR Fact Sheet*. Access at: www.acf.hhs.gov/programs/cb/resource/cfsr-fact-sheet

US Department of Health and Human Services (2000) *Report to the Congress on Kinship Foster Care*. Washington, DC: US Department of Health and Human Services.

US Department of Health and Human Services (2005) *A Report to Congress on Adoption and Other Permanency Outcomes for Children in Foster Care: Focus on older children*. Washington, DC: Children's Bureau. Access at: www.acf.hhs.gov/programs/cb/pubs/congress_adopt/insidecover.htm

US Department of Health and Human Services (2010) *National Survey of Child and Adolescent Well-Being Research Brief No. 15: Kinship caregivers in the child welfare system*. Access at: www.acf.hhs.gov/programs/opre/abuse_neglect/nscaw/reports/kinship_caregivers/rb_15_2col.pdf

US Department of Health and Human Services, Administration for Children and Families (2011) *Synthesis of Findings: Subsidized guardianship child welfare waiver demonstrations*. Washington, DC: US Department of Health

and Human Services. Access at: www.acf.hhs.gov/programs/cb/programs_
fund/cwwaiver/2011/subsidized.pdf

US Department of Health and Human Services, US Children's Bureau (2012)
*AFCARS-Adoptions of Children with Public Child Welfare Agency Involvement
by State FY2003-FY2011* and *Children in Public Foster Care on September
30th of Each Year who are Waiting to be Adopted FY2003-FY2011*. Access at:
www.acf.hhs.gov/programs/cb/stats_research/afcars/adoptchild11.
pdf and www.acf.hhs.gov/programs/cb/stats_research/afcars/waiting2011.
pdf *AFCARS Report #19 for FY2011*. Access at: www.acf.hhs.gov/sites/default/
files/cb/afcarsreport19.pdf

US Department of Health & Human Services, US Children's Bureau (2013)
AFCARS – Adoptions of children with public child welfare agency
involvement by state FY2003–FY2011 and Children in public foster care on
September 30th of each year who are waiting to be adopted FY2003–FY2012.
Access at: www.acf.hhs.gov/programs/cb/stats_research/afcars/adoptchild11.
pdf http://www.acf.hhs.gov/programs/cb/stats_research/afcars/waiting2011.
pdf AFCARS Report #20 for FY2012. Access at: http://www.acf.hhs.gov/sites/
default/files/cb/afcarsreport20.pdf http://www.acf.hhs.gov/sites/default/files/
cb/afcarsreport19.pdf

US Department of State (2012) *Intercountry Adoption: Statistics*. Access at:
http://adoption.state.gov/about_us/statistics.php

Vandivere S., Malm K. and Radel L. (2009) *Adoption USA: A chartbook based
on the 2007 National Survey of Adoptive Parents*. Washington, DC: US
Department of Health and Human Services. Access at: www.aspe.hhs.gov/
hsp/09/NSAP/chartbook/index.pdf

Villalva B. (2012) 'Church adopts 76 foster children out of troubled homes',
The Christian Post, 30 August. Access at: www.christianpost.com/news/
church-adopts-76-foster-children-out-of-troubled-homes-80869/
#IT4Oz3mvfZU9SRmF.99

Vinnerljung B. and Hjern A. (2011) 'Cognitive, educational and self-support
outcomes of long-term foster care versus adoption: a Swedish national cohort
study', *Children and Youth Services Review*, 33:10, pp. 1902–1910.

Wade J., Biehal N., Farrelly N. and Sinclair I. (2010) *Maltreated Children in
the Looked After System: A comparison of outcomes for those who go
home and those who do not*. London: Department for Education. Access at:
www.education.gov.uk/publications/eOrderingDownload/DFE-RBX-10-06.
pdf

Wade J., Dixon J. and Richards A. (2010) *Special Guardianship in Practice.* London: BAAF.

Wallis L. (2006) 'Counting the losses: people who do not pursue their adoption enquiry', *Adoption & Fostering*, 20:1, pp. 48–57.

Walsall Council (2012) *Safeguarding Children: Child appreciation days.* Access at: www.walsallchildcare.proceduresonline.com/chapters/g_chi_app_days.htm

Ward E. (2011) 'Taking the next step: enquirers to National Adoption Week one year on', *Adoption & Fostering*, 35:1, pp. 6–17.

Webster D., Barth R. and Needell B. (2000) 'Placement stability for children in out-of-home care: a longitudinal analysis', *Child Welfare*, 79:5, pp. 614–632.

Wells S.J. and Johnson M.A. (2001) 'Selecting outcome measures for child welfare settings: lessons for use in performance management', *Children and Youth Services Review*, 23:2, pp. 169–199.

Wendy's Wonderful Kids (WWK) (2012) *Website of Dave Thomas Foundation for Adoption.* Access at: www.davethomasfoundation.org/what-we-do/wendys-wonderful-kids/

West Virginia Court Improvement Project (2012) *Data Collection.* Charleston, WV: West Virginia Court Improvement Program Oversight Board. Access at: http://wvcip.com/datacollection.html

Whitaker T. and Clark E.J. (2006) 'Social workers in child welfare: ready for duty', *Research on Social Work Practice*, 16:4, pp. 412–413.

Whitaker T., Reich S., Brice Reid L., Williams M. and Woodside C. (2004) *If you're Right for the Job, it's the Best Job in the World.* Washington, DC: National Association of Social Workers.

Wigfall V., Monck E. and Reynolds J. 2006) 'Putting programme into practice: the introduction of concurrent planning into mainstream adoption and fostering services', *British Journal of Social Work*, 36, pp. 41–55.

Wilson J.B., Katz J. and Geen R. (2005) *Listening to Parents: Overcoming barriers to the adoption of children from foster care.* Boston, MA: Harvard University. Access at: www.hks.harvard.edu/ocpa/pdf/Listening%20to%20Parents.pdf

Wind L.H., Brooks D. and Barth R.P. (2005) 'Adoption preparation: differences between adoptive families of children with and without special needs', *Adoption Quarterly*, 8, pp. 45–74.

Wind L.H., Brooks D. and Barth R.P. (2007) 'Influences of risk history and adoption preparation on post-adoption services use in US adoptions', *Family Relations*, 56, pp. 378–389.

Winokur M.A., Crawford G.A., Longobardi R.C. and Valentine D.P. (2008) 'Matched comparison of children in kinship care and foster care on child welfare outcomes', *Families in Society: The Journal of Contemporary Social Services*, 89:3, pp. 338–346.

Winokur M., Holtan A. and Valentine D. (2009) *Kinship Care for the Safety, Permanency, and Well-Being of Children Removed from the Home for Maltreatment.* Campbell Systematic Reviews. Oslo: The Campbell Collaboration.

Winter K. (2010) 'The perspectives of young children in care about their circumstances and implications for social work practice', *Child & Family Social Work*, 15:2, pp. 186–195.

Wright G. (2012) Personal communication with Susan Smith, 3 August.

Wrobel G.M., Ayers-Lopez S., Grotevant H.D. McRoy R.G. and Friedrick M. (1996) 'Openness in adoption and the level of child participation', *Child Development*, 67:5, pp. 2358–2374.

Wrobel G.M., Kohler J.K., Grotevant H.D. and McRoy R. (1998) 'Factors related to patterns of information exchange between adoptive parents and children in mediated adoptions', *Journal of Applied Developmental Psychology*, 19:4, pp. 641–657.

Wulczyn F. (1996) 'A statistical and methodological framework for analyzing the foster care experiences of children', *Social Service Review*, 70, pp. 318–329.

Wulczyn F. and Hislop K.B. (2001) 'Children in substitute care at age 16: selected findings from the multistate data archive', Chicago, IL: Chapin Hall Center for Children, as cited in Courtney, M.E. (2009) 'Outcomes for older youth exiting the foster care system in the United States', in Kerman B., Freundlich M. and Maluccio A.N. (eds) *Achieving Permanence for Older Children and Youth in Foster Care.* New York: Columbia University Press, pp. 40–74.

Wulczyn F.H., Hislop K.B. and Goerge R.M. (2000) *An Update from the Multistate Foster Care Data Archive: Foster care dynamics 1983–1994.* Chicago, IL: University of Chicago, The Chapin Hall Center for Children. Access at: www.chapinhall.org/research/report/update-multistate-foster-care-data-archive

Wulczyn F., Kogan J. and Harden B.J. (2003) 'Placement stability and movement trajectories', *Social Service Review*, 77:2, pp. 212–236

Zosky D.L., Howard J.A., Smith S.L., Howard A.M. and Shelvin K.H. (2005) 'Investing in adoptive families: what adoptive families tell us regarding the benefits of adoption preservation services', *Adoption Quarterly*, 8:3, pp. 1–23.